Trivializing America

TRIVIALIZING AMERICA

Revised and Enlarged Edition

🖋 Norman Corwin

Lyle Stuart Inc. 🖋 *Secaucus, New Jersey*

Library of Congress Cataloging in Publication Data

Corwin, Norman Lewis, 1910-
  Trivializing America.

  Includes bibliographical references and index.
  1. United States—Popular culture—History—20th
century. 2. United States—Civilization—1945-
3. Arts and society—United States. I. Title.
E169.12.C64 1983   973.92   83-4879
ISBN 0-8184-0389-6

Published by Lyle Stuart Inc.
Published simultaneously in Canada by
Musson Book Company,
A division of General Publishing Co. Limited
Don Mills, Ontario

Queries regarding rights and permissions should be
addressed to: Lyle Stuart, 120 Enterprise Avenue,
Secaucus, N.J. 07094.

Manufactured in the United States of America

To Jack Langguth

Contents

Trivializing America

Introduction

To know our disease, to discover what we suffer from, may be
the only cure.

                                        —Daniel J. Boorstin

It is part of the cure to wish to be cured.

                                        —Petrarch

On July 10, 1985, among hundreds of newsworthy events
around the world, were the following:

Bishop Desmond Tutu, Nobel laureate, charged into an
angry mob to save a suspected police informer from being
burned to death.

An Israeli court convicted 15 Jewish terrorists of murder and
other acts of violence against Arabs.

A Turkish supertanker was struck by an Iraqi missile and
heavily damaged.

Bolivia established full diplomatic relations with mainland
China, and ordered Taiwan's ambassador to get out within 72
hours.

A Greenpeace protest vessel was blown up in Auckland
harbor, killing the ship's photographer.

The government of Sri Lanka freed 643 political prisoners.

13

China and the Soviet Union signed a $14-billion trade agreement.

Egyptian police discovered six tons of hashish hidden under a shipment of tomato paste aboard a cargo vessel bound for South Yemen from Greece.

In Washington the House voted to repeal a nine-year-old ban on American aid to guerrillas fighting the Marxist regime in Angola.

Attorney General Meese refused to rule out kidnapping as a means of bringing terrorists to justice.

The Nuclear Regulatory Commission came under attack for not properly considering earthquake hazards at the Diablo Canyon plant.

Eight major fires in California destroyed 300,000 acres of forests and scores of homes.

A disaster emergency was declared for New York City and several counties to its north, because of an acute water shortage.

—All of this on the same day. But the lead story on two of the three major American network news broadcasts that evening was the announcement that Coca-Cola had decided to go back to its old taste after experimenting with a new one. Had this been merely a flukey aberration in high echelons of broadcasting, it would be remarkable enough, but print journalism joined in the ecstasy. Most of the country's press featured Coke's turnaround on their front pages, at the expense of all but a few of the genuine news stories listed above. The main headline of *The Denver Post*, for example, in type as large as the name of the paper itself, read, "'The Real Thing' Is Back." The banner was fortified, on the same front page, by a six-square-inch depiction of a can of Coke. In two colors.

This, in the country of Joseph Pulitzer, Horace Greeley, William Allen White, Edward R. Murrow and Bill Moyers. This, two centuries after Thomas Jefferson declared that "to the press alone, the world is indebted for all the triumphs that have been gained by reason and humanity."

The values represented in the media's treatment of Coca-Cola's "news" (also reflected by the public—one zealot spent $31,000 of his own money in a campaign to get the company to reverse itself) did not suddenly surface. The truth is that a general erosion of values has been taking place for a long time. The enormity of the free publicity given to the marketing vagaries of a soft drink is, by any rational judgment, fairly sick. But it was only one small, stumbling step in the decline of our national ethos. There have been, and continue to be, frequent hops, skips, and skids in the same direction.

The process is one of trivialization. It amounts to a low-grade, chronic disease. Now and then the symptoms abate, but they return. For the most part, Americans do not know what they suffer from, and those who do are divided about its nature, whether they want to cure it, and whether it can be cured at all.

The gloomiest observers think it may ultimately come down to a question of survival—that our demise is far less likely to be from a nuclear blow (not without destroying whoever deals the blow) than from the wasting effects of trivialization on a broad front. Gloomy scenario or not, it is a syndrome that increasingly concerns artists, scientists, sociologists, government, education, the clergy, and an informed public across a wide spectrum of disciplines and interests.

Demise does not necessarily mean prostration, collapse, being overrun by barbarians, or becoming a colony of Greater China. It does not even mean being dislodged from first place as the country with the most telephones, automobiles, serum cholesterol and gross national product. But when a nation has known greatness and stood as an exemplar to the world, when it has bred giants and accomplished prodigies, when humane ideals have been instilled in its people, when it has aspired, in the words of a state motto, To the Stars Through Hardship[1]—and gradually it turns away from all this and becomes indifferent, complacent, greedy, bored, hungry for kicks, amenable to getting-along-by-going-along, comfortable with mediocrity, its aspirations venal and its governance sporadically avaricious, self-righteous, conniving, browbeating or paranoid, then it approaches a moral nadir.

No doubt there are hazards inherent in speaking of America in terms other than those expressed by Irving Berlin in his quasi-anthem "God Bless America," chiefly the risk of offending patriots who are convinced that we are a country without blemish, problem-free and utterly OK, and that even the budget deficit is beautiful because it is ours. But when I treat, in these pages, of forces in our culture and society that tend to reduce us, to fragment our concentration, erode our standards, fritter away our native genius, and make of our political procedures a kind of National Trifle Association, I do so from a premise that we have been, at moments still are, and could well again become a nation of grandeur, a nation on whom the shedding of divine grace, as entreated in the sixth line of that far superior quasi-anthem, "America the Beautiful," may be importuned by us without having to cross our fingers as we do so.

Some think it is already too late, that the damage is irreversible. I do not share that pessimism, if only on the grounds that to believe recovery impossible is the surest way to make it so. I prefer to think there is enough tough genetic material in the American character for us to rebound. But it will take a strenuous turnaround—a physical, spiritual, psychological, cultural and political reversal requiring the kind of concentrated energy and effort that goes into a massive building project—analogous, in a way, to building a dam that changes the course of a mighty river and at the same time controls flooding and generates energy.

[1] *Ad Astra per Asperum*, the motto of Kansas.

The last part of this volume is taken up with concepts, aspects and prospects of such a turnaround. But long before we arrive at that point—in fact, right away—it is my unrelished obligation to show that the spirit of trivia is abroad just about everywhere, in education, journalism, the arts, entertainment, commerce, advertising, film, television, religion, law, research, philosophy, scholarship, criticism, politics, government, and also in commonly held attitudes toward ethics, sex, and death.

First off, it is only proper to define trivia. It has a genial etymology, coming from the Latin *tri vium*, a crossing of three roads—the sort of place where Roman idlers and gossipers gathered to exchange small talk. The derivation goes straight to the core of its meaning: smallness and unimportance.

But a curious inversion sometimes takes place, for in addition to making little of big things, trivialization can also make big of little things. A classic example out of ancient history was the Trojan war, fought for ten years, we are told, over a woman. No war is ever trivial, but the cause can be. In the case of Helen, at least the soldiers on both sides knew what they were fighting for.

However, the venue in these pages is not the Troy of Aeneas, it is the United States of America; and a logical place to start is with that Mississippi of trivia broadly known as Entertainment, of which we have a greater volume than anywhere else in the world—a steady flow of distraction-hunting and sensation-seeking unprecedented in variety and unparalleled in cost.

1 ✐ Entertainment

Where Life becomes a Spasm
And history a Whiz
If that is not Sensation
I don't know what it is.

—Lewis Carroll

There is a joke that goes, Why are ten pallbearers needed at a rock funeral? Answer: Eight to carry the coffin, and two to carry the radio. It is not much of a joke, but it illustrates a phenomenon of the times—the inundation of America by a rising flood of entertainment, to such an extent that millions have become waterlogged. So pressing is the need for distractions that hikers, amblers, joggers on the street and at the beach and in the country, and shoppers at the supermarket cover their ears with headset radios and listen as they ambulate. It is not enough for some spectators to be present at baseball and football games, watching the action; they listen to other games going on at the same time.

But sports, already a massive industry both *in loco* and on the air, are only a fragment of the universe of entertainment. Every day of the year, in every major city of the country and in many minor ones, attractions are heaped on attractions: movies,[1] plays, concerts, dancing, galleries, museums, night clubs, cabarets, fashion shows, massage parlors, zoos, Disneylands, Sea Worlds, Woodstocks, festivals, pageants, touring, horse racing, dog racing, car racing, drag racing, roller-skating derbies, mudwrestlers, circuses, amusement parks, arcades,[2] recordings[3]—and on top of all that, around-the-clock programs on radio and television, ramified at home by ancillary tapes,[4] discs, cartridges and cables.

And then come private and semi-private entertainments—hobbies, puzzles, partying, swap meets, sociables, smokers, bees, balls, picnics, clambakes, fishing, bowling, skiing, tennis, golf, card games, bingo, gambling. So pervasive is the concept of entertainment as daily necessity that home furnishings now include wall units known as entertainment centers, consisting of modular cabinets and shelves accommodating stereo, phonograph, tape decks and other performing hardware.

Such mass absorption in glomerations of entertainment could signify a lively, curious, fun-loving populace, affluent enough to afford the costs and fees entailed, rewarding itself for hard work well done, enjoying the benefits of a sound, salubrious culture. And while this is to some extent true, most of our amusements, recreations, regalements and revels represent avenues of escape, and not always from the harsh realities of life, from intimations of mortality, from a sense of void, but often from boredom. Sheer boredom.

"The average man," wrote Mencken, "gets his living by such depressing devices that boredom becomes a natural state to him" —a variation on Thoreau's better known observation that most men live lives of quiet desperation. But entertainment itself can

---

[1] In 1982, a year of recession and high unemployment, theatrical movies attracted nearly 1.2 billion paid admissions.

[2] In this category alone, the sale of pinball machines in 1979 generated $2.3 billion in revenue. In 1982, video games accounted for $7.7 billion in sales.

[3] About 12,000 record albums are produced every year, with a retail value of nearly $2 billion.

[4] In 1982, there were 4.5 million videotape recorders in American homes. Conservative estimates are that by 1990, there will be 30 million.

become boring through sameness and surfeit. This happens when escapist fare like TV westerns and hospital dramas dominate the listings for a few seasons and then fade away. Stars burn out on earth as they do in heaven.

So here we have the paradox of the most entertained country in the world seeking still more entertainment in an apparently unslakable thirst for sensation. And the exploitation of sensation as style, device and marketable product ranges all the way from home games to art forms to vandalism.

Sensation is everywhere. Special effects of destruction fill the screen; sensational car chases careen across the tube nightly; sensational stuntists like Evel Knievel, and the nutty exhibitionists who scale skyscrapers, enthrall the media; Guinness-record-seekers strain to make the next edition; rock bands whose very names are sensational (The Bangs, The Pits, Cheap Trick, Rat Scabies, Burning Sensation, Social Distortion, Fear, Bad Religion, The Criminals, Jack Mack & The Heart Attack, Cheri & The Hit Men, Huge Killer Bats, Vultures, The Stilettos, The Grenades, Vicious Fish) put on sensational concerts featuring destruction of musical instruments, TV sets, and on-stage Cadillacs.

The Plasmatics smash autos. Less discriminating musicians of punk rock persuasion bite the heads off pigeons. They are masters of programmed vandalism. Far from being unique excrescences of the culture of sensationalism, they are merely the loudest and least respected. Higher on the scale of respectability, to the point of being displayed in great museums of America and abroad, are sensationalists like Arman (Armand Pierre Fernandez) who smashes pianos, burns violins and blows up automobiles. An admiring article in *Horizon* recounts that

> At one point he furnished an entire art gallery exactly like a middle-class suburban living room, right down to the minutest detail, and then axed the place. He called it "Conscious Vandalism."[5]

[5]*Arman* by Jeffery Robinson, *Horizon*, May-June, 1982.

Arman is quoted as believing there is no fundamental difference between accumulating objects and smashing them. If you break a fiddle, for example, "you get something romantic." Because he is "especially fond of strings"—violins, cellos, basses—"he broke them and burned them and put them in Plexiglass, cut up or chipped or charred or smashed to smithereens. The results were so universally romantic that Arman attracted a great deal of notice. From gallery and museum shows he moved up into major museum collections."

Arman's justification for Conscious Vandalism is experimentation:

> ... this destruction was not as much left to chance as it was a series of controlled experiments, changing the state of the object...

Such experiments differ only in degree from the conscious vandalism of three Miami boys who doused a cat with lighter fluid, set it afire to see it "balloon," and then did the same to three sleeping derelicts, one of whom died from the flames. They explained that they "simply wanted to see the men's reactions when they woke up and found themselves on fire."[6] While there is a huge difference between burning a cello and cremating a man, the same impulse is common to this and all acts of experimental arson: the seeking of sensation by changing the state of an object.

If artists themselves set models for vandalism, it should not be surprising that a public follows. Lawrence Alloway, in *Topics in American Art Since 1945*, propounded a formula for coping with widespread disfigurement of public sculpture:

> I propose here Alloway's law of public sculpture. (1) If a work can be reached it will be defaced. (2) If the subsequent changes reduce the level of information in the work, it was not a public work to start with. ... A public sculpture should be invulnera-

[6]*Criminal Violence, Criminal Justice,* by Charles E. Silberman, Random House, 1978, pp. 62-3.

ble or inaccessible. It should have the material strength to resist attack or be easily cleanable. ... One defense ... could be a high level of redundancy which would incorporate frivolous additions and sprayed slogans into the structure.

It is not that defacers have nothing better to do than vandalize, it is that they seek ways to relieve boredom, ways that at the same time satisfy a need for sensation.

Sometimes the sensation consists of doing nothing, or doing the same thing over and over to the point of absurdity. John Cage, radical composer considered by the *New Grove's Dictionary of Music and Musicians* to have exerted a greater influence on world music than any other American composer of the 20th Century (take that, Copland; and you too, Ives), created a thing for piano entitled *4'33"*, which instructs the performer to sit at the piano, fold his hands in his lap, wait for four minutes and 33 seconds, then rise and bow to the audience. This work is one of the milder, certainly the quietest, of Cage's divertissements which aggressively court aesthetic outrage.

Cage is excusable as an *enfant terrible*, but in the quest for kicks, stable and substantial types are not above sensationalism. Pacifica's radio station KPFK, whose progressive stance and responsible programming have distinguished it among the FM population, nevertheless had a run at trivialization when, on September 6, 1981, it devoted a whole broadcasting day to Erik Satie's *Vexations*, a piano piece of 180 notes which takes about 90 seconds to play. Satie, who enjoyed clowning in his titles and indications, had directed that the composition be repeated 840 times without pause. This was dutifully done by KPFK on that Sunday; for 18 hours and 40 minutes Satie's rather dirge-like little opus went on and on and on, over and over, from sign-on to sign-off. In one stroke the station trivialized itself, its franchise, its subscribers and its audience—the latter, by assuming listeners would not regard this stunt as a wasted day, a small joke not worth the inordinate time given to it. The station was back to normal next day—a very good normal—but the memory of *Vexations* will not soon leave listeners who tuned in the station several times during that day, hoping to hear music or news or a discussion, only to be vexed by those 180 lugubrious notes.

Both were minor instances, to be sure, but social boredom and sensation-seeking are present in a great many walks, in all classes, and across a wide span of ages. A seven-year-old boy set fire to a park of mobile homes (and was put on trial for it) out of sheer ennui. Young adults from society families in Long Island smashed a mansion in Oyster Bay just for the hell of it. When Washington's Kennedy Center first opened, concert-goers made off with so many fixtures that even the interiors of elevators had to be redesigned along the lines of Alloway's recommendations.

Sensation is not only fed to the masses, it is force-fed. Not long after the motion pictures *Star Trek, Star Wars* and *The Empire Strikes Back* (all of which dealt heavily in the destruction of populated planets) had swept the country, one of the largest department stores in California advertised the Atari Defender Game cartridge:

> Alien forces have invaded the Earth bringing with them their death machines. Launch your attack rocket . . . then fire your laser cannons! Only you can prevent the aliens from kidnapping your fellow humanoids and transforming them into treacherous mutants.

Most of the ad was taken up by a monstrous creature holding the Earth in his hands and looking at it hungrily as though it were an edible basketball. It can be argued that not even very young kids believe we are threatened by aliens with death machines. But it is not a question of belief, it is the persistent surfeit of sensation to the point where it begins to jade. Joyce Maynard, in *Looking Back: A Chronicle of Growing Up Old in the Sixties*, tells of taking a four-year-old child to a circus:

> . . . she leaned back on her padded seat . . . toughly, smartly, sadly, wisely, agedly unenthralled. . . . We had seen greater

spectacles, unmoved, our whole world was a visual glut, a ten-ring circus even Ringling Brothers couldn't compete with. A man stuck his head into a tiger's mouth and I pointed it out . . . to my cool, unfazed friend, and when she failed to look [I] turned her head for her, forced her to take the sight in. The tiger could have bitten the tamer's head off, I think, swallowed him whole . . . and she wouldn't have blinked.

But a man's head in a tiger's mouth is nothing compared to an inhabited planet in the sights of a weapon that will blow it to shivereens. George Plimpton, author, actor, salesman, made the boast in a commercial for Atari, that a certain TV game was the only one which offered "total destruction of a planet." What circus can offer that?

George F. Will, castigating the movie *Indiana Jones* for scenes in which characters are flogged, roasted and eviscerated, and the menu of an opulent meal includes live snakes, beetles, eyeball soup and monkey brains, called it "an example of the upward ratchet effect of shocking extremism in popular entertainment," and concluded that "This march toward the shocking is producing a generation that would yawn through the parting of the Red Sea."

In the motion picture *My Dinner With Andre*, Wally asks, "Are we just like bored, spoiled children who've been lying in the bathtub all day, playing with their plastic duck, and now they're thinking, What can I do?"

"Yes," says Andre. "We're bored, now. We're all bored." This comes after Andre has spent half the picture telling Wally how he had gone around the world seeking far-out sensations—to Poland, the Sahara, India, Scotland, Yugoslavia, China, Tibet, Israel— "experiencing a lot of synchronicity . . . hallucinating nonstop . . . things were exploding. . . ." But after all that, he concludes

the truth is, Wally, that in retrospect those things I was involved in are all, in a way, disgusting to me . . .

Andre, a director in the theater, at one point echoes Joyce Maynard's allusion to "visual glut" by recalling an impulse he entertained while staging a production of *The Bacchae* at Yale:

> ...when Pentheus has been killed ... and they rip him to shreds and I guess cut off his head—my impulse was ... to get a head from the New Haven morgue and pass it around the audience ... so that the people somehow could realize that the stuff was real, see.

The actress who played Agawe refused to carry a head from the morgue and so it was not used, but Andre clings to the idea:

> I still think it would be wonderful if the perceptions of the audience could be brought to life.

Though light years separate the art of Andre Gregory from that of Herschell Gordon Lewis, producer of gory horror movies, they are disconcertingly close in their views of the need for, and means of, bringing the perceptions of an audience to life. No movie before Lewis's *Blood Feast* showed a tongue being ripped out. No play before Andre's *Bacchae* came close to passing a dead head around. Had this been done, no doubt some of the audience would have fainted, vomited, turned green, and left the theater, just as they did at Lewis's *Blood Orgy*.

Spectators who have been exposed to gristle and gore, to the feel and smell of a cadaver's head, may find lesser sensations so tame they fall asleep in the theater. Wally, himself a playwright, tells Andre that people today have "redefined the theater in a trivial way ... they are deeply asleep. ... I began to feel that there was nothing [he or his actors] could do to reach those people." Thus his theater audience could no more be impressed by lines in the mouths of his characters than the four-year-old girl at the circus could be impressed by the man with his head in the mouth of a tiger.

Although sensation-seeking crosses class lines, motivations differ. The poor, especially in times of depression and high unemployment, when idleness is forced upon them, have plenty of time and reason to be bored; but the day-to-day need to eat, pay rent, clothe the kids and keep warm makes passive boredom a luxury few can afford. In the crunch of poverty, the poor are less likely to feel boredom than anger, alienation, frustration and victimization, and when these feelings build up and are ignited by provocation, they erupt in riots, looting and arson.

While it is true that some poor people, like some rich, seek sensation for its own sake (the poor are more likely to call it "kicks"), and also true that these kicks sometimes take the form of vandalism, their basic impulses are usually quite different from those of the affluent. In a curious way, the rich man's didoes, because they are little more than idle pranks in the face of options not open to the poor, end up by trivializing, whereas the destructive acts of the poor are attempts, however crude and unadmirable, to do the opposite—to enlarge the ego by asserting it, to commit aggression against targets which cannot strike back and which symbolize the stolidity of those who have more than enough. When a poor man lays waste to a schoolroom, or breaks into the Los Angeles Coliseum at night and wrecks a quarter million dollars' worth of electronic scoreboard, his vandalism is an irrational means of getting back at "them." On the other hand, when rich young blades like the society vandals of Long Island demolish a mansion, they are not impelled by spite or perverted logic, they are simply getting their jollies.

Charles E. Silberman, in *Criminal Violence, Criminal Justice*, states the case of the poor:

> Because their sense of self is so precarious, poor people invest considerable energy in a search for excitement ... for activities that can tell them they *do* exist and they *do* matter. The search for "action," to use a more inclusive term, may involve ... [among other things] ... vandalism. ...

Standing between the poor and the rich, the middle class is also interested in destructive jinks. The United States Forest Service reports persistent vandalism by campers and hikers who not only shoot up and tear down needed signs, but hack away at century-old trees for firewood, paint graffiti on rock faces, and deliberately kill magnificent oaks and evergreens by ring-barking (stripping a band of bark around the tree.) These people, euphemistically called "forest visitors" by the Service, can gain nothing by killing a tree, but perhaps it satisfies them to destroy something much bigger than they are, something that would outlive them if let alone. The rich are usually above this kind of malicious mischief, although they sometimes take out their ego needs on lions or elephants in trophy-hunting. At the other end, the poor not only can't go off on big-game safaris, they can't even afford entrance fees to our wilderness areas, let alone the expense of getting to them.

Thus trivialization can be more than a process of diminution by plethora, overstatement, disparagement or mediocritization; it can be both a symptom and cause of private and public malaise. Although wealth is never a lamentable state except in revolutionary situations where to be an aristocrat is to lose your head, some of the rich suffer at times from an affliction not shared by the lower classes, the endemic disease of those who have everything and can afford to try anything: susceptibility to the boredom of surfeit. Indeed our Andre of the long dinner, though perhaps not wealthy, obviously had the means to travel widely in order to experiment with his senses on four continents. Michael Selzer in his book *Terrorist Chic*[7] comments on experimental careening:

> The consequence of a willingness to encounter everything is that you experience nothing. A life that careens wildly from one posture to the next is not enriched by any of them; the self does not grow as a result, but sinks into a deepening promiscuity of being. There is no authentic gratification in this mode of being, but only a combination of listlessness, triviality, identity confusion, and an unappeasable need for sensation.

[7]*Terrorist Chic*, by Michael Selzer, Hawthorn, 1979. p. 194.

By another of those odd inversions which appear in the landscape of trivialization like geology's erratic boulders, some of the rich have yet another singularity: the need to brandish their estate on occasion. The bigger and more ostentatious their entertainments, the sillier and more trivial they become. In New York City one day, David Frost gathered 60 of his friends and took them to lunch—in Bermuda. All 60 were notables of the order of James A. Michener, John Kenneth Galbraith, chess champion Bobby Fischer, cartoonist Charles Addams, columnist Joseph Kraft, critic Clive Barnes, producer Frederick Brisson. Frost chartered the entire front section of a Boeing 747, and made the trip one long champagne flight coming and going. According to Charlotte Curtis's account in *The Rich and Other Atrocities*, when Brisson told his office that he was going to Bermuda for lunch, "they laughed first. When they realized I meant it, they booed." Frost, himself splendid in a borscht-red acrylic seersucker suit, provided, along with canapes, caviar and bubbly, a palmist and a graphologist to keep his guests occupied between Kennedy Airport and Hamilton. The party, which left in mid-morning, was back in New York by 6 p.m.

The tradition is an old one in America. Jacqueline Thompson in *The Very Rich Book*, tells us that circa 1913, Mrs. Stuyvesant Fish gave a high society party in which the guests were required to talk baby talk to each other throughout the evening. At another party, while the guests were watching a ballet, "servant boys dressed as kittens passed out party favors to the women. The favors were live mice and the ladies' reactions were the *real* entertainment."

In 1966 Truman Capote underwrote a masked ball at New York's Plaza Hotel for 540

> diplomats, politicians, painters, writers, composers, actors, producers, dress designers, social figures, tycoons and what Mr. Capote called "international types, lots of beautiful women and ravishing little things"

all of whom had to present red-and-white admission cards at the door. Although Capote himself thought his party "cozy", some of the guests struggled through difficulties:

> Mrs. Loel Guinness, wife of the international banker, was having trouble with her necklaces—one rubies, the other diamonds. They were so heavy, she said, that she thought she'd have to stay in bed all the next day to recover.

In Los Angeles, Jules Stein, ophthalmologist who became head of the Music Corporation of America, hosted 600 celebrities at a three-day party estimated to have cost more than a quarter of a million dollars. Guests arriving from Paris and New York (flights prepaid by the host) were met by the Steins and a kilted band of Scottish bagpipers who skirled away both at the airport and on a bus that carried the arrivals to Stein's then new Sheraton-Universal Hotel. According to Miss Curtis

> Craig Mitchell, the investment banker, rode most of the way with his fingers in his ears.

Again, gems were profusely displayed:

> Mrs. Nils Onstad (Sonja Henie) was there with her white fringe and several pounds of rubies and diamonds.

Mrs. John Shapiro, sister of U. S. Senator Joseph Tydings, and Mrs. John Lauder confessed to each other that neither had brought a personal maid. Mrs. Albert D. Lasker described the event as "the most wonderful weekend in the history of mankind."

Numbers are important to the parties of the rich. They add to the sensation, just as thousands of extras give weight to a movie. Malcolm S. Forbes celebrated the 50th anniversary of *Forbes Magazine* by giving a party described by Miss Curtis as possibly the country's "largest single assembly of working tycoons." Forbes's country house accommodated even more people than attended the Stein festivities—740. To get from the cocktail tent to the dinner tent

couples had to walk down what may well be the most
spectacular passageway ever devised for a single night ... a
430-foot green tent with a scalloped overhang, tartan curtains,
the carpeting overlaid with more tartan and the ceiling aglitter
with thousands of little Italian lights.

There were also four bands of kilted bagpipers, 63 of them
positioned at intervals along the passageway. During dinner an
orchestra and a choir performed, then there were fireworks and
dancing.

It must be said that ostentation and profligacy among the very
rich are not especially American, and that the archives are
stocked with accounts of expensive and thronged festivities. In
ancient times, parties went on for days or weeks, but these were
usually imperial, like Ahasuerus's celebration in Shushan, described in the Book of Esther; or vulgarly lavish, like the
wingdings of ancient Rome, satirized by Petronius in his Feast of
Trimalchio; or the Shah of Iran's week-long gala at Persepolis in
October, 1971.[8]

For the most part rich Americans have been discreet about
their entertainments. Part of this may reflect a disinclination to
attract publicity, for reasons of security; but another part, no
doubt much smaller, may have to do with our antiroyalist
tradition going back to the break with Britain. A still smaller part
may derive from the example of America's political aristocracy,
especially in the early days. The rich Thomas Jefferson, with his
usual meticulousness, entered in his record of the year 1771,
three separate amusements to which he treated himself: he paid
three shillings to hear a concert of musical glasses, half that fee
for an evening of "Dutch dancing and singing", and the same
amount for seeing a live alligator.

[8]My favorite detail of this party was the convenience afforded King Frederik IX and
Queen Ingrid of Denmark, two of the guests, when they went to lunch at the huge
main tent raised by the Shah on the site of the ancient Persian city. According to
Charlotte Curtis, the royal couple walked from their lodging to the curb, climbed
into a Rolls-Royce assigned to them, and motored the 500 feet to the club tent.

Even though Americans have tended lately to elect rich Presidents (FDR, Johnson, Kennedy, Reagan), the examples of modest deportment by Washington, Jefferson and FDR, apparently entered the consciousness of (then) Vice-President Hubert H. Humphrey. At the Forbes anniversary party he remarked in an after-dinner speech that, "in a country afflicted with poverty, wealth is something of which to be ashamed." How that sentiment went down with the tycoons present was not reported, but the applause could not have been loud or long.

There are any number of ways to measure America's development from the time when Jefferson, still seeking entertainment in 1786, paid a shilling to see "a learn'd pig" perform, but one of the most enlightening ways is in terms of the things that people find amusing. There was no Pac-Man in the days of Monticello, no discos, no all-night movies, no DJ's, no walkmans, no porno parlors, no drag racing, no *Saturday Night Live*, no divisional playoffs, no comic books, no horror pix, no Mrs. America beauty contests. On the other hand, there was time to read a book.

2 ✍ "Give Us 22 Minutes..."

The one medium of entertainment that we and we alone have developed to a technical gloss and commercial clout unrivalled anywhere is commercial television. Much has already been written on the subject—indeed it is a favorite target for criticism—but the worst that can be said about it is not that it is a slave to ratings, which it is; or an assembly line for dramatized violence, which is bad enough; or an attic of old movies; but that it is trivializing a whole culture. It does this both directly and indirectly, acting first upon its own audiences, and secondarily, through its influence among other media, on a widening public.

Take the "least worst"[1] of TV's chronic banes—its handling of news. The average local newscast, almost everywhere in the country, is a kind of succotash served in dollops and seasoned by bantering between anchorpersons, sportspersons, weatherpersons and person-persons. And these people had better be good-looking, sparkling or cute—weathermen with party charm, anchorladies with good teeth and smart coiffures, sportcasters with macho charisma. It doesn't matter if they have a news background or not. One of the highest paid anchorwomen in the business was described by the *Los Angeles Times* as "a leading

[1]British critic Max Shulman's phrase for the television of his country.

33

figure in the ranks of those who know next to nothing about news but can expect to make a quarter of a million dollars annually for dispensing it." Walter Cronkite called the cosmetic approach, "the work of packagers who care more about a hairdo than about the news itself." Not long after he said this, a TV station in Missouri proved he was not exaggerating. An anchorwoman named Christine Craft was dismissed by KMBC-TV, the ABC outlet in Kansas City, because, she said, the station's "research" showed that too many viewers thought her "too old, too unattractive and not deferential to men." (She was 37, and was later described in a newspaper account as having "wholesome, outdoorsy good looks... it's hard to see how anyone could think her unattractive.")

A "news consultant" retained by the station, contended that the clothes newscasters wear have more bearing on their credibility than the style and content of their reporting.[2] Over a sample ten-day period, Craft's on-camera wardrobe chart called for 33 specific items, including pearls, a gold chain, a magenta St. Tropez geometric blouse and cream shirt, a light beige Liz Claiborne linen blazer, a madras plaid J.G. Hook blazer with a yellow Clubhouse silk blouse, and a bright red vertical-light-sleeve Evan Picone creation.

It was not Craft's first experience with image management. Earlier, while employed as a reporter for *CBS Sports Spectacular* in New York, she was required by the producers to dye her brown hair platinum and her brows black.[3]

The cosmetic packaging of which Cronkite complained may

[2]Not only a Kansas City consultant. According to Ron Rosenbaum in *Esquire* (Nov., 1982), Dan Rather was told by Van Gordon Sauter, president of CBS News, that it was not just important to *be* what you are on a newscast, you have to be *perceived* as what you are. "'When we talk about the look of the broadcast and bringing it up to date,' Van said, 'I'm not talking about changing your soul, I'm talking about changing your suit!'"

[3]Craft sued Metromedia, owner of the Kansas City station, and a jury awarded her $250,000 in actual damages and $100,000 in punitive damages, but an appellate court overturned the award in June of 1985. She vowed to carry the fight to the U.S. Supreme Court.

make a profit center of the news room, but when a doll is assigned to purvey news, it is not always of high service to broadcast journalism. Beauty may be truth and truth beauty, but today even Keats would agree that it is not all we need to know.

There is something distracting about a phantom of delight who radiates sexuality, filling us in on murder, rape, inflation, corruption, terror, bigotry, turpitude and sports. Newscasting is not a beauty contest. Ghastly tidings delivered by Aphrodite, or dispatches of grave import from an anchorman with a Barrymore profile and the magnetism of a Valentino, tend to lose something in translation; they become an *effect*. When pulchritude and sex-appeal rate as prime ingredients in the dissemination of news, journalism yields to showmanship.

It could be argued that to deny a footing in TV news to anyone on grounds of excess comeliness is to penalize good looks. Actually it works the other way around: plain-lookers are the ones who get passed up, notwithstanding proven competence. Their features just don't come together well enough to satisfy the packager.

Any time broadcast news is twisted or accented by emphasis on personality, "image," bloom, novelty, sensation, or on being first, it is trivialized. The best of the newspeople have always been of earnest purport; none looks upon news as showbiz, as a profit center, but rather as a trust, an obligation to treat with integrity both what is reported and the audience to which it is addressed.

"The only thing that counts," Edward R. Murrow once told his associates at CBS, "is what comes out of the loudspeaker— and what we're trying to make come out is an honest, coherent account of events. It is not part of our job to please or entertain."

That credo has had tough going. Not only are newscasters recruited increasingly out of casting directories, fashion magazines, model agencies and beauty parlors, but the news itself has been minified, often by stations which specialize in news and might therefore be expected to expand rather than compress their formats. Cronkite resented "the hypercompression we are forced to exert to fit 100 pounds of news into the one-pound sack that we are given to fill every night," and was concerned lest the public, persistently being under-informed, will suffer from the effects of distortion and in this way be "led to disaster."

Charles Kuralt was no happier about what he saw and heard. Most news anchors, he said, "cannot think, cannot write, do not know their communities and would not know a news story if it jumped up and messed their coiffures."

George Schlatter, producer of the television program *Real People* (eccentrics, octogenarian charmers, a violinist who practices daily in a public restroom, a group whose specialty is rummaging through the garbage of celebrities, etc.) believes news programs strain to entertain: "Eight minutes of news, interspersed with chit-chat, banter, and a real-people story. It's show biz."[4]

The all-news Westinghouse radio stations have a slogan which for years has been repeated on the air several times daily: "Give us 22 minutes and we'll give you the world." It's true the world has shrunk—but *that* much? Still, Westinghouse's 22 minutes of news, the equivalent in print of two columns in *The New York Times*, are straightforward and banter-free. The same cannot be said for much of television's formula. Critic Howard Rosenberg, after watching the 11 o'clock news on KABC-TV Channel 7 on a night in July, 1981, wrote:

> What excitement there was on Channel 7's late night loose-marblecast! Sober, respectable, credible Warren Olney having lately been transplanted to the land of the sillies, [is] swiftly learning the program.

Olney had announced during a prime-time newsbreak that Christine Lund, anchorwoman then on maternity leave, would be paying a visit on an upcoming news program to talk about her new baby.

[4]Richard L. Strout, for 61 years a journalist in Washington, told a reporter in an interview in 1982, "Television trivializes the news in a disgusting fashion. It's awfully hard to find out the meaning of anything."

Just before 11 p.m., Olney gave it another shot: "Coming up, a terrific surprise from a new mother." Sure enough the 11 p.m. news program included tape of Lund describing her baby's "fat little cheeks."

"Oh, my goodness," said weathercaster Johnny Mountain. . . .

Viewers barely had time to catch their breath before it was revealed that Mountain's wife that very morning had given birth to a son. Later in the newscast Mountain did jokes about his wife and showed pictures of a monkey, which he said was his new son. . . .

If nothing else, this should once and for all settle the hash of critics who contend that TV news is sometimes shallow and emphasizes anchor personalities more than news.

Are Olney, Lund, Mountain and the others chargeable with perpetrating piffle? Certainly they are guilty in part, even if the klatsch may have been the idea of the news director, or an imperative from the station manager. Persiflage has a home on programs expressly made for it; the news need never stray that way. Murrow would have refused, and so would Chancellor, Reynolds, Cronkite, Kuralt, Collingwood, Trout, Sevareid, Ted Koppel, Jess Marlow, Bill Moyers, Joseph Benti. The last, a superb reporter in Los Angeles, was released by Channel 2 News in one of those periodic shuffles usually involving beautification, competition, and the *idée fixe* of some executive rating-watcher, that in order for a newscast to get anywhere in the marketplace, its cast on camera must be chummy, good kidders, "human," and altogether hale and well met. Benti's case was a local outrage, but he stands for scores of excellent practitioners who have been shunted aside to make way for darlings.

Of course the audience contributes its share to the syndrome. And the contribution is reciprocal. Consumers of entertainment, if fed cultural junk food long enough, come to expect it. And they get it.

Dr. Rodney Gorney, in *The Human Agenda*, worries that "a satiated public might lose its capacity and will to discriminate [between a] cultural triumph and a cultural travesty." In much the same way, a public fed on prattle may suffer diminished capacity to weigh the news. If the judgment of an electorate is numbed by trivia, there is no guarantee that sooner or later a candidate unfitted to rise higher than senior salesman in a sharp used-car operation will not become president. It has happened.

J. B. Priestley, novelist, playwright and commentator, wrote, "There is now a vast crowd, a permanent audience, waiting to be amused. They look on more and more, and join in less and less." If indeed this vast crowd wants its reporters to be amusing, sociable, pretty and cozy, then trivialization has done its work.

Naturally, decisions affecting such matters are not made in the newsroom but higher up. They reflect the philosophy of the board room, of dividend-warders whose first loyalty is to the ratings. David Sarnoff, head of RCA in the era of greatest glory for its subsidiary NBC, once put it bluntly: "We're in the same position as a plumber laying pipe—we're not responsible for what goes through the pipe." The fact that this statement was made at all is revealing, since responsibility is never shrugged off for something of which one is proud. Sarnoff was wrong in his choice of preposition, if nothing else: The networks *are* responsible for what goes through the pipe, but they are not always responsible *about* it.

It does not take a philosopher to recognize that responsibility, as a social obligation, increases in direct proportion to capacity and power. But in the instance of the presidential election of 1980, broadcasters showed not the slightest interest in making concessions to western voters by delaying their projected victory for Reagan until the polls closed in California. On the other hand, these same broadcasters are generally willing to impose occasional blackouts at the request of government spokesmen or agencies. Notable exceptions have been *The New York Times* and Daniel Schorr, who in separate actions made history in the Vietnam epoch by refusing to suppress information they felt important for the public to know. Later Schorr reported that one Jerry Nachman, news director of San Francisco's radio station KCBS, proposed to black out a network newscast "so that the audience would not learn, before the delayed airing of a climactic *Dallas* episode, who had shot J.R."[5]

But then CBS, of which Nachman's KCBS is a member, set a standard of a kind when its then president, John A. Schneider, decided to cut away from live coverage of a vital senatorial debate on Vietnam policy to broadcast a fifth rerun of *I Love Lucy*, followed by an eighth rerun of *The Real McCoys*. (NBC meanwhile carried the hearing.) Schneider's decision triggered the resignation, in protest, of CBS News President Fred Friendly. It was one of the least proud hours of a network that had glittered in the Golden Age of Radio, the shortest golden age in history.

[5]In *Channels* magazine, August-September 1981.

3 ✑ Sports

The trivialization that tinctures newscasting is a contagion from the escapism that saturates television's general programming. Parlor games and sports are among the main pathogens. Undoubtedly they have their place, and this sorry old world would be a great deal drabber without them, but their place is not necessarily all over the dial at prime time. There are weekends in the football season when the sport practically takes over, with power of preemption if games go into overtime. Between pro and college matches, the viewer need never get out of his chair for the better part of a day except to fetch another beer or relieve himself of its consequences. On New Year's Day, the parade of bowl games begins early and ends late, stretching, like the old British Empire, across all time zones. And as though live football coverage were not enough, whole taped games are played back later, throughout the season, for those who may have missed them the first time around.

Then there are basketball, baseball and hockey, with their endless regional and national tournaments, and their playoffs followed by playoffs of playoffs; and after them come tennis, golf, boxing, swimming, diving, track and field events, surfing, yacht racing, horse racing, auto racing, bowling, soccer and so on down the line.

Sports are useful, and justify themselves in many ways, but they existed well before TV—as far back as, say, ancient Greece. And if the cameras were suddenly to be denied access to stadiums, courts and bowling alleys, sports would still flourish, although not as lucratively. But TV and radio, unlike the ball park and football stadium, have an obligation to serve more than sports fans. When sports are permitted to hog the listings, which they often do, they become trivial in the same way that too much of *any*thing becomes surfeit and loses importance and value as a commodity.

If such plethora were just a passing condition, like a glut of avocados on the market, it wouldn't be so bad. The avocados get eaten up, and the situation adjusts itself. But trivialization has a price: it can do measurable damage. Early in 1981, *60 Minutes* documented the case of schoolboys in the town of Belton, Texas, who had deliberately been held back for a full year in the seventh grade so that the school could field a bigger and stronger football team the next season. The principal of the school condoned this on camera, and so did the parents of some of the students. The whole thing was ungodly, especially since the Beltonians on the program projected themselves as God-fearing pursuers of the American dream. There was an unforgettable sequence showing the boys in a huddle just before the start of the game, with the coach leading his young gamecocks through the Lord's Prayer. Immediately after "for thine is the kingdom, and the power, and the glory forever, amen," the coach, without pause, shouted, "All right, guys, now go out there and beat their ass!" This inspirational summons was, if nothing else, ungrammatical. No team has a collective ass, unless it be a mascot, and in that case it could not be beaten without offending the A.S.P.C.A.

What these kids learned early, was the importance of winning. Over a two-year period it was their major course; it indoctrinated them in the prevalent philosophy of sports fans, players, coaches, impresarios and owners across the nation: WIN AT ANY COST. Win if you have to deck a batter, spike a second baseman, cripple a pass receiver, fire a manager, cheat on academic requirements, forge credentials, violate codes, retard the education of grammar-school children by holding them back. Ohio State's coach Woody Hayes was so passionate about winning that he punched a player of the opposing team for intercepting a pass. Arizona State's coach Frank Kush was more discreet—he punched one of his own players.[1] Even a nice-guy coach like Gerry Faust of Notre Dame wants to win so badly that a loss is deeply traumatic. "If we won," he said of his high school coaching days, "I took the night off and partied with the other guys. But if we lost, I wouldn't talk to anybody. I was so embarrassed I went right to bed." Like the coach at Belton, though with better language, Faust invoked divine assistance. In a game against Michigan (his first loss at Notre Dame), Faust called for a Hail Mary from the team (35 percent Protestant) before each half, and crossed himself three times before the kickoff.

Viciousness is not only condoned, it is prescribed in the must-win canon. Jim Wacker, coach at Texas Christian University, exhorted his team to play "smash-mouth" football.[2] Vince Lombardi, pro-football coach, had the formula. "Winning is not the main thing—it is the only thing." As the stakes get bigger, Lombardi's maxim becomes maximized until it functions at the highest levels of government. During the Watergate hearings, Attorney General John Mitchell was asked by Senator Herman Talmadge, "Am I to understand that you placed the expediency of the next election above your responsibilities as an intimate to advise the president of the peril that surrounded him? ... all around him were people involved in crime, perjury, accessory after the fact, and you

[1]Bob Oates in *The Los Angeles Times*, 9.25.81.

[2]Mike McGrady in "The Death of Class," *Newsday Magazine*, 1.13.85. In his text, McGrady italicized the *Christian* in the University's name.

deliberately refused to tell him that. [Was] the expediency of the election more important than that?"

Mitchell answered, "I think you have put it exactly correct. In my mind, the re-election of Richard Nixon, compared to what was available on the other side, was so much more important that I put it in just that context."[3]

Similarly, in the minds of the Belton principal, the football coach, and the parents, the expediency of a winning kids' football team was so much more important than the inexpediency of a losing one, that they too put it in just that context.

Normally the state of being a sports fan is not subject to misgivings. Most of the time it is a harmless condition, benign and even beneficial, for it arouses rooting interest, lets off steam, contributes to parochial or civic pride, and, except for games played indoors, gets one out in the open for a few hours. But when fans become obsessive, they shrink into a state of trivialization that can be awesome. An entry in the journal of the Society to Preserve and Encourage Radio Drama, Variety and Comedy, of May, 1979, contained the following appeal:

> I am looking for someone to tape and trade games involving professional and college football, baseball, basketball and hockey, with teams such as UCLA, Rams, USC, Dodgers, Angels, etc. I tape sports at 1⅞ ips, and usually put football games on 2400 [foot] reels. At present, I have several hundred complete games in my collection with Philadelphia teams as well as other games throughout the country.

Considering that new games come along in numbers resembling freeway traffic at rush hour, it is touching to think of a grown man on South 67th Street in Philadelphia, doggedly recording, dubbing and exchanging tapes of hundreds of old ones.

In addition to the tens of thousands of hours spent in transmitting standard sports, there are supplements which critic

---

[3]Nixon himself had said in 1968, "It is necessary for me to establish a winner image. Therefore, I have to beat somebody."—Quoted by Art Spiegleman and Bob Schneider in their book *Whole Grains*.

James Brown calls "trashsport events." One of them involved
contestants who tried to outdo each other at tossing tires or lifting
pickup trucks. Another, called *Challenge of the Sexes*, matched
male and female athletes in the spirit of the Bobby Riggs-Billie
Jean King tennis extravaganza. Brown described *Games People
Play* as

> no more insulting to the intelligence, than, say, any episode of
> *Three's Company* or, for perhaps a better frame of reference,
> *Roller Disco Invitational*. It's just that promoting foolishness
> and frivolity in the name of sports is becoming tiresome.
> Games that we used to play in the park or the backyard are now
> descended upon by television cameras, cloaked in an ultra-
> serious veneer of genuine competition, surrounded by real
> athletes for a little credibility and splashed out over the air like
> the seventh game of the World Series.

The hunger of rabid sports fans is so gnawing and endless, the
need to fill time between beer cans by looking on is so keen that
during the baseball strike of 1981, radio and television responded
to the crisis by broadcasting minor league games to major cities.
It takes dedication for a fan in Boston to follow a game between
Shreveport and Tulsa, but as the old saying almost goes, any
portsider in a storm. Electronic rescue missions filled the void
not only with live broadcasts out of Tidewater and Pawtucket, but
with tape replays of old games. Some newspapers printed play-by-.
play summaries and box scores of games completed twenty years
ago.

The strike was one of the strangest in the whole history of labor
relations. Athletes who were being paid more per day than the
average worker earns in a month, were pitted against owners
whose combined holdings could elect the next five presidents
with a few senatorial campaigns to spare. To insure against
hardship in just such a strike, the owners had covered themselves
with a fifty-million-dollar policy—on which they collected.

There had never been a lull like it in such a professional

commodity as baseball, and to many of the sport's aficionados, it was as though a plague had descended. The summer sun clouded over. Bitter letters showered down upon sports editors; fans sulked, grumbled, threatened to boycott the offenders when play resumed. At the start of the so-called second season, some stars were booed when they came to bat.

A year later, emboldened perhaps by the outcome of the baseball walkout, players of the National Football League went on a strike that lasted 57 days and wiped out half the season. The athletes wanted a decent cut of the $2.1 billion for television rights alone, stipulated in the League's 1982 contract with NBC, CBS and ABC. Again there was moaning and groaning by deprived fans, most of them incensed over the idea that players who were already well paid by blue collar standards should presume to demand shoulder-pad standards so much higher. Little rage was vented against the 28 club owners, but fulminations over having been abandoned by their heroes were expressed in hundreds of letters to editors; and when play resumed, there were symbolic patches of empty seats. For about two Sundays. By the time Super Bowl XVIII came around, the media had taken up the slack, the great hype engine was running again at full blast, and plethora was restored.

The orchestration was tremendous. Eighteen hundred credentialed reporters descended upon Pasadena from all over the country, 13 from *The Washington Post* alone. "Some wars get less coverage," wrote Mike Littwin in *The Los Angeles Times*. "A football game, yet."

When John Riggins, fullback for the Washington Redskins, held a press conference, it was as though a visiting Pope were in town.

> Reporters gathered around as if he were going to reveal a cure for cancer. They don't just gather, they jostle each other. sort of like football, overweight people crashing into other overweight people.

Riggins, like Tom Wolfe's astronauts, had the right stuff. Including the game, nine-and-a-half hours of sports programming was wrapped around Super Bowl XVIII on NBC alone. On the eve of the game Bob Hope presented an hour-long "Super Bowl Party." More than 100 million viewers tuned in for the kickoff.

In some quarters post-game excitement exceeded even the week-long buildup. *The Washington Post* next day carried a six-column headline across the top of its front page, and devoted more than half of that page, plus two full pages inside the news section, to the game. A patriotic advertiser took out a full-page ad featuring a formal group portrait of the Redskins under the legend, in letters an inch high, "The 'Skins capture hearts, minds of the Nation and its Capital." President Reagan's heart and mind were among those captured: not only did he telephone the Redskins coach in the locker room after the game, to banter about the similarity between the names of Reagan and Riggins, but he called next day for a celebration in the District, toward which 34,000 federal workers were granted a two-hour break, with pay, so that they could attend a parade in honor of the professionals. By the time of the parade, there already had been a celebration far bigger and more emotional than anything the capital had seen after a victorious war. Thousands of screaming revelers ran into the streets, hugging and kissing each other, throwing confetti, waving flares and pounding on cars and buses. Traffic came to a standstill in Georgetown, and in a four-block stretch of Pennsylvania Avenue; incoming traffic on Memorial and Key bridges was blocked. By midnight there wasn't a dent-free car to be seen within blocks of the intersection of Wisconsin Avenue and M Street.

Grown citizens were not only joyous, they were hysterical.

"We beat 'em, we beat 'em ... we're the champs," yelled Larry Overton, a school teacher from the District. ... Suddenly he burst into tears. "I have never ... I have never..." he sputtered. "The Redskins are the best thing we have in this town. Every week they try, they do their best and they deserve this."

Before the game, Littwin in Los Angeles had written that, "With the generous help of the nation's media, and with particular thanks to the TV folks, this game has taken on religious overtones." He was quickly corroborated when, on the day of celebration, a priest at the afternoon mass in St. Matthew's Cathedral in Washington, gave a sermon in which he drew an analogy between Jesus walking through crowds in Nazareth and Riggins smashing through tacklers. The priest, according to Blaine Harden in *The Washington Post*, then asked the worshipers to remember the Redskins in their prayers.

But the values of not all sports fans had been trivialized by sports hype. During the interregnums of both the baseball and football strikes, other fans, having had time to think of aspects wider than batting, fielding, earned run averages, yards gained and passes completed, wondered about certain social, ethical and economic ramifications of professional sports. Opinions that would have been howled down as heretical in times of peace, suddenly began to appear in print. Questions were asked: How is it that owners boldly demand, and often get, stadiums built out of public funds, and then go on to make fortunes, using the facilities but never returning a mil of their millions to the taxpayers?[4]

How is it that the press, which levies lordly advertising rates against other entertainment industries—stage, film, music, the dance, etc.—gives acres of free space to sports—space that often includes front-page position? (On October 23, 1981, *The Los Angeles Times* ran 32 pages of sports, 16 of them on the World Series alone). A too-easy answer is that unlike movies and theater, boxing, baseball, football, basketball and hockey are *contests*; they exercise strength, speed, skill and body contact: they create their own pantheons and stock them with gods. It still does not

[4]Yankee Stadium was refurbished for $100 million at taxpayers' expense, to keep the New York Yankees in the Bronx. The Los Angeles Dodgers did very nicely in their deal with the city for occupancy of Chavez Ravine. The Oakland Raiders, in 1982, were granted a "loan" of $6.7 million to move to the L.A. Coliseum, but the Coliseum later said that the loan was never intended to be repaid.

explain the vast disproportion in volume of publicity between the freebie status of sports and the pay-as-you-go requirements of just about everything else. This imbalance is increased by the avid complicity of radio and television, as voluntary marketing instruments for major sports—with, however, an important difference: the newspaper reader, in the time it takes to flip a page, can skip the sports section altogether, whereas the TV viewer has no such option. If the only, or the most legible, channel in the area happens to be carrying a sportscast at the time he tunes in, he may have to wait three hours before he can turn the equivalent of a page. And if the game runs over the anticipated length, it has right of way: whatever is scheduled behind it must yield.

A cartoon in the *Saturday Review* showed a man sitting in front of a TV set, beer can in hand, cigar in mouth, looking with utter astonishment at an announcement on the screen:

THE

TELECAST OF

TODAY'S FOOTBALL

GAME WILL BE

DELAYED UNTIL

THE COMPLETION

OF THE SYMPHONY

PROGRAM

The plaint of that cartoonist, of *60 Minutes*, of the letter-writers, is not against any sport *per se*, nor against watching games on the tube. No sport is trivial when it entertains millions of people and employs thousands of others in activities far superior to manufacturing poison gas, advertising cigarettes or making porno movies. Again, it comes down to quantification. Not for nothing did Cervantes coin the phrase, "Too much of a good thing." Plethora is never healthful. In medicine, the term means a morbid condition characterized by too much blood in the body. In television, it is often too much blood and guts. In sports, it's too much exposure in relation to the rest of the body politic.

The once stirring mottos "Remember the Alamo" and "Remember the *Maine*" long ago passed beyond applicability and usefulness. Today the cry might be "Remember Belton!"

4 ✑ Guesses and Giveaways

Sports are only one of the voltaic piles that generate teletrivia. Others, just as tireless, are the *non*-athletic games—tune-guessing, price-matching, blind-dating and all the rest. Innocent enough fun, and enjoyed by enough people to warrant their existence—but so many games? Played so persistently? At the time of this writing, *Family Feud* was being broadcast on the NBC channel in Los Angeles not once a week, but five times a week.

Giveaway programs in general are like sweet-flavored gelatinous cultures on which greed and hysteria colonize like bacteria. The hysteria is visible to the viewer, but the greed is not so obvious. Not lightly to be forgotten are the quiz scandals of the late 50's, which ended in grand jury indictments. There have been no frauds since then (at least none has been disclosed), but big money, princely prizes, paroxysms of delight at winning, childlike dismay at guessing wrong answers to fribbling questions, tears, shrieks, kisses, ringing bells, rasping buzzers, hours of production and transmission, all come together to fill the public's time with pablum.

Then there are the formula melodramas, exercises in brawn, conspicuous consumption of ammo, auto chases, beatings, knifings, corpses. To the extent that all this is repetitious and predictable, that subtlety is rarer than chateaubriand on a poor man's table, that any useful significance or relation to our lives is nil, these programs, too, classify as trivia.

Even many of the so-called "specials," whose specialness implies relief from run-of-the-milieu programming, tend to follow well-worn paths, and in doing so become as predictable in their way as *Laverne and Shirley* and *Charlie's Angels*. They keep coming almost interchangeably over the seasons: *Bob Hope in China, Perry Como's Hawaiian Holiday, Tennessee Ernie Ford in Moscow, Steve Edwards and Melody Rogers in Dublin, Dean Martin's California Christmas*. The *déja vu* of commercial televison accumulates very quickly, because the industry relies on safely repeatable formulas. Responsibility for content is passed on to viewers with the familiar shrug, "That's what they want to watch." Naturally cliché programming flourishes in this environment and is in no danger of reform, since television is the most insensitive of the media to criticism, the most intractable when it comes to numbers-versus-quality, and the most assiduous in applying Gresham's law, by which the bad drives out the good.

Critic Cecil Smith, deploring the resignation from a particular network series of three gifted people (a writer, a director and a producer) because of interference from memoranda-dispatchers who pressed them for higher ratings, fired a broadside at the chancellery:

> When network executives, mostly lawyers and computer ex-
> perts and advertising salesmen who couldn't create a fire with a
> mountain of matches, drive out the creative people whose work
> occasionally flickers on the tube, we shouldn't wonder that we
> have so low a level of bland and lifeless television.

Conscionable TV critics of Smith's outlook have a trickier task than their colleagues in other media, for they are the only members of their genus who find themselves often having to criticize on two levels simultaneously—the artistic and the cultural. Judges of music, painting, literature, the legitimate stage, the dance, even of cinema, are much less frequently obliged to speak of the sociological ramifications of the works they review, of the ambience in which these works are conceived, or of the processes by which they are produced and exhibited.

For years critics like Smith tried to help raise a reluctant dinosaur from its flounderings in a self-perpetuating swamp by speaking out for the kind of television that Edward R. Murrow had in mind when he warned, "The instrument can teach, it can illuminate; yes, and it can even inspire. But it can do so only to the extent that humans are determined to use it to these ends. Otherwise it is merely lights and wires in a box."

Since Murrow voiced that caution a generation ago, the concern of critics has been that the instrument not only did not teach, illuminate and inspire, but that it has too often done nearly the opposite: lowered cultural tastes, promoted numbing escapism and discouraged originality.

Max Beerbohm, successor to George Bernard Shaw on the drama desk of the London *Saturday Review*, believed that not every art can hope to acquire good critics:

> An art sunk in the slough of incompetence, will cry in vain to good critics to rescue it.

However, this was written just after the turn of the century, when television was not yet in Vladimir Zworykin's thoughts. Were Beerbohm around today, he would no doubt acknowledge that the art of television, as manipulated by the lawyers, accountants, computer experts and advertising men of Smith's notice, cries out for good critics *not* to rescue it, but to leave it alone. They don't *want* to be rescued: they like it the way it is. Good critics are anathema in such circles. The industry prefers reviewers who will go along with the herds and the ratings. Smith's administrators (there are good ones, too, who are not included in his sweep, but they form a minority) are impatient with challenges to the numbers derby and they are unmoved by critical lamentations when a superb program like *Love Among the Ruins* ends up in

Siberia. They are deaf to shouts of anger because the powerful rating system, that much controverted and often suspect rat race of percentages, remains the chief agency by which mediocrity addicts are made and reared and sustained.

Broadcasters are invariably miffed by criticism of their product and practices, and they protest just as invariably that they are only giving people what they want. But the people have been conditioned to want what they want mainly by years of having gotten what they have gotten.

5 ✑ Print

If teletrivia did not flourish at the expense of the traditional arts, and if it did not crowd out serious work, there would be no chorus of deplorers. But it has chomped its way steadily into other media. One would think that the natural enemies of TV, the media most directly threatened by the tube at its outset and hurt by it over the years, would have resisted taking on the coloration of their common adversary. But press and cinema, having been unable to lick it, joined it. The big screen and the printed page showed themselves capable of prodigies of trivialization.

But then the press has been around much longer than competing media, and complaints about newspaper frippery antedate video. Irving Babbitt, educator, grumbled back in the 20's that "whole forests are being ground into pulp daily to minister to our triviality." Newspaper editors have been defined as "men who separate the wheat from the chaff and then print the chaff." For a scathing comment on the preoccupation of the press with crumbs of information, it would be hard to find a passage livelier than one in Tom Wolfe's *The Right Stuff*, a book about the training and careers of American astronauts. He describes a

descent of reporters on astronauts' wives who were waiting at
home while their husbands orbited in space:

> They came crawling in through windows like ravenous ter-
> mites, like fruit flies, taking pictures and yelling questions ...
> the monster Small-Talk Tea of all times ... they wanted a
> moan, a tear, some twisted features, a few inside words from
> friends, any goddammed thing ... Give us anything! ...
> They're interviewing the dog, the cat, the rhododendrons.

It reads like a line in a poem by Karl Shapiro, written ten years
earlier: "They used to come to me, these journalists with humble
pencils. They begged me from their hats: say something big: give
us an execution: make bad weather."

God knows there is sensation enough in legitimate news.
Hardly a day goes by without somebody somewhere saying
something big or making bad weather. But when rhododendrons
and poets are pressed for headlines, then trivialization-by-
magnification is in progress, and the effect is as unwholesome as
any other kind of inflation.

Within three months in 1981, two reporters and a columnist
on three major newspapers were fired because of fabrications or
unsupported accusations. First was a story about an eight-year-old
heroin addict, published by the *Washington Post* and awarded a
Pulitzer Prize in journalism. It turned out to be fiction. Here the
reporter, unlike Wolfe's ravenous horde, did not solicit a moan, a
tear or some twisted features from actual persons; she invented
her own. Second was a yarn about a confrontation between street
youths in Belfast and a British army patrol, which took place only
in the imagination of a columnist for the *New York Daily News*.
This newsman reached into his hat for the kind of event Shapiro
called an execution. In Toronto, which is American by prox-
imity, a reporter for the *Toronto Sun* wrote an exposé charging
that a member of the prime minister's cabinet had profited from
stock manipulations through tips from inside the government. It
was a sensational disclosure, except that there was no proof to
back it up.

In these cases there was a form of retribution, and damage was confined to the embarrassment of writers, publishers and the Pulitzer Prize committee; but how many undiscovered, un-acknowledged or un-redressed breaches of ethics happen all the time? And the object of each of these is usually sensation. Scoop. The making big out of little or nothing. There are heavy precedents for this in journalism, such as one symbolized by William Randolph Hearst's message to the illustrator Frederic Remington. Remington had been sent to Cuba to draw war pictures, in anticipation of an outbreak of hostilities between the United States and Spain. The artist arrived in Cuba, looked around, and cabled Hearst, "Everything is quiet. There is no trouble here. There will be no war. Wish to return." Hearst cabled back, "Please remain. You furnish the pictures and I'll furnish the war." And the publisher proceeded to do just that, to the best of his ability as jingoist. And when after a ten-week war Spain surrendered Cuba, the Philippines and Puerto Rico, Hearst's *New York Journal* bragged "HOW DO YOU LIKE THE JOURNAL'S WAR?"

Each time there has been a wave of political reaction in America, as in the glory days of Senators Joseph P. McCarthy and Pat McCarran, the press by and large contributed to the amplitude and force of the wave by trumpeting each whistle-stop speech and circulating irresponsible charges and smears like cheap currency. The misdemeanors of journalism got so bad in the late 40's that a Commission of Freedom of the Press, subsidized by the *Encyclopaedia Britannica* and Henry Luce, came to the sorry conclusion that the press of America

> can play down the news and its significance, foster and feed emotions, create complacent fictions and blind spots, misuse the great words, and uphold empty slogans ... these instru-ments can spread lies faster and farther than our forefathers dreamed when they enshrined the freedom of the press in the First Amendment to our Constitution ... the press can be inflammatory, sensational and irresponsible....

Some of the particulars in this indictment translate easily to trivialization, in such phrases as "play [up or] down the news" and "uphold empty slogans"—again, the familiar patterns of making much of nothing, or reducing a forest to a tree. But it should be said that reduction by condensation is not necessarily part of the trivializing process, as long as the residue, the essence, respects the truth. No one expects a reporter to perform like a witness under oath by telling the truth, the whole truth, and nothing but the truth, if only because the whole truth might run too long. Quantification cannot always be avoided, especially in the face of limitations of space, and, because of this, sheer proportion sometimes may interfere with so-called objective reporting. Lester Markel of *The New York Times* believed no form of reporting could be totally objective, and argued his case with numbers:

> The reporter, the most objective reporter, collects 50 facts. Out of the 50 he selects 12 to include in his story ... thus he discards 38. This is Judgment Number One.
>
> Then the reporter or editor decides which of the facts shall be the first paragraph of the story, thus emphasizing one fact above the other 11. This is Judgment Number Two.
>
> Then the editor decides whether the story shall be placed on Page One or Page Twelve; on Page One it will command many times the attention it would on Page Twelve. This is Judgment Number Three.
>
> This so-called factual presentation is thus subject to three judgments, all of them most humanly and most ungodly made.

But again, this is not necessarily a trivializing process, any more than the selection of elements in the composition of a painting or a photograph trivializes. *Something* has to be left out, unless you are painting a mural, and even then the subject might not all be contained. It is when the omissions are biased, when the order of paragraphs purposely plays up or down, when the story is buried on page 64 under a corset ad with intent to diminish, or displayed with a flourish on the front page with intent to aggrandize, when objectivity is forsworn and truth dishonored, that journalism, which is one of the few congenitally ethical professions, and which has its own long Hippocratic tradition of duties and obligations, is reduced to small change.

6 ✐ Music and Laughter

If the press is given to bursts of small talk and newscasters prattle on and there are endless feasts of sports, games and trashsports, surely other avenues of communication, other media—art, music, literature—are safe from the nibblings and discounts of trivialization?

Take music, and the uses to which it is put. Muzak—the very name is a corruption—comes to mind at once, because it is the biggest, richest, most pervasive of all forms of musical presentment. It is a $400,000,000-annual-income industry and enjoys 80 million listeners in 26 countries. Except that the operators of Muzak prefer not to call them listeners. "We want people to hear, but not to listen," said a Muzak spokesman.

And the people hear everywhere. Muzak is piped into homes, offices, department stores, beauty parlors, dentists' offices, the Bank of America, General Motors, a henhouse in San Bernardino, the cardiac ward at St. Joseph Hospital in New York, the Bronx Zoo, grand jury rooms, prisons, the Pentagon, the Astrodome, a 39-floor high-rise cemetery in Rio de Janeiro, 103 medical institutions in Los Angeles, elevators, workshops, and Grand Central Station. Neil Armstrong and his companions heard it in the space capsule before setting foot on the moon. A brothel in Stuttgart requested the "light industrial program" (one of four offered by Muzak—others are office, public area and travel programs.) Muzak has dwelt in marble halls: it edified both Richard M. Nixon's White House and his Key Biscayne quarters.

Piped music (though not Muzak's) even pursues ships at sea. On a cruise to Alaska, I had looked forward to being soothed by the sounds of wind and wave and by the grand mutterings of the ship itself; but no, along the promenade deck was a steady mewling from loudspeakers deployed at frequent intervals so you wouldn't have to miss a beat.

The four "programs" presented by Muzak are made up of miscellaneous musical numbers, but the system is far from hit-or-miss. Tunes are dispatched in 15-minute segments; the service to office and factory workers heightens its "stimulus" quotient throughout a 24-hour day "to increase productivity and efficiency, making the unassuming masses—secretaries, clerks and factory workers—work faster. Simon Legree to the tune of 'Tea For Two.'"[1]

"I hate to use the expression," said a marketing vice-president of Muzak, "but we are human engineers." And a colleague of his, an executive vice-president of one of the company's 283 nation-wide franchises, explained, "A company's ... profit depends on only one thing—the output of your people. And if you want more profit you've got to make your people more efficient. In this way Muzak functions as management's tool."

Not all of the 80 million hearers can be relied on to be unassuming and easily engineered. A dean of music called the product "pallid pap that will rot our musical teeth out." Robert Lippold, sculptor, objected to Muzak flooding the area when one of his works was exhibited at the Pan Am building in New York. The objection was overruled by Pan Am.[2] A passenger sitting next to me on a Boeing 747 demanded that some highly

[1]Mary Murphy, "Muzak Makers' Creed: Hear, Don't Listen," *The Los Angeles Times*, 2.26.74.
[2]Cited in *The People's Almanac*, by David Wallechinsky and Irving Wallace, Doubleday, 1975.

expendable music[3] be cut off while the craft was on the runway waiting in line—a long wait—for takeoff. One of Muzak's own officers volunteered, "We know of no value of Muzak to a self-thinking or creative person . . . we [an associate and himself] don't use background music per se. If we need stimulating, the company is in trouble. We have it in our offices because it is our product, but we can and do turn it off. The only time we recommend it for executives is to cover up conversation. Say we are talking about salaries and we don't want the girls to hear. . . ."[4]

Whatever else it may be—stimulus, tranquilizer, aural nipple, tool of executives, Muzak is basically trivializing. It is not simply that it relegates music to the province of wallpaper. Background music need never be banal. When it is used in support of drama, it can greatly enhance without harming itself. Mozart was entirely amenable to such films as *Elvira Madigan* and *The French Lieutenant's Woman*; Ralph Vaughan Williams wrote aptly for *The Invaders*, Arnold Bax for *Oliver Twist*, Sergei Prokofiev for *Lieutenant Kije* and *Alexander Nevsky*, Dmitri Shostakovich for others. In such uses, music collaborates with artists, it becomes an art among arts. But Muzak collaborates chiefly with management: it is used as an aural smoke-screen, a form of jamming, a hormone in henhouses, an emollient in cemeteries. And millions hear. No wonder a senior student, a not unintelligent 22-year-old, came up to me at the end of a class in a university and asked, "What is an opera?" He had never heard the term, much less an opera or a part of one. Muzak is not to blame for his ignorance, but a smokescreen may obscure more landscape than is intended.

Muzak is not the only musical tool of management. Would that it were. There are also singing and instrumental commercials. Themes of the great composers, melodic lines, harmonic progressions, are made part of the sales force; they are given words and transformed into messages from sponsors. When the United

---

[3]Actually Muzak does not service planes or ships. These are independent systems.
[4]Mary Murphy, loc.cit.

States Marines lifted the tune of their marching song ("From the Halls of Montezuma to the Shores of Tripoli") straight out of an opera by Jacques Offenbach, they at least had the decency to steal the whole thing, and the result was admirable and stirring. It has always made me want to enlist. But Schubert, Mozart, Beethoven, Tschaikowsky, are used in no such edifying ways. They are not swiped in toto, like a stolen car. Instead they are minced, they are molested. The film *2001* gave unprecedented circulation to an imposing motif from Strauss's *Thus Spake Zarathustra*, whereupon, soon afterward, the same stern chords, now having become popular, were used in at least four radio commercials that I know of, the products ranging from fried chicken to real estate. Chloraseptic Mouthwash made earwash of the opening measures of Bach's *Toccata and Fugue in D*, and Gallo Wines helped itself to a Mozart horn concerto.

As for the singing commercial, maybe custom reconciles us to everything, but it is hard to know whether to chuckle or groan at the thought of tens of millions of adults being sung at routinely, as though we were little children learning our ABC's. The simple melody to "A-B-C-D-E-F-G" makes it easier for tots to remember what we want them to remember, and you may be sure that that principle has not been lost on advertisers. But how absurd, after all, that grown men and women should be persuaded by jingles to buy a product. We would never tolerate someone *introducing* himself to us musically, and we would be alarmed if a salesman in our home or office suddenly burst into song as he tried to unload on us an insurance policy or a set of encyclopedias. Yet we permit this to go on electronically in our living rooms and bedrooms all the time. Is it just that being an *audience* does that to us? If that is true, then it's especially sad when measured against Walt Whitman's precept that great audiences make great poets.

The revilers of classic-busting commercials number many more than those who chafe at Muzak, but except for a few grumblings in print there is general lethargy and acquiescence.

However, a man in Chicago showed what a single dissident can do. Richard Wyszynski became so irked by what he called "grubby bastardization" of classical themes that he took action on hearing a passage from Ravel's String Quartet played as background for a radio pitch by York Furriers. He wrote a letter to the president of the company, a man whose name, by one of those ironies that make life worth living, was Richard Wagner. Two months passed without an acknowledgment, so Wyszynski fired again:

> Maurice Ravel did not labor in order to serve Gamzo Advertising or York Furriers, and you are entitled to use not a fraction of his work—not to mention the efforts of the performers in recording. ... I speak from a position of ethics and justice.

A month later he heard from an executive of Gamzo Advertising, which handled the Furrier account:

> Any speculation about how Mr. Ravel would or would not consider the use of his music is exactly that—speculation.

For a year there were further exchanges, in the course of which Wyszynski drew support from Ravel's music custodians in Paris and his publishers in America. Eventually the furrier commercial went off the air. It was impossible to say whether Wyszynski's campaign was responsible, since so much time had passed, but in another instance there was a clear victory. It seems that Central Furniture Mart, also of Chicago, offered furniture specials over television to music from Gustav Holst's *The Planets*. This music, unlike Ravel's, was not in the public domain, so Wyszynski alerted Holst's publishers and heirs in London, and Central Furniture was obliged to pay a fee.[5]

Being sung at by salesmen, sometimes sweetly and soulfully, at other times *con brio*, is, at bottom, demeaning both to salesman and customer. So is the simple-minded mini-drama in which a friend or neighbor or kindly philosopher urges a model to Try It.

[5]Reported by Gary Deeb, in "One Man's Classic Battle," *Chicago Sun-Times*, 8.20.81.

Then comes swift revelation: the headache is cured, the stubborn laundry stain erased, the unstable denture held in a grip of steel.

Of course there are many more ways in which audiences are trivialized. Every day of the year, a thousand times a day, canned laughter is fed into America's loudspeakers. It comes from a laugh machine, and is measured by lengths of audio tape—small jollity, medium jollity, jumbo jollity, graded like olives and shunted into the sound track by a solemn man who is paid for sitting at the console of the machine and pressing keys. TV sees to it that none of its comedy goes unappreciated. Prefabricated mirth is supplied along with other elements of production. Sid Caesar said that some of the laughter heard on TV programs today comes from people who have been dead since 1953.

Marvin Kitman of *Newsday* tells of a "sweetening" session, at a moment of which, on the screen, an actor came into a room. That was all—he just entered. To improve the action, the operator of the laugh machine assigned a titter. A fellow worker objected, "There's nothing funny about that." "Yeah," replied the operator, "but he had a funny look on his face."

Arnold Stang, comedian, recalls sitting in a control room with Milton Berle during a similar embroidering. Berle felt that a particular joke needed a Number 4 laugh, but the risibility expert argued it was not that hilarious. Berle insisted on it. When the program was screened the next day and the joke came along, it was garnished with hearty Number 4 laughter. "See, what did I tell you?" Berle beamed. "I knew it was funny."

Trivialization is seldom illuminated by statistics, but Kitman cited some for·canned laughter:

> Statistically, while shows seem to get less funny every year, the number of laughs seems to be increasing. Shows today contain more laughs per minute (LPMs). Neil Simon gets about two LPMs (the record is 4.1) when he's hot, and he's a very funny man. Sitcom LPMs regularly go higher than Simon's, even when they're not funny.

Where do they get the people who do all the laughing? Originally, the laughs came from an Eddie Cantor radio-show audience recorded in 1938. My friend Al had an uncle who attended the show and was [later] heard on a thousand television programs. I could recognize his laugh. His was the one that sounded like a hyena. Al used to tell him he should try to get residuals every time they had him on a show.

Studio audiences attending radio and television comedy shows are inducted in a ritual known as the warm-up, which is as much an exercise in wheedling and coaxing as the commercials which follow in due time. The commercial is designed to reduce sales resistance; the warmup, to reduce laugh resistance. The bodies in the seats are living applause machines. They are not trusted by the producers to respond without priming, or to applaud spontaneously. Hence the ceremony of holding up applause cards.

It is unthinkable that an audience at a stage play or a movie could be worked on by a pitchman in advance of the curtain going up, or before the screening of a main title. If the soundtrack of a film dared to simulate audience laughter, the live audience would pelt the screen; it would resent the notion that the perception and enjoyment of comedy had to be done for it, like an infant having to be fed. Again it comes down to reduction, to a dwarfing process which contributes, if only slightly, to an erosion of morale, to a pinching of our national spirit. Adlai Stevenson once put a question to *The Wall Street Journal*: "With the supermarket as our temple, and the singing commercial as our litany, are we likely to fill the world with an irresistible vision of America's purpose and inspiring way of life?"

If one thinks that the broadcasting industry, with its apparent conviction that the audience is 14 years of age (and a not very bright 14 at that), is alone in its tendency to treat us like simpletons, then it is even more sobering to look around at some of the other arts. The graphic arts, for example.

7 ✑ Art

For the canonization of soup cans, thank Andy Warhol. For the canonization of Warhol, thank doting patrons and matrons of art who will put anything on their walls and pay well for it providing it has been played up enough in the media, bruited enough by bushwhacking critics and connoisseurs, and touted enough by dealers and curators.

Conspicuous among Warhol's *oeuvres* are *Soup Cans*, 16 replicated images of Campbell's soup cans: *Coke Bottles*, 121 of them; *Two-Dollar Bills*, 80 arrayed in four columns; *Car Crash*, 25 duplications of a smash-up; *White Disaster*, 5 exposures of an overturned and burning car (big painting—6 by 9 feet); *Green Disaster*, another car crash, even larger; *Jackie*, 35 identical portraits of Jacqueline Kennedy; a grid of seven-cent airmail stamps; a cluster of 20 repeated Marilyn Monroes; two braces of Mona Lisa; three overlapping Elvis Presleys. These are the principal fly's eye renderings in Warhol's *catalogue raisonné*, and they are not without interest, just as the graphic stuttering of a defective television tube has a certain abstract appeal, unless you are trying to tune in something.

But just as the eye instinctually acts to create form out of formlessness, as when we resolve the shape of a ship or a shoe out of a drifting cloud, so do we tend to ascribe meaning to replications of explicitly representational images. Surely, we figure, there must be a *point* to 121 Coke bottles in seven tidy rows. Was Warhol being scornful of the imperialism of Coca-Cola, whose sign is everywhere in the world? Did his 35 Jackies express criticism of a too-muchness in the lady, at least at the time he painted it? Did the white and green *Disaster* series protest slaughter on the highways? Was his grim *Electric Chairs* (15 of them) a cry against capital punishment? Was his *Race Riot* a voice raised in the struggle for human rights?

Had Warhol kept silent on these questions, or let his interpreters take over as he usually does, it might have been possible to relate such motives and rationales. But the artist himself set us straight, in a discussion with Claes Oldenburg, Roy Lichtenstein and Bruce Glaser in 1964:

> OLDENBURG (to Warhol): When I see you repeating a race riot I am not sure you have done a race riot. I don't see it as a political statement but rather as an expression of indifference to your subject.
> WARHOL: It is indifference.
> GLASER: Isn't it significant that you choose that particular photograph [on which to base the painting] rather than a thousand others?
> WARHOL: It just caught my eye.
> OLDENBURG: You didn't deliberately choose it because it was a "hot" photograph?
> WARHOL: No.

With admirable frankness in one of his own books, Warhol writes: "If you want to know all about Andy Warhol, just look at the surface of my films and paintings and me, and there I am. There's nothing behind it." He alludes, without pique or resentment, to a critic who called him "the Nothingness Himself." His credo on art does not take up much space: "Making money is art and working is art and good business is the best art." He describes his films as "just a way of taking up time." Thus quantification becomes unavoidable: multiple images, scores of them, add up to saying nothing; art is minified and so is the artist.

However one may define the genre of minimalism, trivialization is in the mix, and in good measure. The minimalists have defenders, of course, who flourish alongside their clients, but no small weight of responsible criticism is against them. Harold Rosenberg, in *Art on the Edge*, writes:

> For Warhol [art] is part of ... self-projection ... something to do for gain. By the force of his indifference, Warhol strips painting and sculpture of any shred of transcendence ... he is the prophet of the minimalist art ... that [seeks] to allude to nothing beyond itself. He gives dramatic clarification to minimalism by minimizing the artist, too, and the world he inhabits.

But if Warhol, in his talented and sometimes disarming way (one can enjoy his audacity, mild outrageousness and anarchic flair, just as one can like Chinese acrobats or a well-executed caper in which nobody is hurt and the victim is a piratical monopoly), makes no claims for himself, his apologists are not nearly so bland, and by their divagations and rationalizations they contribute to the trivializing cycle. Peter Gidal, in his book *Andy Warhol Films and Paintings*, writes:

> The Campbell soup cans remain the hardest of Warhol's works to come to terms with because they still seem so meaningless ... and this is a challenge in a world where every fifth-rate television show claims for itself universal truths. ... The repetition of the image leads to exciting moments which are unanticipated in the pure concept of the piece. The differences brought about by the handling make smudges, colour variations, etc., of importance. By thus illuminating the small moments, Warhol escaped from the gutter of obvious meaning in large statements ... and found for himself a niche which in its alienated subtlety is second to none.[1]

[1]*Andy Warhol Films and Paintings*, Peter Gidal, p. 27.

It is a familiar pattern—aggrandizement by denigration of someone or something else, a process we will take up later in some detail. Down with large statements of obvious meaning, up with smudges and color variations. Down with telecasts which claim universal truths, up with Warhol's niche.

Warhol as prophet is not without honor in his own house and country. No matter that, in the words of critic Robert Mazzocco, his work is "without morals or manners, mindlessly banal" and "haphazardly corrupt"; that in its "deadpan sanctification of the billboard and the detergent," among other facets of his products, "you see clearly that a cultural gutter has been reached." Never mind any of that, he is a celebrity, and celebrity is what counts up front.

"Some company recently was interested in buying my 'aura,'" Warhol wrote in 1975. "They didn't want my product. They kept saying, 'We want your aura.' I never figured out what they wanted. But they were willing to pay a lot for it."

They were still willing to pay a lot six years later, even though the aura had faded somewhat by then. In *The New Yorker* of October 12, 1981, there appeared a full-page advertisement of Sony's Beta videotape. It starred Warhol standing behind a giant television monitor on whose tube was displayed a reproduction of one of his portrait-prints—three times life size—of Marilyn Monroe. Warhol is looking straight at the reader, frowning under his shock of very blond hair. In one hand he holds upright a cassette of Sony L-500 Tape, label forward. Beneath the photo is the legend:

ANDY WARHOL GETS PICTURE-PERFECT PICTURES
WITH SONY BETA TAPE.

and beneath that:

Andy Warhol, pop artist par excellence, looked slightly askance when we told him we'd like to transfer one of his "Marilyn" prints onto Sony Beta tape and it would come out a Picture-Perfect Picture.

After all, every one of his prints shows incredible attention to color and subtle tonal relationships. And its hard to imagine any video tape reproducing his vibrant colors perfectly.

But that's exactly what Sony Beta tapes do...

Big business knows its friends, and Warhol is one of them. In the days of Maecenas, the Sforzas and the Borgias, princely support was given to favorite artists, but no heralds were sent abroad to trumpet their celebrity. Today's sponsors, when they have pets in the performing or graphic arts, keep their mutual identities, images and celebrity alive through publicity. In this way General Electric was instrumental in preserving Ronald Reagan through the years when his B-picture skills were not enough to keep him on the casting lists in Hollywood.

But nobody understands better than Warhol himself the magnetic pull of celebrity. In another of his bursts of candor, he wrote:

> Nowadays if you are a crook you're still considered up-there. You can write a book, go on TV, give interviews—you're a big celebrity and nobody even looks down on you because you're a crook. You're still really up-there. This is because more than anything people just want stars.[2]

Warhol of course was not classifying himself as a crook among crooks, just as a star among stars. In that role he has plenty of admirers among the laity. And plenty of company in his profession, too, although few minimalists are as mini-minded as he in attitude, work and philosophy.

Roy Lichtenstein is Plato by comparison. Though Lichtenstein's work also has a stereotyped quality and is openly derivative ("as prepackaged as a cliché," in the words of a friendly commentator), he does not agree with Warhol that good business is the best art, and in fact is critical of public-relations façades:

[2]*The Philosophy of Andy Warhol (From A to B & Back Again)*, by Andy Warhol, Harcourt Brace Jovanovich, 1975.

Most of our communication, somehow or other, is governed by advertising, and they are not too careful about how they tend to instruct us. I think that may have a deadening effect on the minds of people ... it has made, in a way, a new landscape for us ... all this stuff that we're very familiar with, literature and television, radio. So that almost all of our environment seems to be made up partially of a desire to sell products.

Lichtenstein was aware, as Warhol seemed not to be, of the limitations of Pop art, of its affinity for shallowness. "It was hard," he said, "to get a painting that was despicable enough so that no one would hang it—everybody was hanging everything. It was almost acceptable to hang a dripping paint rag." Asked if he thought Pop art itself was despicable, he replied, "Well, it *is* an involvement of what I think to be the most brazening and threatening characteristics of our culture, things we hate but which are also powerful in their impingement upon us."

Nevertheless, as though drawn by the very power of "things we hate," Lichtenstein, for all the skill of his bold brush, remained earthbound. His subjects alone were enough to keep him from taking off: a ringing telephone, with "R-R-R-R-Ring!" spelled out; a closed door, with "KNOCK KNOCK" printed across it; blown up comic-strip characters; an automobile tire; a sock; a spray can; the cover of a composition book; a ball of twine; an electric cord; a sofa; a golf ball; a pointing finger. Most of these are drawn starkly and simply, in heavy outline, without background or shading—minimal to the core. Again, questions: Is he kidding? Are these stunts, like Warhol's eight-hour movie of a sleeping man and his equally slumbrous four-hour study of the top of the Empire State building? Stunts like swallowing 210 live goldfish at one sitting, which was actually done by one of the record-holders in the Guinness book? If Lichtenstein, like Oldenburg with his soft-sculpture toilets, hamburgers and typewriters, and his massive clothespin, standing flashlight, covey of metallic hats, and Giant Cigarette Butts; if Rauschenberg with his stuffed eagles and winged Coca-Cola bottles—if they deliberately created kitsch in order to satirize America's taste for kitsch, then their comment, if not the canvases and sculptures themselves, are exhibits in the case of the United States versus trivialism.

A mirror which repeats spray cans and socks and sculptural hamburgers may be superbly polished, it may be wrought by Cellini and silvered by Revere, but for all that it still reflects trivia.

8 ✑ Trivia Onside and Off

Do house flies breed in Alaska? (No.)

Why does one's reflection in a spoon appear upside down? (Because the concave part acts as a lens.)

What is the meaning of *Biz 'em pupik?* (I've had it up to the navel. Yiddish.)

Can one throw a quysshen? (Yes. It's a 16th-century cushion.)

Can contact lenses be fitted to apotropaic eyes? (Not very well. In Greek art, the apotropaic eye was painted on the prow of a boat to ward off evil spirits.)

What does the "S" in Harry S. Truman stand for? (Nothing. It stood only for the letter itself, and at first Truman didn't even put a period after it.)

Alors. Do you feel any better for knowing these scraps? There are a million others where those came from, and they come at us all the time, for Americans are the most curious people on earth. Never before has information—most of it useless—been such a popular commodity that it makes fortunes for people who assemble and package it as entertainment in books, TV and radio programs, and parlor games. The circulation figures, audience ratings and royalties deriving from *The People's Almanac, The Book of Lists* and their sequels, *Hollywood Squares, The $25,000*

73

Pyramid, The Guinness Book of Records, The $64,000 Question, Information, Please! and, before them, *Uncle Jim's Question Bee, True or False?, Whiz Quiz, Winner Take All,* and on into the far ranges of encyclopedia country, are such as to suggest that America affords the world's happiest hunting grounds for trivial data.

But paradoxically this constant ferment of Q-and-A does not represent a true thirst for knowledge among the masses who watch games on the tube and devour the almanacs. In books, it is the tingle of the exotic that counts, the mild indulgences of astonishment. What matters in TV and radio games is the match-up, the contest, not the substance. The information dispensed makes for scattered and fragmentary knowledge at best, and much of it is freakish and tricky. (Q: Which is farther north—Venice, Italy, or Vladivostok, Siberia? A: Venice.) Very little of this sticks to the ribs. After all, whom does it profit besides ornithologists or ichthyologists to know whether canaries live in the wild state, or that the smallest fish, the goby, seldom grows longer than a half-inch. Ours is not a particularly knowledgeable era, notwithstanding the waves of information that are constantly breaking over us. Even among university students there are still many who spell "there" and "their" interchangeably, write "it's" when they mean its, and assume "Carmen" is a branch of the Teamsters Union.

Yet the trivia which acknowledges itself to be just that, which points to itself by name in such compendia as *The Encyclopedia of Super Trivia* and the parlor game *Trivial Pursuit*, is not in the least damaging, and is exempted from the indictment that arches over so much of our culture. After all, what harm can come from being flapped by breezes of information? It does not matter whether facts so acquired are gone with the next wind. Curiosity has been satisfied, and that is reward unto itself. Samuel Johnson said there was no fact so minute or inconsiderable that he would rather not know it, and as saucy a commentator as Rabelais asked, "What harm [is there] in getting knowledge even from a sot, a pot, a fool, a mitten or an old slipper?"

Still, even self-proclaimed trivia can be out of bounds. The industrious Wallace-Wallechinsky family (*The People's Almanac* and three sequels; *The Book of Lists* and three sequels; *The Book of Predictions*; *Sex Lives of Famous People*) seemingly runs a trivia agency. The fattest and most useful of their volumes is the original *People's Almanac*. At best it functions like the long established *World* and *Information Please* almanacs—a trove of miscellaneous data serving as a research quarry. But unlike these earlier compendia, most of *People's* data is attributed to original or reprinted material from identified contributors—166 of them— and among the entries are not a few piddling classifications whose inclusion brings up questions of taste never prompted by the *World* and *New York Times* almanacs—the inclusion of rankings such as "20 Celebrities Who've Been Psychoanalyzed"; "15 Renowned Redheads"; and "12 People Who Disappeared and Were Never Found." (One of the 12, Patricia Hearst, was found a lot sooner than never.)

The *Book of Lists*, like *The People's Almanac*, is sprightly and entertaining, but it runs out of bounds more often. It extends the *Almanac's* list of redheads to 30, tells us that Red Schoendienst was born on the same day as James Dickey, discloses that Al Jolson's shoe size was nine, lists "Two Famous Hemorrhoid Sufferers" (Napoleon and Fuminaro Konoye), "8 Celebrities Who Have Had Vasectomies" and "11 Women Who Were Cheer- leaders in High School." But the most amazing list is that of "The 15 Most Boring Classics," in which *Moby Dick* ranks second and *Don Quixote* ninth. They are described by the editors, who themselves compiled the roster, as "tedious tomes."

Gilbert Seldes, in *The Public Arts*, speaks of "the process by which we are hypnotized into not thinking." Trivialization is part of that process. It is not necessarily deliberate and certainly not

mean; indeed, as in the case of the Wallace-Wallechinsky string
of hits, it is often disarming and ingratiating. But when a category
in a volume which assumes an encyclopedic posture, demeans
the value of literary classics by branding them tedious, or when it
panders to the voyeur instinct by naming celebrities who have
suffered from piles or whose tubes have been cut, the effect is
erosive. In an era of canned laughter, singing commercials, wall-
to-wall Sports & Games and tides of kitsch, the last things needed
are to put down Melville and Cervantes as dull plodders and
codify tittle-tattle about rectums and genitals.

Having processed thousands of morsels lying around loose in
textbooks, histories, tomes and encyclopedias, the Wallace-
Wallechinsky compilers turned from fact to fancy in their *Book of
Predictions*. Much of the material is interesting, such as 12
predictions made by "a forgotten American oracle," David Croly,
in 1888, all of which have come true (though another dozen have
not) but in this omnium-gatherum once again the editors
seemed not to know where to stop. They occupy long stretches by
quoting predictions that are too silly or banal to justify the paper
and ink used on them. Examples: in 1996, a ship laden with
pearls will be unearthed in a desert area in southern California;
in 2000, people will be able to walk across the Atlantic; the
following year, the Earth will be admitted to an Interstellar
Federation, and aliens will help us to a "new golden Age"; in
2010 the Soviet Union will attempt to change its past by
dispatching "tachyons, particles that move backward in time." At
various other future dates, Muhammad Ali will have kidney
trouble, Fidel Castro will become dictator of Chile, Henry
Kissinger will take up film production, Moshe Dayan will be
swept into "a tumultuous involvement with a woman" (he died
before the indicated time), Brigitte Bardot "will go in for plastic
surgery but not be pleased by the result," and Jeanne Dixon will
receive a gift of jewelry "made from a substance from another
planet." The prophecy that gripped me least is that sometime in

1985 there will be developed "a brand of toilet that uses a sound track that makes a flushing noise whenever the toilet lever is pressed, even though no water is used in the system."

If there were a print award for bad taste, it could easily go to *The Book of Lists #2* for categories such as 8 WOMEN WHO WORE (OR MAY HAVE WORN) CHASTITY BELTS, which includes "the corpse of an unknown woman of the late 16th or early 17th Century"; 5 PRESERVED SEX ORGANS OF FAMOUS MEN, including those of Rasputin and Ishida Kichizo (famous?); 25 WELL-KNOWN WOMEN WHO HAVE HAD ABORTIONS; 12 RELIGIOUS FIGURES INVOLVED IN SEX SCANDALS; and 18 MEN AND WOMEN WHO HAVE SLEPT WITH THREE OR MORE CELEBRITIES. No fewer than 70 sexual partners are named, each person identified by age and profession. In the case of Clara Bow, actress, she is not only listed as having slept with nine celebrities, but the editors add a gratuitous footnote:

> There is a persistent but unsubstantiated story that Clara entertained the entire 1927 "Thundering Herd" University of Southern California football team.

If the story is unsubstantiated, what is it doing in a collection of so-called facts? And even if it were a true story, what is accomplished by printing it, beyond cheap titillation? Clara Bow had been dead since 1965; there is no possible action for libel; it is safe to pollute her memory by a calumny that dishonors even the small name of trivia.

The toilet of the future, which makes a waterless flushing noise, is already here.

9 ✐ Songs Unheard, Films Unseen

Sometimes trivialization takes subtle forms, is unintended, and is not even perceived as a form of diminution. It occurs when cultural and economic forces interact to suppress a medium of expression. There are no villains, yet the effect is the same as though there had been a conspiracy of them. At least two arts, one ancient and the other modern, are victims of this in America. They are poetry and the theatrical documentary film.

The truth is that in an affluent society of 230 millions, which has bred poets of world rank in its past, poetry has been shunted to a status far beneath that of silkscreen painting and basket weaving. The reasons are many and interlocking: poetry's requirement of disciplined readers; the draining of this pool by the low demands of much best-selling literature and high-rating television programs; the reluctance of education to commit teachers and curricula to an art which most academic administrators, with reason, consider moribund; the lure, to poets, of higher yields for almost any other form of published writing; the reluctance of book publishers to lose money on a volume that may, if it is lucky, manage a sale of a few hundred copies to libraries and other poets. A few periodicals still carry verse, and the bi-monthly *American Poetry Review* goes along bravely, but poetry is simply not a living for the writer. Not in an age when only a Kuwaiti owning mineral rights can afford to address himself to the creation of an epic poem the size of, let's say, Stephen Vincent Benet's *John Brown's Body*.

There are those who say that the low estate of poetry is no great deprivation to a dynamic society; that at best, in the most enlightened setting, poetry is not for the swarm but the swamis. Yet critics like Allan Angoff retort, "the nation that cannot hear its best singers is not only deaf: it is in danger. The lark's song outlasts the lark, but surely whatever facilitates our hearing it, serves human freedom."[1]

Whether the combined songs of an exaltation of larks can affect freedom is an imponderable question, considering the limitations of the potential audience for poetry. But no such limits bind the medium of film, where the numbers vault into tens of millions. I once put to the readers of a magazine, whose circulation approaches half a million subscribers, a simple questionnaire: How many in a given list of movies had they seen? The films ranged from good to superb in concept, execution and information; some were moving, some funny, some gripping, some entertaining by any definition of that sweeping word, some inspiring, some motivating, some shattering. There was (and is) not one that a viewer would not profit from seeing, not one that a person would not come away from knowing more, or better understanding what he or she already knows. The list, and a brief description of each film, went alphabetically as follows:

—*Alexander von Humboldt.* The life of one of the greatest and most versatile of all scientists.

—*Ape and Super-Ape.* Comparative behavior patterns among animals and man, beautifully filmed on six continents.

[1]*American Writing Today*, by Allan Angoff, New York University Press, 1957.

—*The Apollo File*. A comprehensive review of the major milestones in the American space program.

—*Attica*. An investigation of the 1971 rebellion at Attica State Prison in New York, in which 43 were killed and over 200 wounded.

—*Buster Keaton Rides Again*. A sweet and sad and funny film, made in Canada in the twilight of Keaton's life.

—*Champollion or Egypt Unveiled*. An historical reconstruction of the deciphering of Egyptian hieroglyphics by J. F. Champollion in 1822.

—*Dead Birds*. Ritual warfare among tribes of aborigines in New Guinea, with powerful implications for societies which make bigger and better wars.

—*Eakins*. A magnificent treatment of the life and work of the American painter Thomas Eakins.

—*The Face of Genius*. The personal and professional life of Eugene O'Neill, including excerpts from his work and estimates of him by people of the theater.

—*The Forbidden Volcano (Le Volcan Interdit)*. A vulcanologist's view of his science as well as of some of the major volcanos of the world, including a descent into a live crater in Central Africa. Unforgettably vivid photography.

—*The Forth Road Bridge*. If anyone thinks engineering and construction cannot be exciting, this picture would correct the notion. It deals with the building of a suspension bridge over the Firth of Forth.

—*The Gentleman Tramp*. The life of Charles Chaplin.

—*George Braque, or A Different Notion of Time*. The painter—man and philosophy.

—*Georgia O'Keeffe*. The grand old woman of American painting.

—*The Great Migration: Year of the Wildebeest*. The subject of thousands of wildebeest on the move in Africa would seem unpromising, but this is one of the finest animal pictures ever made.

—*The Guns of August*. About the genesis of World War I, based on the historical work by Barbara Tuchman.

—*Hearts and Minds*. A withering excoriation of our role in the war in Vietnam.

—*Henry Ford's America*. A wry and incisive history of the Ford dynasty, made by the admirably unstoppable National Film Board of Canada.

—*High Grass Circus*. A touring circus in provincial Canada— its people, their acts, their problems inside and outside of the tent. A masterpiece, beyond challenge.

—*Hospital*. One of Frederick Wiseman's deeply human institutional films. (Others: *Titicut Follies, High School, Basic Training, Juvenile Court*.)

—*The Human Dutch*. The people of the Netherlands. There could not be a more charming and delightful national portrait.

—*Journey Into Self*. Eight members of a basic encounter group sit in a circle and share inward aspects of their lives. A sort of unplotted Ingmar Bergman picture—when Bergman was in top form.

—*Journey to the Outer Limits*. Young people from widely varying backgrounds take a course in wilderness training.

—*King—A Filmed Record*. The career of Martin Luther King, Jr., from 1955 to his assassination, showing the impact of his advocacies.

—*The Legendary Champions*. A cavalcade of heavyweight boxing champions from John L. Sullivan to Gene Tunney.

—*The Life of Anton Bruckner*. A musical biography enriched by stirring performances of his work.

—*Ludwig von Beethoven*. Valuable if only to see the various houses where a restless genius lived and worked; but there is much more.

—*Malcolm X*. The stormy career of the black leader.

—*The Man Who Skied Down Everest*. The most hair-raising descent—and tumble—ever filmed.

—*Marjoe*. The U.S. evangelical circuit, as seen by a practitioner who used rock music as part of his preaching style.

—*A Matter of Fat*. A must film for every person concerned with being overweight. Done with a wit and warmth that never interferes with its vital information.

—*North Star: Mark di Suvero*. Portraits of a sculptor who has been called "the last heroic figure in contemporary art."

—*Olympic Games* (any of six features made on the Games: *The Olympic Day*, *Games of the XXI Olympiad*, *The Olympics in Mexico*, *Olympia-Olympia*, *The Tokyo Olympiad*, *Visions of 8*).

—*Point of Order*. Events of the first McCarthiad (Senator Joseph).

—*Raoni*. On the struggle of Amazonian Indians against exploiters and polluters of their forests.

—*Rebel in Paradise*. Gauguin in Tahiti.

—*Robert Frost: A Lover's Quarrel with the World*. The vision and wisdom of a good gray eminence.

—*Russia*. A tour of the Soviet Union that is wider, deeper and far less costly than a trip. Harrison Salisbury of the *New York Times* is guide.

—*Salesman*. A remarkably dimensional film by the Maysles Brothers, about four men who sell $50 Bibles.

—*Terminus*. A railway station in England. A landmark in the development of the documentary.

—*A Time for Burning*. An actuality film of a crisis over integration in a church in Omaha, Nebraska. Great in every way.

—*To Die in Madrid*. The rise of Franco and the fall of Republican Spain.

—*Volcano: An Inquiry into the Life and Death of Malcolm Lowry*.

—*Walls of Fire.* Three major Mexican muralists, Orozco, Rivera and Siqueiros. Especially Siqueiros.

—*The War Game.* A projection of what would most likely happen in a typical evacuation area of England before, during and after a nuclear attack in the opening minutes of a third world war.

—*Who Are the Debolts? And Where Did They Get 19 Kids?* The family life of the Debolts, who number five biological and 14 adopted children of various nationalities and physical handicaps.

—*The Wild and the Brave.* The phasing out of a white game warden in Uganda, and his replacement by a black whom he instructs in the problems and dangers of the job.

—*With Infinite Tenderness.* The maturing of an autistic child, told in a spirit worthy of the title.

—*The Wolf Men.* Truths about the maligned and misunderstood wolf.

—*Woodstock.* Music, people and events in an epochal three-day gathering of more than 400,000 rock fans.

The results of the questionnaire confirmed my suspicions. Based on mail and voice votes, the average respondent had seen 2.8 of the 50 films. Most of them were angry about it. "I live next door to a major university, and the movie mecca of the megalopolis," wrote one, "yet I see only those films deemed by exhibitors to be commercial."

Another writer: "For those of us who feel culturally and educationally deprived, it would be a joy to watch just about any of the films on the list."

A woman who had seen four of the 50 was deeply vexed: "There is an awful pain of rage and despair that chokes me when I feel cheated and badly used. The realization that so many great films have been made but are nowhere to be seen, is one of those times."

The most seen by any one reader was eight films, by a woman in Riverside, California; but she felt this was no reason for her to be pleased: "I'm really rather ashamed of myself, because I consider myself an aficionado of the medium, and thought I was more exposed than I appear to be."

These responses, and others like them, indicate that a good many people yearn for a chance to see films of the calibre and content of the 50. But the creators of such films face rugged and discouraging obstacles, the meanest of which are financing and distribution. Not even the extraordinary achievements of David and Albert Maysles, and the honors that have come to them, have been proof against such hazards. In an interview with Roy Levin, published in *Documentary Explorations*, David Maysles told of the problems of *Salesman*, one of the select 50:

LEVIN: Did you personally finance *Salesman*?
MAYSLES: Yes, almost every penny our own money.
LEVIN: Have you gotten your money back?
MAYSLES: No, not at all.
LEVIN: Have you been able to get national distribution?
MAYSLES: We distributed ourselves in half a dozen cities.

Ed Pincus, producer, had an even more melancholy account of his film *Black Natchez*:

LEVIN: So you haven't really made any money from it?
PINCUS: No. We often distributed it free. Maybe we might have made a little money, but not very much.
LEVIN: Were you able to support yourselves?
PINCUS: No, no. Not at all. Nobody got paid salary on the film, except toward the end, one of the assistant editors got something like $30 a week.

The Canadian producer Alan King, interviewed by Alan Rosenthal three years after completing A *Married Couple*:

ROSENTHAL: Has the film covered its costs yet?
KING: No. It will eventually, in Canada and England. What will happen in the States is very much up in the air, but I am not terribly optimistic.

Frederic Wiseman (included in the 50), on financing *Titicut Follies*:

Q: Was anyone willing to back you financially?
A: Not in the beginning. I had to get credit from the labs, borrow equipment, and borrow money from the bank to buy the film.

Don Pennebaker, on his film *Monterey Pop*:

Q: How did you handle the distribution?
A: We went to a couple of major companies and asked if they would distribute it, and they said it didn't interest them.

The wonder is that these films get made at all. But once they are made, they take us into worlds that are sometimes as remote and unsuspected as the whorls of Jupiter, sometimes as close as next door; they inform, interpret, investigate, stimulate, recreate; they heighten our perception of our times, our mores and ourselves; they refresh and sharpen our sense of history; they are argufiers and persuaders, docents to the arts, preceptors to the sciences; they alarm, calm, arouse, edify, explain, influence, motivate. Whatever else they may be and do, they communicate through the universal language of the moving image, a tongue not very unlike the lingua franca of music; at their best, they dispense with the high services of dramatist and artificer, and address humanity and its condition by speaking to us directly. Those are no mean errands.

Yet for all of that, most of these films gather dust in vaults, and have been followed into those dim chambers by at least as many more fine documentaries produced since the 50 were made. A few of them were shown on television, but only eight—probably the ones seen by the aficionado in Riverside—were shown in theaters, and then very sparsely. And that is particularly sad in these cruel times, because more often than any other vehicle, the documentary film is inspired by compassion, or energized by a crusading sense of justice. In a time as callous and cynical as the 80's, it is heartening to realize that at least one medium cares—

about the handicapped, about the rights of minorities, about underprivileged children, endangered animals, drug addiction, pollution, the environment, victims of all kinds of predation. One can only watch with awed admiration the performance of documentarians who lavish time, energy and funds, sometimes cashing in their insurance policies or borrowing money to complete their films, sometimes risking health and even life, to do work which they hope will accomplish some good through disclosure, interpretation, argument or just plain truth-seeking.

Compassion is a singular and pervasive force in their films. Not only *homo sapiens* but elephants, wolves, whales, apes and other species have come under their broad umbrella. Robin Lehman's *End of the Game*, Nicholas Noxon's *Last Stand in Eden*, William Mason's *Cry of the Wild*, Michael Chechik's *Greenpeace Voyages to Save the Whale* are only a few of the best examples. The plight of the handicapped generated several films: *Best Boy* is a moving account of a 52-year-old mentally retarded man who leaves home and the protection of parents for the first time, to start toward a more independent existence. *Leo Beuerman* is about a man with a cruel deformity, whose quiet self-sufficiency gives him the stature his body lacks. *Other Voices* is about the attempts of a dedicated doctor and his staff to help four young mental patients in a home-like therapeutic environment. A *Way Out of the Wilderness* shows what happens when severely handicapped children are treated with patience and tenderness. *Survival Run* follows a blind marathon runner and his co-runner, a sighted guide, in a thronged race over an extremely rugged cross-country course. There is only one fall. The two run as one, and finish not last. It lifts the heart.

Membership in this group belongs as well to the films of Joe Saltzman, especially his *Why Me?* concerning the physical and psychological traumas of breast cancer; *The Very Personal Death of Elizabeth Schelt-Holt Hartford*, dealing with a luminous old woman struggling to live on welfare; and two documents relating to victims of violence—*Gunshot* and *Rape*.

Among films sympathetic to neglected minorities, there are several on the Indians of the Americas. *Annie-Mae, Brave Hearted Woman* is about an Indian activist, a sort of Norma Rae among her people, who unfortunately did not, like the labor organizer, triumph in time for the closing credits. Instead she was murdered under circumstances as bitter as the lot of the Indians for whom she struggled. *God Is a Woman* is not theosophic, but about the Cuna Indians of southern Panama. *The Divided Trail* is about Chippewa Indians living in Chicago. *The Other Side of the Ledger ... an Indian View of the Hudson Bay Company* demonstrates that the Canadian Indian's lot is not an easy one either.

There is hardly an area of art, science, music, history, politics, sports, geography, law—hardly an area of human interest and concern which does not attract the documentary-maker. But while his metier may be the last reliable refuge of social concern in the media, there is a sort of chasm between, let's say, the home audience that watches *60 Minutes* on television and the people who would never think of going to see a Cousteau picture or *The Politics of Poison* in a theater. Each week, *60 Minutes* presents what is, after all, the equivalent of three documentary shorts, almost always of sharp social significance. The series is a hit; it ranks consistently high in the ratings, and is no stranger to the number-one position. But when 1982's Oscar-nominated short documentaries were screened competitively in a single showing for members of the Academy, only 147 of 3,600 eligible voters turned out. "Such good work, so little chance of major public attention," wrote critic Charles Champlin in a review headed, "Short Films: An Air of Sadness." The sadness lay in the seeming indifference of the very people one would expect to be the most interested.

If one has young children, and searches through newspapers for a good movie to take them to on a weekend, films of this character show up about as frequently as an eclipse of the sun. Even among entities which care about works of high quality, there are blind spots when it comes to the documentary. The Janus Film Festival featured an eight-week showing of what it called "foreign and American film classics." They *were* classics. Sixty-three of them. But not a single non-dramatic movie was among them, as though there were no such thing as a documentary classic.

This means, again, that wonderful pictures are made but not seen. The fault, if it can be called a fault, rests partly on certain educational failures, but mostly on the disinterest of motion picture exhibitors. Yet they cannot be blamed for not wanting to book a picture that will not pay back its rental or take care of overhead expenses. There is no chance for documentaries to draw big audiences so long as audiences are not exposed to them. And without big audiences, there is small encouragement to raise money to produce such films; and so the cycle is closed.

The cultural and educational loss to America is impossible to measure, but it cannot be small. Exposure to these and similar films might have stirred the interest of young people in new disciplines, inspired young and old to do collateral reading, heightened attention to the humanities, made people more aware of the realities of the world. Then perhaps there might have been a reversal in the direction of taste—an upgrading rather than the opposite—and the effect of this would have been felt in all the media—especially in television, where it is sorely needed.

Still, in the persistence of the documentarians there is something brave and hopeful. For so long as we can make documentary films that are outspoken on crucial issues, and are critical, when need be, of government, business, labor, the courts, the military, the professions, and, not least, ourselves; so long as *60 Minutes* and programs like it can go on exposing frauds, knaves, crooks, creeps, rackets, ripoffs and high bunglers; so long as men and women of principle and good heart and clear conscience and fast film can go on creating documentaries that enlighten, serve the public interest, and exercise the better angels of our nature, then it will not be all that easy to send our republic to the dogs no matter who is elected president.

10 ✒ "Supp'd full with horrors"
—Macbeth, V. 5.

While few people know what films they have been missing, millions know what they are getting. The successes of American movie makers historically are too many, too solid, too famous to bear remark here; indeed if it were possible to compound a graph of technical and artistic achievement across the decades and around the world, American cinema would rank high—some think highest. But the world is not static, and factors complex enough to dizzy a computer can and do change public values, tastes, proclivities and choices. Phenomena like credit cards, punk rock, weather satellites, moon landings, *Hustler* magazine, Twiggy, and Mobil editorials were unanticipated a generation ago. And so were extrapolated comic strips like *Star Wars*, demonological kitsch like *The Exorcist*, feature-length stag films like *Deep Throat*, and movies contrived expressly for display of violence and horror. All of these movies in varying degrees make small if any demands on the intelligence and sensibilities of their audiences, and in this sense they narrow down both the scope of their enterprise and the expectations of their public. And they do this very successfully. Their work is full of action, effects, and atmosphere: everything is there but ideas.

A case in point, and a conspicuous one, is George Lucas, creator of the runaway hit movies *Star Wars, The Empire Strikes Back*, and, with Steven Spielberg, *Raiders of the Lost Ark*. It may be considered sacrilege by votaries of Lucas to suggest that he has more in common with the makers of good horror films than with the luminaries of top rank to whose company he has been raised by his commercial and critical triumphs. He has little in common with Gance, Bergman, Griffith, Fellini, Eisenstein, Capra, Ford, Renoir, Zinneman, Milestone, Von Sternberg, Buñuel, de Sica, Losey, Kurosawa, Huston or even with Francis Ford Coppola, with whom he grew up in films and with whom he shares footing on the peak.

Lucas's virtues are strong and far outrun his lacks, which may be transient, but in those pictures which established his reputation and fortune, Lucas depended on many of the same devices used in the better horror movies—shock, special effects, and disintegration. Whole planets blow up in *Star Wars*; whole people blow up in the horror pictures: it is a matter of degree. Lucas is not without grace and wit, but so are some of the goremeisters. There are tokens of ideas in Lucas's extravaganzas, like the high-toned malarkey about "the force" in *Star Wars*, but these notions are simplistic, just as the substance in most horror films is naive and decrepit.

Joe Saltzman, in *USA Today* ("Lucas Films: An Empty Way Station?")[1] praises Lucas for his technical brilliance and skilled story-telling, but asks, "Is that all there is? And why?" Noting that Lucas is under obligation to nobody but himself and has the freedom to do whatever he likes with his money and talent, Saltzman cautions that

> For Lucas to throw away his obvious skills on films that do little else but amuse is a tragic waste of talent. ... Since few critics are able to resist the hypnotic appeal of a Lucas film, someone should say to [him]: Congratulations on another amazing piece of movie-making, but don't stay too long at the inn. The

[1]September, 1981.

journey ahead may be more difficult but in the end, it would be much more satisfying to yourself and to your public. It would be a pity if an artist of your stature and ability fails a brave new generation just as hungry for ideas and meaning as any generation before it.

The comparison of Lucas movies to good horror films rests on the assumption that there *are* good horror films. The genre is not without its examplars (*Frankenstein, Dracula, Psycho, Dressed to Kill,* etc.) but in the high and rising tide of trivialization, the shilling shocker has reached an advanced state of deliberate repulsiveness.

In a volume on the history of B-picture production in Hollywood, *Kings of the B's,* Todd McCarthy and Charles Flynn present, among others, the filmmaker Herschell Gordon Lewis. Mr. Lewis stands at the head of a class of schlocksmiths, both for the vividness of his art and the forthrightness of his exegetical comments. He chose to shoot his first film, *Blood Feast,* in Miami, which he favored as a production site because the unions had not yet "despoiled the territory" and there was "an ample supply of talented people who would work for very little money."

Seeking new frontiers in cinematic gore and gristle, Lewis hit on the inspiration of ripping the tongue out of a character's mouth. First he had to find a girl whose mouth size would accommodate a sheep's tongue which had been bought for the purpose. The tongue was stored in a motel refrigerator, but when the power went out for most of one day and the room "began to smell gamey," the tongue was drenched in Pine-Sol so that it would not, in Lewis' words,

> smell us out of the entire motel. .... Into this girl's mouth we crammed the tongue, [cranberry] juice, gelatin, and stage blood. The lunatic [in the film] pulled out the sheep's tongue, along with all the stuff that hangs out behind it.

It was a new first in cinema. No film had ever shown a tongue being ripped out before. Pride of originality was also felt in a new way of showing how people die:

No one had made films in which people die with their eyes open, not shut. ... No one had made films in which blood and gristle show at the end. People died very neatly. *Blood Feast* I have often referred to as a Walt Whitman poem—it's not good, but it's the first of its type and therefore it deserves a certain position.

Q: You, then, were years ahead of Sam Peckinpah in that respect?
A: Oh, yes. Peckinpah's blood is much more watery than ours. Yes, he uses exploding devices in the clothing but that's because Peckinpah shoots people. We *dismember* them![2] It's elementary that when you dismember somebody, it's a lot more repulsive than simply to shoot them cleanly. We had people dying in ways that are now regarded as very much "in." ...

Q: Do you have any imitators or competitors?
A: They are legion! They are legion! There are many people who feel that the road is paved with gold. Just as they followed us into the nudies, they follow into gore.

Lewis arrived at his standards not without some grounding in esthetics. He was aware of Whitman, although not favorably disposed toward his poetry, and knew the source of the famous phrase about disbelief:

The audience ... going along with what Coleridge called a willing suspension of disbelief, is challenging you at all times. ...

Demographics also figure in his calculations:

While we were cutting *Blood Feast*, my partner and I looked at each other and said, "What are we going to do with this picture?" ... People who were coming into the cutting room, looking at it on the Moviola, couldn't watch it ... because it was repulsive psychologically. And I thought, maybe we do have something here. ... We decided to open in the Bel Air Theater in Peoria, feeling if we drop dead in Peoria, no one on earth will ever know—it's a different planet.

[2]Lewis's italics.

Lewis explained that it is not easy to tell, from a drive-in clientele, how a picture will go:

> It's hard to get an audience reaction, especially in Peoria, where they bring in five people inside the car and three more in the trunk.

The film opened on a Friday, and the next night Lewis drove down to the Bel Air in a driving rain to find traffic backed up down the highway and state police on hand to handle the crowd.

> I knew we had something. ... *Blood Feast* was a runaway winner. ... It started an entirely new category of filmmaking. ...

He was right about that. Since *Blood Feast* about 700 horror films have been made, with many variations on gristle and gore. In *The Incredible Melting Man* the audience is treated to a decapitation in which a man's head is torn off and tossed into a river. The camera follows it down the river and over a waterfall; it smashes against some rocks and breaks open; the brains spill out and float away.

In *The Thing*, a corpse sprouts a pair of jaws from its chest, and, to appease the hunger of the producer if nobody else, the jaws chew off the arm of a doctor. The same film claims the distinction of what journalist Eric Kasum thought must be "the most terrifying and repulsive autopsy sequence in movie history, a putrid monster's guts that pour out of the created innards of [an] extraterrestrial creature."

Tom Burman, a makeup and special-effects veteran of three dozen horror movies, tells of producers who "actually want to graphically sever someone's head and show the trachea breathing and the carotid artery spurting blood. It covers up story weaknesses."

Steve Miner, who directed Parts 2 and 3 of *Friday the 13th*, told Kasum that he became involved in films as a writer of children's comedies, but they did poor business, "so I started killing the kids, and people love it."

Another bloodbath picture that did very well at the boxoffice was *The Texas Chain Saw Massacre,* which in 1981 alone, seven years after its release, earned $6 million. In one of its scenes a woman is impaled on a meat hook and left to die. The tableau of a victim dangling in her death throes worked so well for the makers of the film that it was later selected by them as

> the film's most exploitable [read "salable"] moment. It was reproduced in ads and posters all over the world—presaging the violence-against-women theme that has permeated TV and movies ever since.[3]

Tom Savini, special effects artist admiringly known in the trade as The King of Carnage, has many grisly reels to his credit, including passages in *Friday the 13th, Maniac, Dawn of the Dead, Deranged,* and *Eyes of a Stranger.* He is quoted as saying that although he personally has never chopped a hand off, pulled an arm out of a socket or shot someone in the head, he has enjoyed inventing ways to do it on film. An article about him in a craft magazine[4] notes that two weeks after filming began on *Eyes of a Stranger,* three murder scenes were added to the script to accommodate his skills. In one, a rapist-murderer gets shot in the forehead and "loses half his brains through the back of his head." In another a decapitated head rests on the bottom of an aquarium tank. In a third, there is "a realistic rendition" of a throat being slit.

Artists of high and secure reputation are not strangers to the genre, going back to Robert Weine (*The Cabinet of Dr. Caligari*), Val Lewton (*Cat People*), Fritz Lang (*M*) and Alfred Hitchcock. The latter's *Psycho,* in which a woman is murdered while taking a shower, is regarded by cineastes as the benchmark film that legitimized the display of violence to general audiences. But none of the old-timers enjoyed the special skills of expert head-smashers, blood-spatterers, disembowelers, and decomposers.

[3]*"The Real Texas Chain Saw Massacre,"* by Ellen Farley, and William K. Knoedelseder, Jr., in *The Los Angeles Times,* 9. 5. 82.
[4]*On The Set,* July, 1980, p. 34. Unsigned article.

Among successors to Hitchcock to whom his mantle has descended is Steven Spielberg, who like George Lucas can make any movie he wants. He chose during the height of the horror cycle to make *Poltergeist*, in the unreeling of which a character rakes flesh from his face, down to the bone. In *Raiders of the Lost Ark*, Spielberg's special effects men disintegrated faces and bodies into amorphous pools of gunk.

Gore merchants have champions and defenders, some highly placed. Although critic Linda Gross found *The Texas Chain Saw Massacre* "despicable . . . degrading . . . a senseless misuse of film and time," and *The Philadelphia Inquirer* inquired, "Why are droves of people plunking down $3.50 for what amounts to the privilege of throwing up?" and *The San Angelo* (Texas) *Times* suggested that the state legislature take steps to have the film "deported to Arkansas or somewhere," *The New York Times's* Vincent Canby found redeeming art in it. Stan Kaminsky, author, believes that horror pictures in general relieve the pressures of everyday life: "We are inundated every day with news of senseless brutality, killings, and terror. When we see a thriller we do get frightened, but because there is a plot that gets resolved, we are also allowed to feel relief—a feeling we don't get often in real-life situations of terror."

Robert Hoffman, professor of psychology at Adelphi University, thinks depictions of violence are good for us: "Violence is there for a reason. It's good to let the heart beat fast and let the adrenalin flow. Being scared, being concerned about one's safety, is a part of life—a normal emotion you should experience. There are people who never get stimulated or scared or excited. That's unhealthy!"[5]

Perhaps certain theories are unhealthy too. Being scared and concerned about one's safety is not necessarily a boon, as anyone who lived through the destruction of Beirut, Dresden, Warsaw, Manila, Nanking and Nagasaki can testify. To Jews rounded up

[5]Quoted by Maureen Early in *Newsday*.

at midnight for deportation to Nazi concentration camps it was not helpful for the heart to beat faster and the adrenalin to flow. There are hundreds of ways to relieve the pressures of everyday life, including sports, games, reading, listening to music, walking, jogging, and making love. So it is a curious notion that in order to escape from tensions created by daily increments of brutality, killings and terror, we go to see films of brutality, killings and terror.

The effloresence of the horror-terror genre, its support by the public, and rationalizations in its defense, are evidence that standards have been shrivelled to the point where emptiness becomes profitable when framed in a context of sensation. Maureen Gaffney, producer of educational films at the Media Center for Children in New York, addressed this very point: "The trouble with most horror films made now is that there is no serious content. They reflect no myths, they have no center. They are just pure sensation, but that is a reflection of our times because so many adults are living lives of pure sensation."[6]

Devotees of horror films are unlikely to be convinced that watching a good documentary might be time better spent for them, and certainly better for their young children, than attending *The Corpse Grinders*. It is a little like trying to persuade an addicted smoker that the weed he burns may be as deadly as eating poison mushrooms, though it takes a bit longer to do mischief. But if one still wants to de-program a horror fan from his jollies, perhaps a good point of departure would be to refer him to Herschell Gordon Lewis's description of a peak in his film *Blood Orgy*:

> The maniac pulls the eyeball out of a girl's head and *squeezes*. And you see the knuckles tighten, and you see this eyeball all the time. And finally it bursts, and this inky black glop squirts out all over the place. I have seen people faint, vomit, turn green, leave and go to the washroom because of that scene.

[6]Quoted in "Have Horror Films Gone Too Far?" by Elliott Stein, *The New York Times*, 6. 20. 82.

No light is shed in the interview, from which this fragment is excerpted, on the commercial fortunes of *Blood Orgy*; but William Friedkin's *The Exorcist*, a film of incomparably richer texture and bigger budget, which enjoyed not only Friedkin's direction but a cast of such stars as Ellen Burstyn, Jason Miller and Max Von Sydow, also made people faint, turn green, and go to the washroom. Nothing as gross as a squashed eyeball, but leprous lesions on a child's body and the spewing of pea-green vomit in a priest's face were among the excitements. *The Exorcist* was one of the greatest box-office smashes of all time, supported by audiences far beyond Peoria and other such geographical pockets.

Once again the driving forces are novelty, sensation, and being first—Lewis with patented thick blood, Friedkin with a girl's head that turns full circle. Thousands cheer.

Friedkin, interviewed while *The Exorcist* was posting new highs at the boxoffice, said, "There are only three reasons to make a movie—to make people laugh, to make them cry, and to frighten them." Possibly he did not include a fourth reason—to make them think—because in some circles that is the same as frightening them.

11 ✐ Law

In Waterloo, Nebraska, in 1910, it was illegal for a barber to eat onions on a working day between the hours of 7 a.m. and 7 p.m. In the state of Louisiana in 1914, the legislature ruled that no woman could wear a hatpin which protruded from the crown of the hat more than one-half inch. In Alabama in 1923, a section of the state code prohibited the placing of salt on a railroad track. An Indiana statute of 1926, decreed that bed sheets in hotels throughout the state must be at least 99 inches long and 81 inches wide.[1]

We cherish these ordinances for their quaintness, although their point in time, as the saying goes, was not very far back. But in the fall of 1981, a Superior Court justice in Yorba Linda, California, ordered 12-year-old Carrie McGonigle banished from an adults-only condominium because a homeowner's association insisted on a minimum age limit of 14 years for tenants. The judge upheld the right of the association to enforce this stricture, and ruled that Carrie, who occupied the $118,000 property with her mother and two teen-age sisters, must get out by January 1, 1981. He further decreed that until the child reached her 14th

[1]*It's The Law,* by Dick Hyman, Doubleday Doran, 1936.

98

birthday, she could visit with the mother on week-ends and legal holidays.

On the scale of national concerns this was a minuscule matter except to the McGonigles, and among the bricabrac of jurisprudence it ranks with the onion-eating, hatpin, salt, and bed sheet regulations. But such ordinances inflict no irreparable damage, whereas silly judgments, which trivialize the spirit if not the letter of law, can hurt. "Any laws but those we make ourselves are laughable," wrote Emerson—one of his looser maxims—but Mrs. McGonigle was not laughing. "The judge might as well take Carrie out and shoot her," she said. "There is no way she is going to live any other place but with me."[2]

As law itself is extensible and flexible, so are concepts of trivialization within it. In equity, a demurrer may succeed on grounds that the matter in dispute is trivial and therefore below the dignity of the court. But this doctrine has seasons when it is fashionable and when it isn't, times when it is treated as an absurdity. Fifty years ago, if a student sued to enjoin a school from prohibiting long hair as part of a dress code, the case would have been thrown out of court. Not so in recent years. A key obstacle to the implementation of what had long been considered trifling rights was removed by the United States Supreme Court in 1969 when it ruled that five Des Moines schoolchildren (ranging in age from eight to 15) had a right to protest the war in Vietnam by wearing black armbands to school and in the classroom. School officials had forbidden them to do so, and the children (through representation, of course) sought injunctive relief on the ground that their constitutional rights had been violated. The Court found that peaceful demonstration without disruption is protected by two constitutional amendments—the 1st and 14th—as a symbolic form of free speech. The court went on to say that neither students nor teachers lost their constitutional rights of free expression at the schoolhouse gate; that "state-

[2]Associated Press dispatch, 10.8.81.

operated schools may not be enclaves of totalitarianism"; and that pupils both in and out of school are entitled to basic rights which the state is obliged to respect.

Since that time federal courts have decided that male high school students may wear their hair at any length or in any manner; that girls cannot be required to keep their hair at "one-finger width above the eyebrows"; and that dungarees cannot be prohibited under the school's dress code.

In Massachusetts, a federal court granted an injunction to a high school teacher against action by school authorities to discharge him because he had used the term "mother fucker" in a classroom—a term which he said he could not "in good conscience" promise not to use again.

In Vermont a federal judge agreed to review a student's charge that school officials had been unreasonable and arbitrary in administering grades and dismissals. Other courts have taken up matters such as the wearing of goatees by prisoners in a state jail; the right of a prisoner to have access to a typewriter; the obligation of a state prison to employ a Muslim chaplain on the same footing as Catholic, Protestant and Jewish chaplains.

Naturally not everybody in and around the halls of justice has been happy about the courts even admitting such matters to their dockets, let alone having found for the petitioners. Supreme Court Justice Hugo L. Black, who himself was involved in a hairlength case, wrote:

> The only thing about it that borders on the serious to me is the idea that anyone should think the federal constitution imposes upon the United States courts the burden of supervising the length of hair that public school students should wear.

Two of Black's colleagues on the high court, Justices Frankfurter and Jackson, used a term to describe judicial regulation of matters they considered too trifling to consider. The term was trivialization. A justice of the Court of Appeals of California, Macklin Fleming, in a treatise on "The Adverse Consequences of Current

Legal Doctrine on the American Courtroom,"[3] expands the definition:

> Trivialization sets in when the language of fundamental constitutional right begins to be routinely used by the courts to justify judicial regulation of administrative decisions of the smallest moment—with the consequence that a sort of Gresham's Law operates under which bad judicial decisions drive the good ones from public notice. The result, as with the boy who cried wolf too often, is to give the entire body of constitutional law a somewhat inconsequential and frivolous cast.

Whether the judicial decisions operating under Fleming's version of Gresham's Law are good or bad depends on the eye and bias of the beholder. The American Civil Liberties Union, and the majority of the United States Supreme Court in the famous *Tinker vs. Des Moines School District* and other cases of like stripe, would disagree with Frankfurter, Jackson, Black and Fleming. There is no end of rhetoric and persuasive argument on both sides; but there are other and far more grievous forms and processes of judicial trivialization that are never called by that name. They occur in staggering abundance, all the time, and what they diminish is first of all truth, and, along the way, equity, honesty, logic, morality, integrity, decency, personal reputation and, in the end, humanity. Not always, of course, do they lay waste, and not everywhere, but they occur in sufficient quantity and frequently enough to support a bill of indictment. And such a bill has been presented in a 280-page book entitled *Injustice For All*,[4] written by Anne Strick.

Strick's thesis is that our adversary system of law subverts true justice, and she is at pains to construct from both historical and current sources a critique and rationale so compelling that a Harvard professor of constitutional law, a Pulitzer-Prize-winning historian, a former university president, a former state attorney

[3] *The Price of Perfect Justice*, by Macklin Fleming, Basic Books, Inc., 1974.
[4] G.P. Putnam's Sons, New York, 1977.

general and a former justice of the United States Supreme Court variously praised it as original, arresting, comprehensive, incisive, something "every lawyer should read," and an innovation with potential to stimulate "a second renaissance in judicial administration."

Fine praise, but it was odd that, with the exception of a few jurists, a law professor or two and an occasional lawyer, apparently nobody in the state and federal courts, nobody in journalism and the humanities, had ever taken a good hard look at the adversary system; nobody had done what jurists in particular are trained and equipped to do—judge the system in a systematic way, and publish the results.

Strick hammers away at the adversary system's fierce, sometimes barbarous emphasis on *winning*, and on the premise, stubbornly maintained with full knowledge of its falsity, that truth will be revealed and justice served as a matter of course.

> This is sometimes called the fighting theory of justice, and it underlies both the conceptual framework and the procedure of our law. Each side must present *not* all it knows, but only its own "best case"; must assail the opposition; must attack and counter-attack, "discover" and avoid discovery.
>
> Nearly all members of our legal profession hold this adversary method to be desirable; in truth admirable—in fact, a very jewel among the world's judicial systems. Yet there is little evidence that either its sources or its claims, its underlying assumptions or its implications, have been much explained at all. Ever.

So far from this, according to Strick, that the figures are shocking. On the logical assumption that ignoring or neglecting a thing is the ultimate means of trivializing it, discussion of the adversary system has been minimized almost to the vanishing point. Strick discovered that out of 125,000 volumes in the University of Southern California Law Library (as of March 1976), not one single book was devoted to the adversary system of law; UCLA's Law Library held 248,646 volumes and again not one dealt with the subject. The Los Angeles County Law Library, together with its eight branches constituting the largest law library in the country, was no different except that its collection numbered over a half-million volumes. A compendium, *Law Books in Print*, which listed material by subject as well as title, contained 347 categories ranging from "Abbreviations" through "Zoning," but "Adversary System" was not among them. Of the two college texts which *mentioned* the subject either in chapter headings or an index, one devoted one and a half pages out of 1415; the other gave it two pages out of 1048. Yet in the opening chapter of the second text, *Civil Procedure, Cases and Materials*, the authors wrote:

> A distinctive element of the procedure for resolving legal controversies is the adversary system. This element is indeed essential to the whole subject, and unless it is understood it becomes well nigh impossible to explain, much less to justify, most of our procedural law.

Toward understanding it, Strick goes into what one law dean called "the abuse, mishandling and puerilities of cross-examination"; into surprise and character attacks; suppression and falsification of evidence; demeanor of lawyers; tone and mime skills; eyebrow-lifting; "listen-to-that" shrugs; triumphant punctuations like, "That will be all!" when no great point, or none at all, has been scored; abuses of plea bargaining; naked judicial bias and inadequacies; attacks on the credibility of witnesses who are known by the attackers to be honest; and so on and on into a jungle of legal atrocities.

Once more the "win system," with powerful side chains in sports and politics, stands unassailable. Complaints against it are not new. The French knew something about it. "You're an attorney," wrote Jean Giraudoux. "It's your duty to lie, conceal and distort everything, and slander everybody". Anatole France said with equal cynicism, "Law in its majesty equally forbids the rich as well as the poor, to sleep under bridges, to beg in the

street, and to steal bread." But whatever the geographical and
historical derivation of our laws and our attitudes toward jurisprudence, we in America have managed to work them into the Win
Ethic with such assurance and professionalism that nobody,
apparently not until Anne Strick, thought to examine the
question or take a count of the books in which this vital
procedure, this "essential element," does *not* appear.

It took a non-lawyer—who had been introduced to our trial
system in what she calls "a spectrum of unrelated matters"
sometimes as plaintiff, defendant, witness, juror, but mostly as
observer—to devote five years of study and inquiry to write the
first extensive disquisition on the process. Not that the inequities
and improprieties which she indicts had gone totally ignored by
fellow laymen, but they were usually barely mentioned, and then
in a summary way. For example, David Cort in his astute little
volume, *Revolution by Cliché*, fires a short clip:

> The adversary and appeal system of procedure is the worst
> possible way to find, collate, and present the truth of any
> situation. Most people have come to recognize the law as the
> deadly enemy of justice.[5]

Karly Llewellyn, in *The Bramble Bush*, wrote that the hardest job
for the student in his first year of law school is

> to lop off your common sense, to knock your ethics into
> temporary anesthesia. Your view of social policy, your sense of
> justice—to knock these out of you . . . you are to acquire ability
> to see only, and manipulate, the machinery of the law . . . it is
> an almost impossible process to achieve the technique without
> sacrificing some humanity first.[6]

Judge Fleming, too, acknowledged "the disruptive tendencies
latent in the adversary judicial process." But perhaps the most
illuminating insight into the deformities of the adversary system,
if only because the most personal, came from Wayne D. Brazil,

[5]*Revolution by Cliché*, by David Cort, Funk & Wagnalls, New York, 1970.
[6]*The Bramble Bush*, by Karly Llewellyn, Oceana, Dobbs Ferry, New York, 1960.

who left a lucrative law practice and took up teaching because he felt he had been damaged and scarred by many of the things he was obliged to do to give his clients competitive representation.

In an article, "The Attorney as Victim: Toward More Candor About the Psychological Price Tag of Litigation Practice,"[7] Brazil claims that the weapons used commonly by litigators may do as much psychic damage to their users as they do adversarial damage to their targets. He shares Llewellyn's distress over the concept of manipulation, and identifies the victims as people, data, documents, words, doctrines, precedents, institutions—"virtually everything that can be moved to serve some purpose." The human subjects are even more numerous, and include clients, witnesses, opposing counsel, judges, clerks, jurors, expert consultants, court reporters, and colleagues. Among devices of manipulation are intimidation, contrived tantrums, distraction, ingratiation, predation, deceit, suppression of critical documents when the litigator can get away with it, subterfuge, emotional posturing, pandering to vanities, exploiting fears, generating confusion, and hiding as many selected skeins of evidence as possible.

Brazil's main thrust is that a system which "virtually compels" this kind of unethical and unhealthy behavior invites disrespect for itself and develops undesirable psychological characteristics in those who operate the system.

> Something is psychologically askew. ... I believe "money" and "winning" are the primary motivations of a high percentage of litigators who are most comfortable with ... the current system. The people who seem ... best adapted to its pressures are not people to whom justice and esthetics are the paramount values, but are people who thrive on competition and doing battle, who are thoroughly engaged by gamesmanship, who love the taste of victory, and to whom the power and status that accompany wealth in our culture are very important.

They measure success, he goes on, not by fairness of result but in how much more they got for their clients than they were entitled to, how much better they did than other attorneys might have done, or than opposing counsel did for *their* clients, and how much money they made. "Woe to the peaceful," he laments, "woe to those to whom victory is less important than justice."

Brazil could not stand himself in the role expected of him by his peers; he felt uncomfortable, dissatisfied and unhappy, and did not respect the results of his work. So again and again the pathogens turn up—the processes of reduction and trivialization.

In the following confessional excerpts from Brazil's article, tokens of quantification appear frequently—words and phrases which plainly connote a scaling down. I italicize them:

> My manipulations and concealments not only *eroded* my self-respect, but also subtly discolored my feelings about others. The human subjects ... were converted in my eyes ... into something different from me, *something less complex and sacred*, something like ... *inanimate objects* in my environment that I move around ... to satisfy myself ... the people I manipulated ... *tended to become children* in my clouded psychological vision—children in the old pejorative sense of *only partial people*. ... It must be very difficult to regularly view others as *incomplete* and manipulate them without gradually coming to view oneself that way ... (a) tendency to objectify and *devalue* others, invites a general cynicism and sense of alienation from the entire social fabric.

Challenges to the adversary system and concern about legal ethics have surfaced before in American law. Sixty years after the Declaration of Independence, a Baltimore attorney named David Hoffman presented Fifty Resolutions to guide the professional conduct of lawyers. In 1854 one Judge Sharswood gave a series of lectures on legal ethics at the University of Pennsylvania, and 33 years later the precepts he staked out were, with slight modifications, encoded in the Canons of Professional Ethics of the Bar Association of Alabama. These canons progressed, in no great hurry and with no great change, to become in 1908 the canons of the American Bar Association (ABA).

But all these canons did not help much in the long run. After another half-century passed, the ABA in 1964 appointed a Committee on Evaluation of Professional Standards which, after six years of hard labor, produced a code found useful by many state legislatures and supreme courts. Then in 1977 a Commission on Professional Standards was established, and in 1980 it delivered a set of Model Rules of Professional Conduct.

These rules are fine as far as they go, but the trip is relatively short, and the stops are local. Instead of engaging the deficiencies of the adversary system on a broad front, they are concerned with such important but nevertheless stratified issues as mandatory disclosure, client perjury, correction of false testimony, conflicts between present and former clients, disqualifications within a law firm, and whether a lawyer should refuse to go along with conduct proposed or demanded by a client. Whether the latest model rules of professional conduct will work any better than previous codes remains to be seen, but in the meantime it will do no harm, and may do much good, if the voices of Strick and Brazil and others of like heart and conscience are heard in the land. Heard louder and oftener.

12 ✒ Sex

Revolutions, even exalted ones, usually dissipate their force through excess, resistance, bumbling proselytes, fanatics, or any of these in combination. The American sexual revolution is no different. While it would take nimble rationalizing to call it exalted, it did sweep away accumulations of hypocrisy, guilt, intolerance and censorship, and few resisters besides hard core puritans, Victorian throwbacks, rednecks, pietists and professional Comstocks would insist that there was absolutely nothing redeeming in the relaxation of laws and language, and the loosening of rigid strictures in art.

Yet there were losses in the gains. Schlocksmiths and porno people quickly moved in; "adult" no longer meant only a person who has attained majority, but a customer to whom prurient matter is legally marketable; explicit sex and all its moving parts migrated from burlesque to the legitimate stage, from the stag film shown only at smokers and sleazy conventions to wide-screen multi-million dollar productions exhibited in major and minor houses everywhere.

Few Americans would willingly return to the days in the late 50's, when a Cleveland woman was sentenced to seven years in the Ohio Reformatory after police, searching her apartment for other material, came upon "four little pamphlets, a couple of photographs and a little pencilled doodle" judged to be lewd and lascivious. Yet when the sexual revolution ended that kind of judicial atrocity, the first to benefit from the new freedom were not customers who sought and bought dirty doodles and lewd pamphlets, but merchants, hucksters, entrepreneurs, porno publishers, X-rated producers and mafiosi who made fortunes out of sexual commodities. Today upwards of 150 million copies of "adults only" magazines are published each year.

"Thinkers prepare the revolution," wrote Mexican novelist Mariano Azuela, "bandits carry it out." While by no means all purveyors of sexual material belong in the phylum of bandits, the point was quickly reached where even friends of the revolution began to think wistfully of sexual rituals practiced in days not long past. Bradley Smith, introducing *The American Way of Sex*, savors a moment of nostalgia before plunging ahead with texts and illustrations covering and uncovering American sex, pre-Columbian to post-Hefnerian:

> It is worth considering that the sight of a bare-breasted native girl in the *National Geographic* or the drawing of a corset-clad woman in the Sears Roebuck catalogue, may have offered as much visual sexual stimulation as the present gynecological spreads in *Penthouse* or *Hustler* magazines. Only fifty years ago it took flowers, candy, multiple dates and a "line" of conversation to get a girl into bed. Perhaps there was more pleasure in the slow buildup of three or four sequential dates, of a quiet dinner party with champagne in a private dining room and then the ultimate seduction, than the present first date, cocktail and/or a joint, followed by mutually agreed-upon sex.

Again, the trivializing action of plethora. The question may be put, if sex is universal and necessary, how can there be too much of it? It is close to being a silly question, for there are many benign natural elements which can be harmful in overabundance—too much water in floods, too much sunshine in drought, too many people for the great globe itself.

There is actually an algebraic formula to determine how many people have lived on the earth from the time man evolved. It is a dignified equation, one that would delight Euclid and depress Malthus, to the effect that N-1, minus N-2, over R, equals two parenthesized sets of symbols over eight other characters, and it comes out that, of the grand total of people who have ever lived, the present population is around 4 percent.

If we were to apply the same sort of formula to estimate the quantity of sexual matter in print today, as compared to the accumulative total of everything that has been published since printing was invented, the figure would have to exceed 95 percent. And this notwithstanding the occasional flourishes of erotic literature in earlier times.

The most dramatic leaps have come within the past generation, not only through an astronomical increase in print of all kinds, and more people around to read, but because of what must be acknowledged to be a revolution as valid historically as that of the industrial revolution.

Leading the transformation was not erotic sculpture, paintings, nude centerfolds or X-rated movies, but print—the medium which pervasively established itself beyond the control of censors. Dr. Alfred C. Kinsey's *Sexual Behavior in the Human Male* came out in 1948. Ten years later, Albert Ellis's *Sex Without Guilt* championed the right to enjoy sex, and condoned practices long considered taboo. At that point there was meager scientific or forensic support for his position, but it did not stay meager for long.

The court decisions detoxifying the infamous smuggle-through-customs titles like *Lady Chatterly's Lover, Fanny Hill,* and *Tropic of Cancer* encouraged fleshly novels and instructional books, and these rode in on a rising tide together with compilations of erotic art such as the Kronhausen, Bradley Smith, Grimley, Gerhard and Rawson volumes, the Hindu, Roman, Greek, Chinese, Japanese and Persian collections, the explicit works of Rowlandson, Rops, Von Bayos and Hokusai, and manuals such as *The Joy of Sex, The Picture Book of Sexual Love,* and *The Photographic Manual of Sexual Intercourse.* Meanwhile the photographic nude became so common as to approach the condition which the French call *toujours perdrix*—partridge at every meal. Few bookstores except those specializing in religion, science or the occult, are without representations of nudes in some context or other. All manner of occasion, both legitimate and flimsy, is used to present the photographed nude. Notable among the legitimates are Muybridge's *Studies of the Human Figure in Motion,* the quasi-abstract perspectives of Bill Brandt (much admired by Picasso, Braque and Henry Moore), and the chastely svelte models of John Rawlings. But since Brandt and Rawlings, the terrain, and most of the specializations, have gone pretty much downhill.

It was another glut, another case of overload. This time created by forces above and beyond the court decisions: the impact of Freud; the influence of Havelock and Albert Ellis; two world wars and two Asiatic wars, each of which introduced American troops to cultures whose sexual attitudes varied widely from their own; the weakening of religious and sectarian authority, especially among younger people; the pill; anti-establishment movements; the emergence of cohabitation, abortion and homosexuality as mentionable subjects in polite society.

It is always possible that, by some seiche-like oscillation of social mores, sexual repression and moral vigilantism may be re-asserted. It is even conceivable, though one may well shudder at the prospect, that a draconic Ayatollah, if in power, might execute Hefner, Guccione and Flynt, or at least stop their presses. But the one thing that is not reversible, the plethora that is here to stay, is the extent of scientific inquiry into sexuality. Almost all of it is relatively new, and could no more be undone, even if one wished it, than we could undo the physics and inventions that went into the building of the atom bomb.

The Masters and Johnson report, published in 1966, lists 333 scientific papers culled from throughout the world. Of this number only 13 were published before 1910, and only two of these in America. The remaining 320 are all products of the past two generations, most of them of the past 20 years. This corpus is the element that will not go away, unless the torch be put to all tracts and treatises, and I have not yet met anyone who will side with the arson squads of *Fahrenheit 451*.

None of the foregoing has anything to do with whether one prefers the company of Little Annie Fanny to Anita Bryant. But as it relates to trivialization, all of these plenitudes—graphic, literary, scientific—produced a kind of surfeit, a boredom, an offhandedness, the sort of syndrome that led Erica Jong, herself a practiced hand at erotica, to say, "My reaction to porno films is as follows: after the first ten minutes, I want to go home and screw. After the first twenty minutes I never want to screw again as long as I live."

So jaded was the reading public with new hardbacks on sex that when late in 1981 an exceptionally amusing and informative compendium was published—Albert B. Gerber's *Book of Sex Lists*—bookbuyers were not much interested. The text is lively, resourceful and at times provocative, with enough outcroppings of bad taste to keep pace with lesser works of light vein and similar substance, but by the time it appeared, both the subjects of *lists* and *sex*, which had enjoyed brisk book sales not many months before, had been played out.

Not in the least played out, however, was double entendre, a practice that came in through the open door of the sexual revolution, and which now enjoys numbers unprecedented in the history of TV and standard print. Specimens:

In a quarter-page ad offering condominiums for sale, two cartoon figures, a man and woman shaped like eggs, wear leis around their necks, and are apparently Hawaii-bound. The underlying text starts off with large bold type:

GOOD EGGS
GET LEI'D
(and then some)
Country Club Condominiums

The connection with eggs and Hawaii turned out to be an Easter egg hunt to be held on the grounds of the condo development, with a first prize of two trips to Hawaii. This ad did not run in *Playboy*, where it would have blended into the background, but in a daily newspaper.

A two-page display advertising an airline, pictured the body of a Boeing 747 stretched out across the width of both pages. The embellishing legend read, "You've Got to Have a Good Body to Go Far in This Town."

A full-page color ad for Campari in *Newsweek* (3.30.81) carried above a portrait of the actress Geraldine Chaplin, a caption in dense 24-point type:

GERALDINE CHAPLIN TALKS
ABOUT HER "FIRST TIME."

followed by an "interview":

CHAPLIN: To be perfectly blunt, it was a bit disappointing. Oh, it was good ... but not at all what I had expected. In fact, I couldn't for the life of me understand why all my friends thought it was such a big deal.
INTERVIEWER: Miss Chaplin, you'd be surprised how many people feel that way. So don't be embarrassed ... just tell me what happened.
CHAPLIN: It all started at a party in Madrid. I felt a tap on my shoulder and when I turned around there stood this wonderfully attractive young man.
"Campari?" he asked.
"No," I said, "Geraldine."
He laughed and ordered a Campari and soda for me. ...

Perhaps the chief complaint against America's double entendre standard is that it is so simple-minded; it requires little if any collaboration from the reader or viewer to be understood. To the degree that genuine wit enters the balance, the quotient of snicker and smirk is reduced or eliminated. A good example lies in one of the coarsest of all Shakespeare's sexual allusions. It occurs in Act II, Scene 5, of *Twelfth Night*, when Malvolio starts to decipher the letter he believes was written to him by Olivia:

> *By my life, this is my lady's hand:*
> *This be her C's, her U's, and her T's;*
> *and thus makes she her great P's.*

Eric Partridge, in his treasurable *Shakespeare's Bawdy*, either missed or did not acknowledge the allusion, but it is to me beyond question that the C, U, T, coming together as *cut*, a common synonym for the female orifice,[1] alludes to the source of the lady's great pees. Here instead of trivializing a sexual joke, Shakespeare does the opposite—he expands, by exercising the reader's imagination and sense of humor.

For some products and advertisers the double entendre is too slow, too indirect. The Jōvan Perfume Company advertised a set of "Sex Appeal" essences with bursts of prose including, "Perhaps the strongest appeal ever made to man. Primitive as a jungle. Pulsating as excited love ... this unique blend of ... special stimuli arouses anyone within reach. Spray lavishly where your pulse beats strongest ... or anywhere else where your imagination takes you ... because someone you know needs it. And everyone you know wants it."

The same company went further in a full-page color ad in *Vogue*, featuring a severely cropped closeup of a man's hand on a woman's knee. On the fourth finger of the hand is a wedding ring. Beneath ring and knee is printed, "The only musk oil dedicated to the proposition."

Compared to this, the hair dye Clairol was relatively chaste in

[1]Roger Blake's *Dictionary of Sexual Terms*, p. 53.

its famous headline, "Does she, or doesn't she?"

In an idle moment I once drew up a list of names for perfumes to supplement those regularly found in the pages of *Vogue* and *Harper's Bazaar*. They had a crude progression from mild to just beyond the point on the scale reached by Jōvan: Parlor Pink, Virgin Glow, Slightly Kissed, Opening Move, Mantrap, Torrid, Yes, Hurry!, Brass Tacks, First Offense, Sheer Disaster, and Statutory Rape.

A wry commentary on sexual teasing in ads appeared in a four-inch space on the front page of a massive classified ad section in *The Los Angeles Times*. It started out with the single white-on-black word S E X in letters three-quarters of an inch high, then in small letters beneath it, "Now that we have your attention" ... and it went on to advertise diesel Volkswagens.

All of this of course is very mild when compared with explicit sexual matter in print and on film, but in the latter the material is clearly labelled: *Hustler, Playboy, Penthouse*, etc., and on the screen *R-* or *X-rated*. No such candor distinguishes sex-oriented ads and commercials pushing real estate, airplanes, jeans, liqueurs, perfumes, beer, clothes, cars, and whatnot. In a comment on gratuitous sex on TV, Norman Lear asked

> Do we really need young women in bra-less sweaters running and bouncing across a set because someone has said that dinner is ready? Do we need the same young woman jumping up and down in her bra-less sweater when she is told that dinner will consist of *lamb chops*? "Not lamb chops?!" Jump, jump ... This sort of TV behavior is not motivated by the artistic needs of the writer or the director or the actress. It is motivated primarily ... by the needs of the three networks to win in the ratings. ...

Essentially the broad, teasing sexual approaches of advertising and the even lower manifestations of some TV comedy trivialize a natural, powerful and universal life force because, in big and little ways, they remove sex from its due context of social and ethical relationships—as though eroticism had little or nothing to do with love, sympathy, need, comfort, or anything else of human depth or substance.

13 ℐ Religion

Of all systems of abstract thought, religion has the widest spread. It overlooks life, death, morality, ethics, justice, divinity, speaks for creation, superintends the cosmos, deals in myths and mysteries, mediates the soul, accommodates hope, fear, power, charity, devotion, mercy. Yet for all of that, much of it is steeped in trivia.

The same writ that alludes to Arcturus and his sons, and to loosing the bands of Orion, dwells on the number of brass sockets, staves of shittim wood and twined linen hangings in the construction of an altar; it inveighs against anklets, wimples and crisping pins in the dress of women; fusses over dietary and architectural details, rites of purification, stipulates physical defects which exclude a priest from office, sets the exact number of oil lamps and cakes of shrewbread to be placed in the holy of holies.

Goodness and mercy, green pastures, still waters, restoration of the soul, transit of the valley of the shadow of death, eternal life in the house of the Lord, are gathered into six sentences of a single psalm, yet there are tedious rounds of hair-splitting, and mysterious configurations such as the numbers 666 and 144,000 which occur in consecutive verses of The Revelation. "Here is wisdom," is written by way of introduction to the first figure; concerning the 144,000 we learn only that "they"—not otherwise identified— were not defiled with women, they were virgins; that they followed the Lamb wherever he went, and that they, and they alone, were able to learn a new song sung by the "voice of harpers harping with their harps." (Rev. 14: 1-4). Biblical commentators, after many calisthenics, still cannot satisfactorily explain these numbers.

Veneration and trivialization constantly cross in religion. The 1807-page compendium, *Exhaustive Concordance of The Bible*, by James Strong, S.R.D., LL.D., actually lists every last *a, an, as, are, be, but, by, for, from, he, hers, his, I, in, it, me, not, of, on, she, that, the, thee, unto, upon, was* and *were*. The placement of each of these words by chapter and verse is meticulously arranged in an appendix of 18 parallel columns per page of fine print, page after page after page—an Amazon of trivia, useful to nobody, but laid out in full because each article, pronoun and preposition is, after all, in the *Bible*, and the Bible, like Everest, is *there*.

Still, this is an inoffensive and pure-minded form of trivia. Sacredness, like taste, is beyond dispute. A hair of the prophet, a shroud, an ark, a wall, the black stone of Mecca, a capitalized pronoun—so long as the sanctity in which believers envelop such articles and particles is not imposed on non-believers by fire, sword or mandate, no harm is done. Gourmands of the spirit, no less than of food and drink, are entitled to their indulgences. The trivialities of pilpulism, the waste of time and breath in wrangling over how many angels can dance on the head of a pin, are too trifling to frazzle the fabric of a whole society. It is when the *concept* of a divinity, of a godhead, of God, is itself petty, when the ineffable is rendered not only effable but picayune, that trivialization causes damage by lowering sights and values. And while whittling God down to anthropomorphic size and character is practiced universally, there are certain uniquely American ways of doing it which employ showmanship, salesmanship, mass media, gimmickry, and entreprenurial messiahship.

There is an ancient Hindu merchant's prayer which asks for advantageous trading, high interest and great wealth, and it is so unblushingly cheeky that we smile when we read it:

> Indra, may I gather wealth from my purchases! ... With my prayers, I sing this divine song, that I may gain hundredfold! ... May what I get in barter render me a gainer! May the accruing of gain be auspicious ... (may I) gain wealth through wealth ... may Indra place luster into it for me.[1]

The exclamation marks are in the original prayer, and at this distance we may be charmed or amused by the earnest insistence of the votary. He is merely asking for fat profits. He does not claim that he knows the Vedic gods personally, that he has met Indra face to face, been anointed by heaven, or armed with divine authority.

In contrast to this candid Hindu, Americans who pray to gain wealth through wealth, tend to brag about God's personal confidence in them. Nelson Bunker Hunt, Texas billionaire, a Croesus on the world level of Paul Getty, the Greek shipping magnates and the Saudi oilmen, is foursquare for religiousness. "The important thing to have," he said at an investment seminar for millionaires, "is a spiritual environment in this country that will mean we can keep the money we make." Not long before, he had tried to corner the world supply of silver, and had lost so heavily that he had to be bailed out by a government-approved loan of $1.1 billion. It took a consortium of banks to do it. Earlier, Hunt had also been deep in oil and soybeans. In his many investments he had no doubt hoped for God's blessing. In turn he gave his own blessing to William R. Bright, founder of the Campus Crusade for Christ and director of a $49 million evangelical complex that included a "Christian Embassy" and a travel agency. Hunt's benediction took two forms—money, and a

[1]*The Prayers of Man*, by Alfonso M. Dinola, Heinemann, London, 1962, p. 191.

declaration that Bright was "the closest thing to Jesus on earth." The object of this praise was in no position to dispute it, since he himself announced that he was "commissioned by God to save the world."

One of Mr. Bright's strategies for saving the world was the formation of a constellation called, with stunning fatuity, "History's Handful." Its goal was 1000 donors willing to donate or raise $1 million each. Bright harvested $170 million from History's Handful by the middle of 1980. Nelson Bunker Hunt alone gave $10 million, but on Bright's scale this was modest. According to *Newsweek*,[2] at a "Christian briefing" in Houston

> Bright explained how (donors) could be enshrined in his "Golden Globe Hall of Honor." For $100 million, a donor can become a "world sponsor"; for half that, a "hemisphere sponsor," and for $25 million, a "continental sponsor." A mere $25,000 buys only the sponsorship of a single earthly mission.

The director of financial planning for Bright's Great Commission Foundation, William C. Wagner, explained the compatibility of Holy Script with holy scrip:

> The Bible is the inerrant word of God—the undisputed book on financial success. There are some 500 verses in the Bible on prayer, but there are over 2000 on money and possessions.

At the same investment seminar, John W. O'Donnell of Newport Beach, Ca., one of the foremost tax-shelter advisers in the country, had a supply-side view of the Creator: "The Lord is the all-time capitalist, not a socialist."

A clear line of descent, or ascent, from the Hindu merchant who prayed to gain a hundredfold, to the modern investor, was indicated by David Jackson of Denver in the course of a lecture on barter-trading as a way to avoid taxes:

> The Good Lord has entrusted assets to you and made you an agent. The master has a duty to cooperate with you. He will

[2]June 16, 1980, p. 55.

indemnify and compensate you. Real estate agents get 7 to 10%; attorneys, maybe 33 to 40%. God has said you can have a 90% agency. With generosity like that, don't you feel bad about limiting it to 10%?

Oftener than not, American evangelists profess to know God very well and to have inside tracks to Jesus, but the one who knows God best would appear to be Morris Cerullo, self-proclaimed "Prophet of God," whose Third World Crusade appearances have attracted more than 100,000 congregants to a single service. He claims in his autobiography, *From Judaism to Christianity*, that he met God face to face in Paterson, N.J., and was lifted into heaven, where he encountered "The Presence of God" in the form of a six-foot-high flaming ball.

> My eyes were drawn to the place where the glory of God was standing in the heavens, and right where He had been standing, there was a hole in the sky in the form of two footprints. It was as if someone had taken a knife and cut a hole in a great big cake of cheese and one could see right through it. ... I knew what I had to do. I put my feet in the indentations that had been made by the Presence of God, and to my utter amazement, my feet fit perfectly into those footprints. They were the exact size.

This trumps the story of Cinderella's shoe, and for the first time reveals that God has the foot size of a short, stocky man.

Cerullo shares with the religious millionaires of the investment seminar an appreciation of God's power to indemnify and compensate. His World Evangelism organization bought the El Cortez Hotel in San Diego for $7.5 million and sold it two years later for $12 million. Early in 1982 a corporation financed by Cerullo announced plans to build a $50 million hotel-con-dominium resort on the Smoky Mountains of Tennessee. But spreading the word of God and making big deals in real estate are only two of Cerullo's interests. Others include a lively antago-nism toward women's rights, homosexual rights, and the rights of the elderly because they all fit in with the sinister evil forces designed to tear down the structure of our society as Satan makes his last great spectacular onslaught.

Whatever one may think of Satan, who is unpopular in all but a few exotic cults, he is a large abstraction, adversary to God himself, physical opponent of the Archangel Michael, prominent in the Books of Isaiah, Job and the non-canonical Enoch, and a luminous figure in pages of Aeschylus, Sophocles, Seneca, Dante, Milton and Goethe. But Satan, too, has been trivialized to accommodate American prophets and statesmen. One might expect Morris Cerullo to believe Satan is busy making tracks in a spectacular onslaught, but what of a U.S. Army general, later to become Secretary of State, who speculated that the erasure of 18 minutes of Richard M. Nixon's voice from a Watergate tape might have been the doing of a demonic force?

Satan and his associates, like God and Jesus, have been scaled down to petty activities. Larry Gohorn, former president of General Automation and a participant in the great investment seminar, declared that in 1978 God commanded him to "get the banking system operational," and told a reporter in 1981 that he had been "personally attacked by demons."

Alexander Haig was not the only one to think that demons had been nasty to President Nixon. Billy Graham, evangelist closest to the White House in the era of conservative presidents, was shocked by Watergate—not because of the criminal conspiracy which it exposed, but because Nixon, whom Graham had thought to be "every inch a Christian gentleman," had used so many expletives. Graham blamed it on sleeping pills and demons.

> Even the Greek word for them both is the same. My conclusion is that it was just all those sleeping pills, they just let a demon-power come in and play over him.

Small wonder that fundamentalist Christians in some of the western states early in 1982 circulated rumors that Procter &

Gamble's corporate symbol of a crescent moon with a bearded face, in profile, looking at a group of 13 stars, was connected with satanism and devil worship. The company was hard put to find where the rumors originated. A woman in Phoenix said she heard about the supposed link between P & G and Satan at a fundamentalist Christian seminar. Other sources cited the Trinity Broadcasting Network of Tustin, Ca., producer of Christian TV programs delivered to 1.3 million viewers by cable, as the responsible party. Trinity denied it. Finally P & G gave up its moon, stars, and suspect eidolon.

Religious broadcasting is highly profitable, and resoundingly successful both in terms of affluence and influence. The Christian Broadcasting Network (CBN), which has a $20 million production facility in Virginia Beach, Va., draws more mail than all three commercial networks combined, and receives income estimated to exceed $1 million per week.[3] Jerry Falwell's Moral Majority sermons are carried by 395 TV stations and 500 radio outlets. The Southern Baptist Radio and Television Commission, seeking to take advantage of "new opportunity," drew up plans for a 105-station denominational network. National Catholic Telecommunications announced it was "adding another dimension to the church's work, to reach out more effectively." The United Methodist Church publicly instituted a $25 million campaign for what it called "TV Presence and Ministry."

These major Christian denominations went about the broadcasting business with relative sedateness, compared to the gimmickry of the evangelists. Among the latter group, Oral Roberts, founder of Oral Roberts University, offered his broadcast audiences a "blessing-pact plan" through which he would "earnestly pray" that any gift given to his ministry will be returned "in its entirety from a totally unexpected source," and promised that if, after a year, this did not happen, the donation would be immediately refunded with no questions asked. In 1983 Roberts

[3]*Watch Magazine*, August, 1980.

moved to higher ground following a seven-hour conversation with Jesus in which Jesus gave him "marching orders" and chided him and his supporters for dragging their feet with donations for a three-building medical complex Roberts was installing in Oklahoma. "When," Jesus asked with apparent impatience, "when are you and your partners going to obey me? When?"

The partners alluded to were "prayer partners," whom Jesus instructed Roberts to ask for $240 each. In return they would receive 48 tapes containing Roberts' commentaries on books of the New Testament, plus 14 special blessings that included money and success. Though Roberts did not quote Jesus on the cause of cancer, he advised his prayer partners in a 12-page fund-raising letter that "I have become keenly aware of how Satan is trying to take control of the cells and cause them to multiply out of their divinely placed order." As to the size of the suggested donation, Jesus was quoted verbatim: "Tell them this is not Oral Roberts asking [for the $240], but their Lord."

Roberts is but one of many preachers who exchange goods or tokens for tithes. Among others were revivalist A.A. Allen, who sold pieces of his original revival tent as "Prosperity Blessing Cloths," and guaranteed possession of these swatches to reward the buyer with good health and economic security. Dr. Frederick J. ("Reverend Ike") Eikerenkoetter II, likewise offered a "prayer cloth" for healing purposes.[4] "Money," he said, "is God in action."

The money is very good. Jesus might be appalled, but then there were no investment seminars or transmitters in Jerusalem. His ministry did not divide its time between sports and the word of God, as does Gannett-owned radio station KPRZ in Los Angeles, which features local and nationally syndicated ministers and gospel music six days a week, but on Saturday carries Stanford and Notre Dame football games, and, in season, the entire Los Angeles Kings hockey league schedule. The station's general manager explained, "By carrying Kings hockey, we have

[4]*Religion in American Society*, by John Wilson, Prentice-Hall, 1978.

preempted some of our Christian advertisers because, frankly, the revenues are greater. We're still committed to the Christian format, but we're also committed to making money."

It follows that if God is trivialized, Jesus is next in line. Bruce Barton, advertising nabob (Batten, Barton, Durstine & Osborne), assured America in his best-selling book, *The Man Nobody Knows*, that Jesus

> . . . was a salesman at heart . . . he would be a national advertiser today, as he was the great advertiser of his own day. . . . Take any one of the parables no matter which—you will find that it exemplifies all the principles on which advertising textbooks are written . . . his language was marvelously simple . . . all the greatest things in life are one-syllable things—love, joy, home, hope, child, wife, trust, faith, God. . . .

What Barton neglected to mention was that all the meanest things in life are one-syllable things too: hate, sin, greed, lust, pain, whore, slave, pimp, bawd, crook, rape, rage, gloom, doubt, war, fiend, ghoul, brat, pox, plague, throe, curse, woe, groan, moan, stroke, death. And some of the greatest things in life are polysyllabic . . . happiness, beauty, brotherhood, kindness, amity, benevolence, charity, consideration, patience, plenitude, wholesomeness, prosperity . . . they make a long list, longer than the monosyllables so close to Barton's Jesus.

Jesus might not be pleased to learn that he would be big on Madison Avenue; that Billy Graham compared his Sermon on the Mount to President Eisenhower's first foreign policy address; that Jerry Falwell advertises over TV the *Jesus First LP Album*; that Ken Foure, featured speaker of "Spiritual Emphasis Week" at Grace College, an evangelical Christian school in Indiana, was a used car salesman who, in his own words, "switched the pitch to Christ."

Of course, not only Christian evangelists have found fat pickings in America. Imported faiths, some of them as exotic as an albino dzeggetai, have reaped riches from this fertile land. To name only one, there is Mahataj Ji, a teen-age guru whose shepherding in America earned him a fleet of sports cars, a Rolls-Royce or two, and a $22,000 British Jensen touring car used especially for festivals.

And why not? If so many other things in American society are marked down like goods in a bargain basement, in order to keep merchandise moving and cash flowing in, why not God? Exaltation and edification are all very well, but there is a time and place for everything, and it is only sound to keep prayer cloths and blessing-pact packages circulating where they can do the most good. To trivializers God is a resource and religion is a technique, and the combo is unbeatable.

14 ✑ Downgraders

So far, with the exceptions of a war fought over a beauty queen, and trendy vandalism, the trivialization discussed here has been on the whole good-natured and intended to entertain or make money. But there are meaner aspects, in which trivialization is malicious and intended to injure—where the process of rendering unimportant consists of sharply reducing the subject. It happens often in criticism and is by far the ignoblest form of that art. The very terms that describe it deal with quantities—verbs like belittle, discount, detract, minimize, cut down to size, nullify. It's an old approach. When the critic of *The Musical Courier* disliked Debussy's *Pélleas and Mélisande* at its first performance in New York, he called it "a nasty little noise." *The New York Times* brushed off Bizet's *Carmen* as "little more than a collection of chansons . . . as a work of art it is nothing." Brahms was accused of "mousey obsequiousness" in his fourth symphony. The *New York Herald* judged Wagner's *Siegfried* "a chaotic mass of triviality and filth"; Schoenberg was called, variously, an amoeba, a beetle, a gnat, a Schoen-bug, a maggot, a mollusk and a mosquito. His highest rating at that time was woodpecker. The critic Lawrence Gilman said of Stravinsky, "He is the nearest any composer has ever come to achieving almost complete

127

infantilism." Wordsworth held all of Walter Scott's poetry worth less than four shillings. Alfred Kazin called Thomas Wolfe a "professional hillbilly."

Trivialization by diminution is not confined to the arts and entertainment, as might be inferred from these examples. It has important political uses, too. When Westbrook Pegler, a syndicated columnist whom older readers may recall with anything from admiration to nausea, wanted at one time to show his scorn for singers and actors whom he felt were too liberal as well as overpaid, he trivialized their professions:

> A singer emits certain sounds from the neck, that's all . . . an actor utters recitations written for him; he bawls, whimpers or whispers, and stands here and there according to minute directions after long and patient instruction.

But denigrating singers and actors was not taxing for Pegler. He could transcend that level of abuse, as for example when he set out to scourge a great scientist, a task that might have given pause to most of us:

> Albert Einstein, whatever it is he has added to the sum of human knowledge, did what he has done because he couldn't help it, and has received beautiful rewards in the coin that he values most . . . a posturing old fellow, delighting in a show of homely and spectacular modesty.

Pegler was not unique in this subspecies of criticism. Whole disciplines have been dismissed in a sentence, just as Pegler did with Einstein. Here is a comment by Harry S. Truman, on modern art:

> I am of the opinion that so-called modern art is merely the vaporing of half-baked lazy people. There is no art at all in connection with the modernists.

Again quantification. No art at all.

One can trivialize an art, a profession, and ultimately one's own self-reliance. Simply suspend your judgment and give yourself over to the sirens of publicity and celebrity, and the work of making choices is done for you. With a coincidence that suggests poetic justice, the word "sell" and the first syllable of "celebrity" sound identical. In the old days, celebrity was something to celebrate, but in our time it has been modified by the ad agencies and the media, until it has become a commodity routinely sold in the marketplace, and used in turn to do more selling.

Celebrity endorsement is a form of condescension, because it says in effect, "Look, average consumer, you have nothing resembling national identity, whereas I have lots of it, so how can you be expected to judge for yourself which product among many is superior? Leave that to me. I am rich and worldly; I get around; therefore I know." Orson Welles is a man of considerable substance; he has been around a good deal—so when he tells us that a certain wine is never sold before its time, we had better listen and remember the name of the wine. Bob Hope sells with agile impartiality the products of Texaco and California Federal Savings & Loan, and God knows what else, and whatever he sells is worth buying because he is selling it. Why bother reading the ingredients on the label, why bother testing the product, why bother asking your next-door neighbor whether she's tried the brand and it satisfies her? Celebrity knows best.

The trivialists keep coming on. They are heard and seen and read by millions. They are elected to office. Increasingly to high office. With a kind of cheerful consistency they make little of big, and big of little. "If you've seen one redwood tree you've seen them all," makes little of big. To make big of little you take down a portrait of Lincoln on a wall of the White House, as Reagan did when he moved in, and replace it with one of Calvin Coolidge. All three were presidents, but Lincoln's stature heavily overshadows the others. Conceivably, it would be uncomfortable for a small president to have a great one looking down on him.

Trivialization is, among other things, insulting. Not just on the obvious level of Pegler calling Einstein a posturing old fellow, or the *London Times* kissing off Chopin as "a composer of attractive trifles." Terms of ethnic derogation like Wop, Yid, Nigger, Chink are ugly but not contractive, whereas calling a black man "boy," or a member of the yellow race a gook (the literal meaning of which is dirt or grime) *is* contractive. Yet even these terms, for all of their contemptible quality, are direct. Almost as bad are indirect insults to one's intelligence, such as the original campaign of the tobacco companies to get women to smoke. Typical was an ad showing a man puffing a cigarette while a girl appeals winsomely, "Blow some my way." That campaign and others like it succeeded; women now smoke by the millions and get lung cancer by the tens of thousands. To be fair, the "Blow some my way" approach was made before the Surgeon General first linked smoking to cancer. But what is to be said in defense of an ad campaign in which a woman smoker is paid the compliment, "You've come a long way, baby," suggesting arrival at some long-sought, treasurable goal?

In a sense we are insulted when vast oversimplifications are made to educate us, as when *Life* Magazine decides for us that Mozart's *Don Giovanni* is the greatest single work of art in the history of the world. It insults us when *Time* calls *Star Wars* the greatest film of the century. It insults our intelligence when some publication, I forget which, announces that Catherine Deneuve is the most beautiful woman in the world. It insults us when Dr. Edward Teller, father of the H-bomb, takes out a two-full-page ad in the *Los Angeles Times* to proclaim in all seriousness that he was the only victim of the Three Mile Island disaster, because he suffered a heart attack on reading what Jane Fonda had to say about it.

The ultimate in the way of trivialization, whether intentional or not, is to get rid of the offending subject altogether. Vanishment. This is done by conveniently forgetting, denying, treating with indifference, expunging from the record, proscribing, reducing people to numbers or things, or, in extreme cases, exterminating. Most of these methods are too familiar to require illustration, but there are always interesting excursions.

H.R. Haldeman, when asked in 1981 about the transcript of a conversation with Nixon in which they discussed hiring thugs in 1971 "to beat the shit out of May Day protesters," replied that he "did not care much" about ten-year-old tapes.[1]

P.G. Wingate, retired vice-president of the Du Pont Company, writing on environmental pollution, declared that "about the best Congress can do about acid rain is to let it rain."

James J. Kilpatrick, syndicated columnist, disposed of one of the most alarming of a series of Surgeon General's reports on smoking and cancer by suggesting that:

> The high incidence of cancer among heavy smokers may be explained not by the chemistry of nicotine but by the personality of the individual. Maybe heavy smokers are more susceptible to stress, and maybe the stress triggers cancer.

Patients in hospitals are often regarded by nurses and staff workers as categorical types and referred to by diagnostic label rather than by name. Carol Taylor, in her book *The Horizontal Orbit*,[2] tells of having lunch with seven nurses, of whom three invariably referred to their patients by their conditions—the craniotomy, the skull fracture, the diabetic. The other nurses, while they did not use names (they were dining in a public place, and could be overheard) used descriptive phrases—"sweet old lady, just a kid, nice guy but weird"—which at least recognized the patients as human beings. The author wondered whether there might be a relationship between a nurse's habit of talking about her patients as persons, and her ability to treat them as such.

Usually the erosive effect of trivialization is subtle and accumulative, but occasionally it can be quick and sharp. In another hospital episode recounted by Taylor, a man whom she calls Mr. L was waiting on a bench outside a radiation room, along with another patient. He was to have his right elbow X-rayed. The girl at the desk, after a long time on a telephone,

---

[1]*The Los Angeles Times*, 9.25.81.
[2]*The Horizontal Orbit*, by Carol Taylor, Holt, Reinhart & Winston, 1970, p. 13.

looked at a slip of paper and called out, "Who is the right elbow?"
Mr. L. recalled:

> to my surprise I sprang to my feet, and claimed to be the elbow
> she was looking for. It's unbelievable. The system keeps me
> waiting for 57 minutes, then it addresses me as something less
> than human, and what do I do? Leap to my feet and claim to
> be a right elbow.

When television was first introduced in South Africa, a
reporter for Springbok Radio, a commercial outfit, opened an
interview by requesting: "Would you please not mention television in the course of your comments? We are asking all our
interviewees to refrain from discussing it." His employers were
afraid they would quickly be done in by the competition, and
apparently thought that if TV were not mentioned it might go
away.

But all of this is small change compared to the gainsayers of
historical fact. Five American right wing organizations in
concert offered to pay $50,000 for proof that the holocaust of
the Jews and other minorities in World War II actually took
place. A survivor of Auschwitz, Mel Mermelstein, took them
up on it and they reneged on their offer, so he sued. The
bravado of the defendants quickly dissipated, and they settled
by paying Mermelstein $100,000, plus apologies. But denial
of these unspeakable atrocities persisted elsewhere to such an
extent among the hate-mongering canaille for three full
decades after Hitler, that in 1981 the American Nobel laureate
in literature, Czeslaw Milosz, could not refrain from alluding
to it in his acceptance speech at Stockholm:

> We are surrounded today by fictions about the past. ... The
> number of books in various languages which deny that the
> Holocaust ever took place, and claim that it was invented by
> Jewish propaganda, has exceeded 100. If such an insanity is
> possible, is a complete loss of memory as a permanent state of
> mind, improbable? And would it not present a danger more

grave than genetic engineering or poisoning of the natural environment?

Such complete loss of historical memory is never amnesiac, but as deliberate as the original decision to commit genocide. And if people choose to remember only that which suits their taste or temperament, as though history were a menu from which one picks only palatable dishes, then we do indeed face the dilemma posed by Milosz. It is the beginning of a philistinism that spreads to art, science, and morality.

Forget *Carmen*. Dump Einstein. Ignore the hazards of smoking. Throw out modern art. Sweep Watergate under the rug. Stop imagining there ever was a holocaust.

Trivialization, like greed, knows no bounds.

15 ✑ Death

In *Hearts and Minds*, perhaps the most polemically powerful documentary film ever made, there is a moment in which General William Westmoreland, commander of American forces in Vietnam, tells an interviewer, "The Oriental ... doesn't put the same high price on life as does a Westerner. Life is plentiful, life is cheap in the Orient. As [their] philosophy of life expresses it, life is not important."

Unfortunately for the effect of the general's statement, it directly follows actuality scenes of anguished grief such as seldom appear on a screen—a mother trying to crawl into the open grave of a lost son, to be buried with him; a South Vietnamese child sobbing and moaning piteously before the portrait of his father, killed in action.

It is typical of spread-eaglists to belittle outsiders, especially if they are enemies. But chauvinists should think twice before committing anything to the record, as Westmoreland did, on the subject of comparative cultures and their respect for life. For it is neither common nor fashionable to honor life in much of the world, including our part of it. On the contrary, the main emphases are on agencies of death and destruction. The world's two most powerful nations spend more on arms than on anything else. America's costliest collective enterprise during consecutive administrations was an undeclared war for which men were drafted to kill people they did not know in a place they would rather not have been, for a purpose they were not sure about. In the course of this, civilians on both sides were massacred. We are supposed to be above that sort of thing even in declared wars, but we weren't; and American perpetrators when tried for their crimes, were either slapped with paper towels, acquitted, or pardoned after sentencing.

A military court found Lt. William L. Calley guilty of the premeditated murder of 22 unarmed men, women and children at Mylai. The verdict, not the crime, was considered repugnant by many Americans, and he was pardoned.

A song, *The Battle Hymn of Lt. Calley*, was recorded and sold a quarter of a million copies. It apotheosized a wholesale killer in a heavenly setting:

> *When I reach my final campground in that Land Beyond the*
> *Sun,*
> *And the Great Commander asks me, "Did you fight or did you*
> *run?"*
> *I'll stand both straight and tall, and this is what I'll say:*
> *"Sir, I followed all my orders and I did the best I could—*
> *Count me only as a soldier who never left his gun."*[1]

Calley's shooting spree took place thousands of miles from mainland America, in a context of a bitter and protracted war. But what of peaceful America in the context of a college campus in the same Ohio known as the State of Presidents? On May 4, 1970, National Guardsmen who should never have been called out, fired into a crowd of Kent State students who were peacefully demonstrating against the invasion of Cambodia. Four students were killed. Several townspeople in neighboring Kent told reporters later they were sorry only four had died.[2] Still later a grand jury investigating the killing returned no indictments

---

[1] Quoted in *Star Spangled Kitsch*, by Curtis F. Brown, Universe House, 1975.
[2] Dr. Laurence J. Peter, in his compendium of quotes subtitled *Ideas for Our Time*, cites one Dr. Paul Williamson, father of a Kent State student, as warning his son, "Avoid revolution or expect to get shot. Mother and I will grieve, but we will gladly buy a dinner for the National Guardsman who shot you."

against the National Guard, but several against students and faculty.

There was no way in which the Guardsmen could have sorted out those four students from the rest of the demonstrators. But then the military mind does not stop at such frills as selectivity. Retired Army Colonel Charles Beckwith, commander of the aborted raid to release the American hostages in Teheran, later set up an anti-terrorist consulting firm to service corporations and governments. He kept on his desk a plaque reading, "Kill 'em all. Let God sort 'em out."[3]

To condone murder is to honor death and trivialize life. If America puts the high price on life that Westmoreland claims, it becomes harder than ever to explain the not-long-past lynchings,[4] the tenacity with which registration of guns is resisted, the street crowd in Manhattan which gathered to watch a demented man teeter on a window ledge 20 stories up and urged him to leap to his death; the trigger-happy cop who shot and killed a naked, unarmed man in Los Angeles; the 40 teen-agers who mugged, robbed and stripped a young man, chased him through Times Square throwing cans and bottles at him, then hounded him into a subway station where in desperation he leaped onto the tracks, fell against the third rail and was electrocuted. "The crowd howled with laughter," a witness told reporters, "They thought it was a big joke."

In south central Los Angeles, on a night in August, 1981, a 67-year-old man ran out of gas, walked to a nearby service station, bought a can of fuel and was returning with it to his car when four young punks stopped him, forced him to hand over $400 in cash, then poured gasoline over him and set him on fire. He died in agony while the four sauntered off down the street.

In California's San Gabriel Canyon, a good Samaritan motorist stopped to help three youths get their car out of the mud. They shot and killed him.

[3]Jennings Parrott, in *The Los Angeles Times*, 11.8.81.
[4]There have been between 4500 and 5000 lynchings in the United States since 1885, when records were first kept.

In Baltimore a 34-year-old man was walking along a dark street with his fiancée when her purse was snatched by a bicyclist. The man gave chase, was grabbed by three teen-agers, thrown to the ground, and shot dead.

City after city, crime after crime, senseless killing after senseless killing—as casual as shooting clay pigeons. Vicious cruelty is never pretty, but like other forms of expression it comes in several shades. It is deadliest when planned and executed deliberately as an instrument of policy, like the *schrecklichkeit* of the Nazi high command. Savagery is all too common in the torture of political prisoners by extremists of left and right, but when it is exercised offhandedly, as in the impromptu incineration of the motorist who ran out of gas, it is a symbol of total disregard for human values and life itself. Murder becomes a matter of small account, trivial, hardly worth thinking about, certainly nothing to be sorry for. A teen-age murderer, asked if he had any regrets, replied, "I didn't know him. Why should I feel sorry about what happened to him?"[5]

In a society inured to trivialization, death and disintegration are spectacles and sensations not far removed on the scale of thrills, from the tingle of plummeting descent on a roller coaster, the tickle of voyeuristic pornography, or fascination with the lethal hazards of auto racing, where every so often cars collide with each other or smash into the grandstands. Most of the ingenuity of special effects in films is given over to annihilation, to blowing people up, ripping them apart by gunfire, cremating them (*The Towering Inferno*), crushing them (*Earthquake*), devouring them (*Jaws*), beating, whipping, raping and torturing them. Even Jehovah was cast as an extremely wrathful destroyer in *Raiders of the Lost Ark*.

Much of this appetite for violence has been blamed on American TV, not only by church groups and the Moral Majority, but by people who are not above making use of it

[5]Cited in *Criminal Violence, Criminal Justice*, by Charles E. Silberman, Random House, 1978, p.48.

themselves in their work. Richard Condon, author of *The Manchurian Candidate* and *Prizzi's Honor*, told Michael Selzer (*Terrorist Chic*, p. 173):

> With TV, people from the age of three on just hunger for blood and pain and prodigious brutality of the crudest kind. TV has produced savage, simpleminded people, don't forget. And there are 215 million of them in the United States, and I don't exclude myself from that number.

No doubt TV has contributed much, if not most, to the climate of this aberration, but it is too easy to blame only that medium. Print is not without sin. "The press," wrote Sisyphus in *Commonweal*, "peddles crime and catastrophe." Walter Mears of the Associated Press believes wire-service reporters emphasize superficial conflicts because they are weaned on fires and accidents. "If you don't know how to write an eight-car fatal on Route 128 [Boston] you're gonna be in big trouble."

However, the worst exemplar, and the one least seldom blamed, is not a medium of communication but the government itself. The grand scale of its operations makes it a vast and unavoidable presence, like the atmosphere around us, so that everything it does permeates and affects our existence. Certainly deadly parallels suggest themselves, like that of mass murder. Lieutenant Calley indiscriminately shot 22 men, women and children at Mylai. But the government indiscriminately A-bombed 200,000 non-combatants in Hiroshima and another 150,000 in Nagasaki.

Burglary: The government was behind the Ellsberg and other break-ins of the Watergate era, and Watergate itself.

Perjury: President Eisenhower lied to the world about the U-2 incident. Lyndon Johnson lied about Tonkin Bay. Nixon lied about Watergate.

Bribery: The Abscam scandals—Congressmen willing to sell out to rich Arabs; the Reagan administration proposing modification of a federal law prohibiting corporate bribery overseas.

Many countries have criminal records worse than our own, but the concern of this canvas is not trivialization in Germany, South Africa or the Soviet Union; it is the trivialization of America. And part of the overall picture is the way we feel about violence and death as materials of entertainment.

Attraction to the spectacle of death is an arrived-at taste. The ancient Romans acquired it the way any people acquire any spectator sport—by programming. They were fed gladitorial fights-to-the-death and Christians vs. Lions as circus acts under the heading of Entertainment. Americans are not the first public to be offered shows in which killing is sport, merely the first to turn a whole country, through films and television, into a colosseum of infinite tiers.

Thomas Mann was only partly right (about the Romans, at least) when he wrote in *The Magic Mountain*:

> ... the ancients knew how to pay homage to death. For death is worthy of homage ... severed from life, it becomes a spectre, a distortion, and worse. Death, as an independent power, is a lustful power, whose vicious attraction is strong indeed; to feel drawn to it, to feel sympathy with it, is without any doubt at all the most ghastly aberration to which the spirit of man is prone.

Mann could not have been thinking of homage to death in terms of the ancient plebes—80,000 at a time—who flocked to the arena of the Flavians to see blood and guts spilled on sunny afternoons. He was no doubt alluding to the dignity with which death was treated by ancient Hebrews, Egyptians, Periclean Greeks, by peoples who have raised tombs and temples to heroes and loved ones—Mausolus, the Taj Mahal, Westminster Abbey, the tomb of the Medicis, the Invalides.

By no means all Americans, either historically or today, are infatuated by the "lustful power of death." Lincoln at Gettysburg spoke of "these honored dead"; his countrymen were as sober and grieving at the funerals of Franklin D. Roosevelt, the Kennedy brothers, and Martin Luther King as they were at that of Lincoln

himself. Arlington National Cemetery and the solemnly beautiful acres of the Punchbowl in Honolulu are properly hallowed
ground.

But Mann could have been describing film and TV entrepreneurs and millions of their viewers flourishing 60 years after
The Magic Mountain, when he called our century's "vicious
attraction to death" just what it is—"a ghastly aberration." As a
mode of trivialization it is among the deepest symptoms of moral
decay in this or any other age.

16 ✐ Education

Nobody except degenerates like Hitler and his bravos, and occasional nobs like Baron de Mandeville, comes out flatly against education. Not these days, anyway. Mandeville, an aristocrat, was convinced that dissemination of knowledge for the working poor should be kept within their occupations because "the more a shepherd, a plowman or any other peasant knows of the world, the less fit he'll be to go through the fatigues and hardships of it with cheerfulness and content."

Hitler, whose awfulness might have been entertaining as high camp had it gone no farther than *Mein Kampf* and not programmed itself into a holocaust, scorned universal education as "the most corroding poison that liberalism has ever invented for its own destruction," and was explicit as to the kind of education he wanted for German youth: "A violently active, dominating, intrepid, brutal youth—that is what I am after. ... I will have no intellectual training. Knowledge is ruin to my young men."

In America, on the other hand, lip service to the glories of education, and degrees of glory itself, have long been attached to the process. It has been called the apprenticeship of life, a companion no enemy can alienate, a solace in solitude, an ornament in society, a refuge in adversity, the cheap defense of nations, a debt due from the present to the future, our only political safety, and the most important function of the state.

And our society has put its money where its mouth is. In the 1970's alone, federal support to public education amounted to 227 billions. Small wonder it has been thought of as the established church of the United States. A visiting Englishman, product of a quite different system, assessed education as one of America's major religions, replete with its own orthodoxy, its pontiffs and its noble buildings.[2]

Yet though education is the nation's third ranking industry, it, too, has been and is being trivialized from within and without, by steady whittling away to the point where the very words themselves, trivia and triviality, appear like symbols woven into a tapestry. "Teaching," wrote William Arrowsmith, himself a teacher, "has been fatally trivialized by scholarship which has become trivial."[3] Robert M. Hutchins, once Chancellor of the University of Chicago, spoke of the need for "the elimination of triviality from the elementary and secondary schools."

Notwithstanding billions spent on schooling, the reward for teachers has been notoriously low compared to other professions. Barely to keep up with inflation, teachers have had to strike from time to time. President Kennedy spoke of

> modern cynics and skeptics who see no harm in paying those to whom we entrust the minds of our children a smaller wage than is paid to those to whom they entrust the care of their plumbing.[4]

There was a time when criticism and discussion of education, to say nothing of debate, were staged on high ground, and compounded into a formidable literature. Never mind Plato and Socrates; there were poets like Matthew Arnold, scientists like

[2]Sir Michael Sadler, *The New York Times*, 9.1.56.
[3]In *Matrix*, '67.
[4]Address at Vanderbilt University, May 19, 1963.

Thomas Huxley, churchmen like Cardinal Newman, philosophers like John Locke, historians like Renan, statesmen like Jefferson, essayists like Emerson, critics like F.R. Leavis, novelists like C.P. Snow, all of whom had strong positions and advanced them with such skill and polished language that even today they reward the reader who enjoys good rhetoric. Positions were argued by distinguished adversaries, and some of the issues involved are still unsettled: humanism versus utilitarianism; liberal education versus scientific training; knowledge of Shakespeare versus knowledge of quantum mechanics.

Academia has always been vexed with problems of method, curriculum and emphasis, but these are legitimate concerns of education, and do not represent trivialization. However, when a school declares a holiday because its football team wins the big game; when courses in frivolous subjects take up time and space; when students are admitted to major universities without knowing the difference between *there* and *their*, or cannot recognize the contradiction in a sentence like, "There should be no prejudice against negroes and other lower races"; when there is an air of patient sufferance in the classroom, as though the enrollees were serving time to get a degree; when scholarship is forced to unseemly lengths and postures in order to satisfy austere dicta of publish-or-perish; when tenure is granted or denied on bases other than the merit of the teacher, then education joins all those other systems and processes on the long casualty list of trivialization.

A century and a half ago, John Henry Cardinal Newman, lecturing in Dublin on the aims of education, defined them as raising the intellectual tone of society, cultivating the public mind, purifying the national taste, applying true principles to popular enthusiasm and aspiration, giving enlargement and sobriety to the ideas of the age, facilitating the exercise of political power, and refining the intercourse of private life. Nobody of good will and intent can cavil about those objectives, but all of us may well mourn the disappearance of most of them from the sights of academe today. The good Cardinal would settle deeper in his grave if he knew that the principles applied to popular enthusiasm are currently channeled into athletic programs, that the intellectual tone of society is so low as almost to defy being raised, that the public mind is cultivated chiefly by advertising and publicity, that the fixed aims of popular aspiration are material success, celebrity, and political power, that the ideas of the age, while sometimes large and sober, are more often mean and confused, that the exercise of political power is facilitated chiefly by the media, and that to "refine the intercourse of private life" would be generally construed to mean improving sexual techniques.

Early in 1982, a man named Billy Don Jackson, who had been a football star at UCLA, found himself in court. He had been voted the team's "most inspirational player" by his teammates, and had received an award for "best spirit and scholarship." He left the university in his junior year, and a few months later got into an altercation with a drug dealer and stabbed him to death. He pleaded no-contest to a charge of voluntary manslaughter and was sentenced to a year's jail term and five years of probation, with an important condition attached: that he take remedial instruction to "increase his ability to read and write so that will never be an embarrassment to him again."

The prosecutor was satisfied with the verdict, but made a comment that Cardinal Newman might have pondered with morbid interest: "My God, they brought this kid to one of the top universities in the country and it takes a court order for him to properly learn to read and write."

Among those who attended the trial was UCLA's football coach, Terry Donohue, who regretted "how sad this thing is," and pledged to help Jackson "in any way possible for the future." It was fine for the coach to show interest and sympathy, but what was and remains missing from the picture is an explanation from the Chancellor of UCLA as to how (we know *why*) a student who could neither read nor write could be admitted and stay for three years in a citadel of learning whose chief purpose, as Francis Bacon put it 400 years ago, should be "to dignify and exalt knowledge."

Jackson was far from alone in his lack of literacy. Statistics cited by the MacNeil-Lehrer Report in April, 1982, placed the number of illiterates in America at 25 million, with another 10 million who cannot read or write well enough to answer a want ad. The pool of illiteracy was estimated to be *growing* at a rate of one million each year.

Certainly universities are not to blame for such a dismal condition. They do not teach illiteracy. The responsibility rests with national priorities which, at bottom, create matrices for everything political, economic and cultural. And if a country gives higher priority to aiding corporations like Lockheed and Chrysler than to aiding education, then it should hardly surprise us when an eighth of our population cannot read a newspaper or write a letter.

Money, being the root of both good and evil, is capable of either nurturing or blighting educational growth. The nurturing function is obvious, but the process of corruption tends to be subtle and sometimes takes many forms, all of which have the effect of trivializing education. One of these is subsidization, either open or covert, by government and industrial agencies including the CIA, NASA, the Atomic Energy Commission, and chemical, pharmaceutical and electronic corporate giants. In the late 60's, when the dollar was much less frayed by inflation than it became later, the military establishment poured 758 millions into defense-contract research at 12 universities,[5] the research being done in campus labs by university personnel. An additional 288 millions were spent at the same addresses on "classified" contracts.

Nearly 20 years later, Du Pont, Mallinckrodt, and other such houses, having been quick to notice the commercial implica-

[5]M.I.T., Cal Tech, Stanford, Harvard, Illinois Tech, George Washington, John Hopkins, Pennsylvania, Texas, California, Cornell and Princeton.

tions of the New Biology, put millions into university research on molecular genetics and other aspects of biotechnology. Under the heading, "The Big Bucks of Biology," *Newsweek* (April 6, 1982) reported a conference of the presidents and top scientists of M.I.T., Cal Tech, Stanford, California and Harvard to deal with the hazards of "turning science into the handmaiden of industry and corrupting the nature of basic research. ... The fear is that profits and not truth will guide science."

One of the side effects of subsidizing the new biology was to make millionaires out of a few select professors, and to promote others to high corporate office while still teaching.

At UC Davis, according to *Newsweek*,

> students complained that Raymond Valentine, who is vice-president of [a company named] Calgene, abruptly switched their projects after they'd spent two years on them. In some cases, charges biologist Raymond Rodriguez, "grad students have had their projects changed to serve commercial interests."

Complaints of this order apparently had little effect, because late in 1983, *The New York Times*, in an article by Katheriene Bouton, reported that it would be difficult to find even a single scientist among leading university researchers who was not affiliated with a powerful corporation. "The university-industry waltz," Bouton called it. And the dance goes on. In return for agreements to deliver patents or licenses deriving from special studies, Du Pont has given Harvard Medical School $6 million, Celanese and Bristol-Meyers made like arrangements with Yale; M.I.T. was dealt $8.5 million by W.R. Grace, and Monsanto spread $50.5 million among three universities.

This situation recalls one of Cardinal Newman's lodestar lectures in which he attacked the insistence by influential forces of his time, that education should be confined to "some particular and narrow end, and should issue in some definite work, which can be weighed and measured." Newman's opposition to this connects by a long fuse to an explosive comment by Robert

Hutchins, made in an address at the University of Chicago in 1967:

> To confuse education with training and the transmission of information, and to conceive of the university as the instrument by which we become prosperous and powerful is to guarantee, insofar as an educational system can affect the outcome, the collapse of civilization.

Defenders of subsidization argue that it expands, not contracts, specialized areas of education. In some instances, where a university imposes no-strings-attached conditions on corporate endowments, a case can be made for the defense. But there is no defense for the barbarity of slashing educational funds as was done by the Reagan administration, both directly and by fobbing off responsibility to state and local governments under the high-sounding principle of "The New Federalism." At the same time that Reagan and his neoconservatives were fattening the Pentagon's budget, enriching already flush corporations through a tax-credit dodge of breathtaking audacity, and slashing taxes for the Warbucks element, preparations were going forward to liquidate the Department of Education.

A significant expression of the indifference, if not hostility, of the Reagan policy toward the educational needs of minorities was the shutting down of the only institute of higher education for American Indians—Deganawidah-Quetztalcoatl (D-Q) University, near Davis, California, a polytechnic school which had prepared Indians for jobs in industry. It was cut off from federal support at a time when unemployment among Indians was the highest for any group in the country, including blacks.[6]

Reagan's New Federalism was described by Henry Steele Commager (*L.A. Times*, March 14, 1982) as an intrusion upon

[6]D-Q University in 1977 was awarded the highest accreditation rating of the Western Association of Schools and Colleges, and in 1981 a 41-member United Nations delegation toured D-Q and found it "a university of the people...a people with a culture that is centered upon love of fellow mankind." According to David Risling, D-Q's president, the Reagan administration was anxious to evict the school and sell the property as surplus land.

an area historically off-limits to government meddling:

> Why should education, which is more obviously the concern
> of the whole people of the United States than any other public
> authority, except defense, be reserved exclusively to the states?
> What, after all, is local about education? Why should Amer-
> icans take for granted that there should be 50 educational
> systems, 50 curricula, 50 standards of educational compe-
> tence, 50 levels of appropriations, all varying widely not only
> from state to state, but within each state? ... why should there
> be 50 standards of education in a nation that does not have 50
> standards of voting or office-holding or of military service, or—
> and this is important—of political philosophy?

Then, quoting Chief Justice Earl Warren in the historic *Brown
vs. Topeka* case to the effect that education is today "the most
important function of the state ... the very foundation of good
citizenship," Commager concludes:

> If this is true—and who can doubt it is—why should there be
> 50 standards of education to prepare for a single standard of
> citizenship? Are we one nation or 50?

The answer is that to a true trivializer, a single high standard of
education is less important than lowering a deficit. Small
intellect often resents large capacity in others, and it is not
surprising, therefore, to find numbered among the sayings of
Ronald Reagan the naked question, "Why should we subsidize
intellectual curiosity?" That question is as bold a statement of
philistinism in education as has ever come from an American
public official above the level of sheriff. For it is precisely the lack
of stimulation and deadening of curiosity that has drawn the
heaviest fire against education all through our history, a barrage
that continues to this day. It is what prompted Jefferson to say,
"State a moral case to a plowman and a professor. The former will
decide it as well, and often better than the latter, because he has
not been led astray by artificial rules"; and which caused the
Adams of *The Education of Henry Adams* to write, "nothing in
education is so astonishing as the amount of ignorance it

accumulates in the form of inert facts ... the chief wonder of education is that it does not ruin everybody concerned in it, teachers and taught alike"; and which drew from that most assimilable of American philosophers, Will Rogers, the observation that there is nothing more stupid than an educated man once you get him off the things he was educated in.

Criticism of education continues to accumulate. But at what are such disparagements aimed? At the study of medicine? Law? Engineering? Business? The school of nursing? Physics? Geology? None of the above. They are aimed at the humanities. For it is safe to attack the teaching of the humanities. They have no army. Medicine is watched over by the hawk's eye of the AMA; the law has regulatory agencies and superstructures; chemistry and biology are nurselings of industry; but the liberal arts have few knights to enter the lists for them. One of these paladins, oddly enough, was President Lyndon Johnson, who when he signed the Arts and Humanities Act in 1965, noted that "Somehow the scientists always seem to get the penthouse while the arts and humanities get the basement."

For a while, before Reagan spread his roc's wing over the realm of education, the humanities were permitted upstairs, to mingle with moneyed company. As of this writing they are not only back down, grovelling in the sub-basement for a living, but holding out tattered hats for pennies from the private sector.

17 ✑ Mediocrity

Trivialization, mediocrity, kitsch and conformity are profitably compatible. Their harmony is unrehearsed, each arriving at its station in our culture by a separate path.

Mediocrity is a business, like making low-quality shirts for low-income consumers at a low price. With this important difference—mediocrity cuts across all arts and professions, all layers of society, all politics, law, government, art, science, religion, industry. While there are scattered islands and archipelagos of excellence in each domain, mediocrity is like a continental mass. Not only in America, of course. But we have the distinction of being the only country that is proud of it, the only country where mediocrity rules by fiat, as in the structured mediocrity of most of commercial television, and the planned obsolescence of many manufactured products.

Only in America, so far, has anyone in high office called for mediocrity as a national desideratum. Senator Roman L. Hruska of Nebraska, defending the nomination of G. Harrold Carswell for Justice of Nixon's U.S. Supreme Court, against criticism that he was mediocre, stated

> Even if he were mediocre, there are a lot of mediocre judges and people and lawyers. They are entitled to a little representa-

tion, aren't they, and a little chance? We can't have all Brandeises and Frankfurters and Cardozos and stuff like that there.

The Senator need not have worried. The representation is blanket and perennial, and always working. Russell Baker, journalist, came to believe that being no brighter than anyone else is a social asset among Americans.

There is a certain negative comfort in the thought that every country has its Hruskas; that among nations in Europe which are far from backward the cry is an old one. Napoleon and Pascal, to name only two, complained about small-mindedness in France; in England John Stuart Mill glumly noted "a general tendency throughout the world to render mediocrity the ascendent power"; in Germany Schopenhauer was sure that mediocrity was in league against excellence, not only to resist but to suppress it. Still, Americans themselves are the first to admit that the famous inscription of welcome at the base of the Statue of Liberty might well have been extended to include not only the tired, the poor, the homeless and the tempest-tost, but the lacklustre. James Fenimore Cooper warned against a "tendency to gravitate toward lending a value and estimation to mediocrity that are not elsewhere given." A century later, President Hoover fretted that we were in danger of developing "a cult of mediocrity." In the 60's, Robert Osborne, essayist and cartoonist, wrote angrily in *The Vulgarians*, "We are settling by default, as no great nation has ever settled, for a conforming, unthreatening, median, massive mediocrity." He also warned against accepting "dangerously simple answers," thus anticipating by a generation the most widely voiced criticism of the Reagan administration in the 80's.

Though writers are conspicuous among Cassandras of mediocrity, they have company. Charles Brower, president of B.B.D. & O., felt we are living in "the great era of the goof-off, the age of the half-done job, of waiters who won't serve, carpenters who will come around some day, executives whose mind is on the golf course, students who take cinch courses."

Crawford Greenwalt, head of Du Pont, believed society itself is injured when people "sacrifice identity in the damp laundry of mediocrity." Anthropologist Margaret Mead was appalled to find people "working hard to be as mediocre as possible."

Mediocrity is, above all, comfortable. It makes modest demands on the powers of perception and ratiocination, and none at all on creativity. This translates itself into business opportunities—to supply instantly recognizable and assimilable goods, whether they are pictures, music, books, gifts, novelties, whatever.

If it is hard to think of something original in the way of a birthday greeting, there is corporate help. Various services are ready to take care of it for you—one of them by dispatching a messenger to sing your sentiment for a fee. If you are from a small town and visit New York City, and want either to impress the distinction of your travels on friends back home or remind yourself perpetually of the exhilaration of looking down from the torch of the Statue of Liberty, or from the top of the Empire State Building, you buy a Statue of Liberty thermometer, or a bronze model of the Empire State. A Philadelphia manufacturer sells 500,000 tiny replicas of the Liberty Bell each year. Disneyland averages 560,000 pairs of Mickey Mouse ears annually sold over the counter. Elvis Presley belt-buckles sell briskly in Memphis; tri-cornered hats in Colonial Williamsburg; bags of salt in Salt Lake City; peanuts in Plains, Georgia. Souvenir shops throughout the country take in upwards of two billion dollars a year.

A discriminating tourist could find a dozen objects that better express the character of Washington, D.C., than an ashtray with the Capital Dome pictured on it. In buying the ashtray to give as a gift, the tourist knows it is not unique, because the shop has cartons full of identical copies; but uniqueness is not a consideration, either for him, or, in all likelihood, the prospective recipient. For a bringer of gifts does not want to worry whether the offering will be scorned as tasteless, naive or inferior; he chooses friends as he chooses gifts, on his own level.

To the consumer reared in mediocrity, travel souvenirs are pieces of time, place or history just as a Prudential insurance policy is a Piece of the Rock. During the presidency of Lyndon Johnson, an enterprising Texan sold little jars of water from the Pedernales River, water which had been sanctified by flowing past the Johnson ranch. When Mt. St. Helens erupted, merchandisers packaged and sold thousands of plastic envelopes, each containing an ounce of volcanic ash. Tokens of this kind present no hazard, but when *ideas* are bottled, when problems are stuffed into little packages, when answers to critical questions are turned out like souvenir ashtrays, mediocrity no longer frolics in the fun house, but exerts a heavy presence everywhere.

The relationship between kitsch and mediocrity is more causal than casual, since a country that embraces stereotypes in art, religion, music, education, entertainment and economics, will accept political stereotypes too. It is no accident that Soviet paintings, sculpture, architecture, design, journalism and literature are as stolid and dull as the country's political establishment. In America, fortunately, there is too much raw assertiveness and competition for that particular type of ossification to set in, but mediocrity and stereotypicality are nevertheless fed by deep springs in our culture, by the levelling effects of media, by celebrity worship, the trivialization of education, the proliferation of kitsch, and the power of money to sway, if not buy, elections.

Only a mediocre culture could have tolerated for so long, and with more approval than disapproval, the degradation of its liberties by Senator Joseph McCarthy and the cadre of political troglodytes who flourished in his time. Only an electorate of poor-to-middling judgment could have shrugged off Nixon's early record and elevated him to the presidency, and then repeated the mistake four years later. Only political parties numbed by hype, and too passive to demand reforms in our primary, nominating and appointive systems, could have picked super-mediocrities like Ford, Carter and Reagan to begin with.

"One has to come to grips," said James Michener in an interview, "with why we pass up the great men to be president. We pass them up because we don't want first class men in that position; we want somebody who is a stupid bum like us. We really are in quite serious trouble."

The trouble he speaks of is a uniformity which often is mistaken for blandness, when in fact it can be quite dangerous. For uniformity, when imposed by state or religion, ultimately becomes a silent destroyer, like a wind carrying poisonous radiation across a continent. Historically without exception, conformity has strengthened ruling cadres by identifying loyalty with conformism. Many times in our own past this has happened—in the Sedition Acts of 1798, the Bolshevik scare of the 20's, the Alien Registration Act of 1940, the loyalty tests and decontaminations of the mid-40's, and, worst of the lot, the craven anti-communist hysteria under Truman and Eisenhower, when witch-hounding blacklists and purges riddled government, church, film, radio, TV, education, law, medicine, labor, the armed services, and many occupations theretofore untouched by heresy-hunts. Not only did persecution of political pariahs damage careers and lives, but by smothering dissent, it wiped out resistance to the mediocritization that had become endemic through manipulation of public temper and opinion. Andre Siegfried, French economist and historian, wrote in 1965 that in America public opinion "is both more spontaneous than anywhere else in the world and also more easily directed by efficient propaganda technique than in any other country." The unpleasant truth is that for most of this century, we have lived with what amounts to a one-party press in a two-party country, and only when the war in Vietnam became so malignant that the bankruptcy of our position was obvious to all but a war-obsessed president and a core of unshakable doctrinaires did the monolith crack.

Orthodoxy, sacred as it may be to subscribing theologians, is the fast friend of mediocrity, since it removes incentive to think. An army is a model of orthodoxy; it is made up mostly of bodies which act on command; whatever thinking is necessary to its functions is done for it. The same applies to communicants of all fanatical religious and social orders (Khomeini in Iran; Jim Jones in Guyana). No wonder Isaiah scorned ritual and Jefferson hated priests who "so disfigure the simple religion of Jesus."

The ultimate in trivialization is to reduce the capacity and will of people to think for themselves. In that exercise mediocritization has always had its strongest support, corroboration and collaboration.

18 ✐ Pilpul

Quibbles. Pilpul. Argle-bargle. All are forms of trivialization, involving disputation over trifling niceties. Smallness of detail may suggest that hair-splitting is a pastime of simple types, of rustics and bumpkins, but nothing could be further from the truth. Cavils and quiddities come much more often from refined, perhaps overrefined, intellects.

No one can deny the scholarship and dedication of the *mishnayim* and *shass* who for generations met to study and explicate the *Mishnah, Gamara, Talmud* and other canons of Jewish law and tradition. Yet for all the breadth and dignity of their inquiry, they were not above wrangling at great length over such matters as the simple injunction in Exodus 16:29, limiting travel on the Sabbath: "... let no man go out of his place on the seventh day." A faction led by Rabbi ben Nuri argued that if a man falls asleep on a journey and does not know the Sabbath has begun during his sleep, he may with impunity proceed 2000 cubits, a little over half a mile, in any direction. But another sage insisted the traveller may move only four cubits, or about six feet, whereas Rabbi Judah believed that in either case, once the man chooses a direction, he may not change it.[1]

[1]*The Mishnah*, selected and edited by Eugene H. Lipman, Norton, 1970.

Not much has changed in circles of high haggling. A volume on the work of the American painter Barnett Newman,[2] includes an exchange of pilpul between Newman and the art historian Dr. Edwin Panofsky. The latter, commenting on contemporary works of art, alluded to Newman's canvas entitled *Vir Heroicus Sublimis*:

> I find myself confronted with three different interpretations of the curious form *"Sublimus"*: Does Mr. Newman imply that he, as Aelfric says of God, is "above grammar"; or is it a misprint; or is it plain illiteracy?[3]

Newman responded:

> Ernout and Meillet, the authorities on Latin etymology, in their famous dictionary, give *"sublimus"* as a collateral form (*Doublet archaique*) . . . of particular importance is the fact that *"sublimus"* was used by the Roman poet Accius (170-86 B.C.) who is quoted as using this construction, by Cicero.
>
> It is not for me to argue over Panofsky's Latin . . . it is enough to point out that he does not know quite as much as he thinks he does. He should, therefore, be flunked not only for bad research but also for poor scholarship . . . One would think that by now Professor Panofsky would know the basic fact about a work of art, that for a work of art to be a work of art, it must rise above grammar and syntax—*pro gloria Dei.*[4]

Erudition is a legitimate goal of scholars, teachers, critics and philosophers, but it can be niggled to bits by overparticularity. There is a tendency among deeply read critics to dispute minor details while misreading the main event. Bernard DeVoto occasionally did this. He castigated Pare Lorentz's documentary film *The River* for having gone only down only one bank of the Mississippi, and was offended by the use of the word "elsewise," a mild variant of "otherwise," in a major documentary broadcast. "A discriminating mind," he proclaimed "could not possibly have written 'elsewise'."

[2]*Barnett Newman*, by Harold Rosenberg, Abrams, 1978.
[3]*Art News*, February, 1961.
[4]*Art News*, May, 1961.

Another pilpulist attacked an all-star four-network dramatic broadcast commemorating the ratification of the American Bill of Rights, because the cast had too much name-power and the production generated too much energy through its integration of sound and music. "All that the occasion required," he wrote, "was a Chief Justice of the United States Supreme Court reading aloud the first ten amendments to the Constitution."

Pauline Kael, film critic, was certain Genevieve Bujold could never become a star of the first rank because she had the wrong nose. Richard Schickel, writing in *Time*, decided Marsha Mason was "not really attractive enough to make one forgive her inadequacies as a performer." John Simon told a Filmex audience, "To have a beautiful film about supposedly beautiful human beings portrayed by a Barbra Streisand or a Liza Minelli ... is an offense as colossal as if the dialogue were all four-letter words. I cannot adjust myself to ugliness just because ugliness enjoys enshrinement by public bad taste."

Vincent Canby took up one-sixth of a review in the *New York Times* deriding names that Richard Brooks had given to two characters in his movie, *Right Is Wrong*. One was Patrick Hale. "If that name doesn't make you fall on the floor in a fit of laughter, nothing in the film will ... the level of wit is best gauged by such character names as Patrick Hale and that of the female vice-president, who is called Mrs. Ford."[5]

Karl Shapiro, writing with the intensity of *mishnayim* calculating the number of cubits one may travel on the sabbath, analyzed an allusion by the poet Yeats to "nine-and-fifty swans":

> What is the purpose of this strange and unnecessary form of enumeration? Is it only a piece of romantic Irish parlance, a graceful decoration of a numerical fact? Not at all. In the first place, "nine-and-fifty swans" means something that "fifty-nine swans" does not, if only for the reason that nine-and-fifty swans is metrical. Whether Yeats took an actual count is beside the point; we gather from the poem that the birds rose in the air before he was finished "counting." He has found, I think, the

[5]*The New York Times,* 4.16.82.

best, if not the inevitable number. One might conceive of fifty
swans, perhaps, but not quite fifty-nine swans, and certainly
not sixty-nine or nine-and-forty swans. I do not know how to
explain this except by saying that forty in most contexts is an
obese word and fifty a *lean* word. In Cummings' poem about
Buffalo Bill the number-shape onetwothreefourfive gives the
number of pigeons shot down in a single burst. There would be
no art evidently in shooting down four pigeons and too much
in shooting down six. The phrase nine-and-fifty does not
represent the root meaning 59, but rather . . . all the effects on
the senses of that mysterious number.

Shapiro, like the *mishnayim*, was sincere and not specious in
attaching weighty significance to numbers, nor was he putting
anyone down. On the other hand, preciosity when used for show,
is a form of one-upmanship. As in a turning camshaft, every
upstroke produces a corresponding downstroke: The one-upsman
succeeds only at someone's expense.

The writer who labors at elegance and preens himself on
arcane language, knows that he is placing a screen between
himself and his reader. A professor of English at UCLA, in a
book review published in *The Los Angeles Times*, used the noun
tralatition. He liked it so well that he came back two paragraphs
later with the adjective *tralatitious.* Tralatition cannot be found
in the *Random House Unabridged,* the *Heritage* or the *Webster's
Collegiate* dictionaries, but it is listed in *Mrs. Byrne's Dictionary
of Unusual, Obscure and Preposterous Words,* which is where it
belongs. It means metaphorical. It is an uncommonly inept
word because its first two syllables are "tra la," and I doubt if any
noun that wants to be taken seriously can recover from that.

Just as madmen do not think they are mad, and bores think
they are fascinating, pedants are never aware of their pedantry. A
professor who teaches at Northwestern, wrote an article on
Readers Theatre, an institution which deals essentially with
people getting up on a stage and reading texts from books or
plays. The piece bears the title, "Readers Theatre: Spatio-
Temporal Interpenetration," which is warning enough. Instead of

clarifying the object, it obscures it through phrases like, "changing ratios of auditor-event relationships ... the body in sounding gives the paralanguage to language ... multisensory impingements ... teledynamic environment ... interpenetration of sight and sound will become congruent to the original flexibility of the rhapsode to play upon the sensorium of the listener ... the creation of meta worlds beyond the immediate place of spatial temporal occupancy." Not that theory is unwelcome, but in a journal intended for student actors and directors, it should not sound like a psychoanalytic text.

The connection between pedantry and trivialization may seem remote, but anything which does a disservice to language, to a subject, to the capacity of a student to assimilate, anything which spoils the fun or inhibits the sense of adventure implicit in every learning process, ends by reducing the teacher, those he teaches, and what is taught.

Intelligence has little to do with it. Pilpulists, bores and pedants can be very bright; indeed, as they plod from point to point, most of them are. It's just that they lack discrimination and proportion, both of which translate into values. William Arrowsmith, writing in *Matrix*, '67, was sure that

> Socrates could no more make associate professor these days than Christ could be elected Pope. Our scholars are tame, inturbulent and decent men, and their scholarship is like them. We are losing touch with what is greatest and most turbulently useful in our past, and what is worst, we don't seem to know it.

More discouraging than tameness, is that when scholars do occasionally strike out on bold new salients, they take us, oftener than not, in directions that lead nowhere, or to places we'd rather not go, or toward some impossible goal. One such excursion demonstrates how subtly trivialization works in areas like social philosophy:

For twenty weeks at Berkeley and UCLA, various notables of the arts and professions met in symposia to discuss the substance of what they considered an important study by Dr. Joseph Meeker, a book entitled *The Comedy of Survival*. The doctor's thesis is that in the interests of survival, we must turn from what he calls "the tragic mode," which he says has dominated our civilization. to embrace what he calls "the comic mode," through which we can live harmoniously with our environment. No one can quarrel with that objective. But Dr. Meeker defines comedy as

> a philosophy which permits people to respond with health and clear vision despite the miseries the world has to offer. Its mode is immediacy of attention, joy in small things, the avoidance of pain whenever possible, the sharpening of intelligence, complexity in thought and action, and strategic responsiveness to novel situations.

This was hailed by many thoughtful people as a truly valuable formula for survival, and no one in those 20 weeks of confabulation demurred. Yet under scrutiny the proposal turns out to be not only antic and vague but dangerous. It trivializes elements and forces which it would be much safer to respect. In the order in which Dr. Meeker laid them down, the following considerations arise:

Avoidance of pain sounds attractive, but it easily translates into avoidance of responsibility, a running away from the very realities to which we must be educated, and against which we would do well to be forearmed. Taken to a logical extreme, avoidance of pain is justification for the drug culture. Seeking anodynes is far less useful for survival than seeking solutions.

"Joy in small things," is a luxury to be indulged only after we have taken care of the big things like peace, freedom, public health and solvency. Victims of famine and war, driven from their homes or reduced to eating rats and insects, take very little joy in small things.

Dr. Meeker advocates "immediacy of attention" as another precept of the comic mode. We snap to attention fast enough when gas prices go rocketing and the lines form; we are instantly aware when Argentina invades the Falklands; or Mexican fruit flies or killer bees invade southern California; we don't have to be alerted to the dangers of nuclear waste.

Sharpening of intelligence? Whose standard of intelligence? Hitler was intelligent. Nobody could be sharper than the lords of OPEC. The Mafia has some of the best business brains in the country.

What are the values of "complexity of thought and action"? Some of us are already so complicated in thought and action that it takes therapy or divorce courts or Dear Abby to straighten us out.

Dr. Meeker urges us to realize that

> the major threats and sources of pain are inherent in the nature of things, and are not merely errors of judgment that we can correct by human manipulations, personal commitments, or by some form of moral rearmament. Good guys and bad guys seem to share the same leaky boat, and it becomes harder to worry about who the villains are, as we discover that we are *all* victims.

Alas, it does not become harder to worry about who the villains are, it becomes easier every day. And there is little to be said for sharing a leaky boat with bad guys. It is much more sensible to pitch them overboard and patch the leaks.

"Perhaps," Dr. Meeker suggests, "we should spend less time trying to transform the world that surrounds us." When Porgy in *Porgy and Bess* sings, "I got plenty of nothing and nothing's plenty for me," we understand him but we don't want to emulate him. It seems an extremely poor ambition to change ourselves to fit the world that surrounds us—a world of unprecedented greed, cruelty and terror, poisoned by chemicals and radiation, polluted by smog and noise, overpopulated, its masses dancing like some species of super-monkey on strings pulled by cartels, lobbies, capital, labor, the Kremlin, the third world, the market, the military, the oligarchies and the oiligarchies.

Dr. Meeker also believes that disasters such as physical and biological events, failing institutions, new strains of disease, nuclear accidents, accumulated wastes and

catastrophes that we have not prepared for, remind us convincingly that we are not in control of our world, and our welfare is not essential to its processes. Painful as that lesson will be, it can teach us the basic humility and acceptance which is needed to transform a tragic view of life into a comic one.

Nowhere is mention made of preparedness except for the single negative, "catastrophes that we have not prepared for." The doctor proposes accepting earthquakes, physical events such as famine, and failing institutions, with basic humility—a proposition that invites submission and sufferance, and honors such doctrines as Laissez-Faire, Render unto Caesar, You Can't Fight City Hall, Blessed Be the Meek, Roll with the Punches, Take It Easy, Laugh It Off, and the Satchel Paige imperative, "Don't look back, because someone might be gaining on you." To which is now added, "Don't look ahead, either."

These are hardly constructive recommendations. What they do is to trivialize the problems of today's world, and that is like saying to someone who is slipping off the edge of a precipice, "Remember! Basic humility! Goodbye and good luck!"

19 ✒ Research

Control of fire, invention of the wheel, shaping of tools, development of writing, domestication of animals, organization of government are among the recognized major building blocks of civilization. Usually absent from such lists is research, from which comes everything about us—the commonest appliances, the light we turn on, the fillings in our teeth, vitamin capsules, television, the automobile, the glasses we wear, the paper in this page, freedom from polio; all are the results of basic or applied research.

Of the pillars and arches supporting society, research is relatively recent, dating from the 16th century in Europe. Francis Bacon was one of the first to urge organized research toward investigation of nature and the study of scientific laws. But it was not until the 1800s that research took hold, chiefly in America. Since then research of all kinds has burgeoned until today the initials R & D, for research and development, are as common and familiar as EKG and IOU. Every major city's directories list from a dozen to half a hundred research companies, and no important industry, science or university is without a formidable research arm, with the military the biggest R & D spender of them all.

Research has been called a necessity, a gamble, a state of mind, an art, a craft, and an organized method for keeping us reasonably dissatisfied with what we have. It is the device we use when we want to find out what device to use. It works to solve problems, dissolve myths, enlarge, confirm, negate, instruct, persuade. It can open or close hypotheses, penetrate to the pith of matter, carry us into worlds beyond our own; it can unbraid the helix, peel layers off the mysteries of origin, swing on the hinges of time.

It can also be trivialized. In staggering proportions it is assigned to such tasks as marketing research, to find out why people will or will not buy a certain cold tablet, deodorant, weight reducer, car, cigarette, sanitary napkin, razor, gasoline, soft drink or brand of salmon. More money is poured into the shape and color of bottles and packages, the names and logos of products, the style and trim of automobiles, the groupings and preferences of TV's public than is invested in cancer research or consumer safety.

Even though marketing research is often trained on the weaknesses or vanity of the consumer, and even though the euphemisms of the marketplace are sometimes distressingly coy ("To women," counseled Dr. Ernest Dichter, expert in these matters, "don't sell shoes—sell lovely feet!"), there is nothing utterly debasing or contemptible about any of this low level stuff—it's a living, and in a free market there is no reason why a manufacturer should not try every resort short of dishonesty and misrepresentation to gain an edge over competition. Nobody gets painfully hurt by claims that four out of five prefer Scrunchies over any other caramel nut bar or toilet paper, even though the statistical base for the claim may be open to question. But in some other areas of research, the results may turn out to be any of

several unsavory things, and sometimes all of them at once—
inaccurate, misleading, reversionary, prejudiced, fatuous, downgrading and, for some individuals, devastating.

The least heinous and most widely practiced subspecies of
research are those of audience measurements—the familiar
rating systems known as Trendex, ARB, and Neilsen, with their
Overnights, Multi-Network Area Reports, Storage Instantaneous
Audimeters, and Sweeps. None of these techniques, and the
slavishness with which networks and advertisers act on their
results, are in good odor with the people who make programs for
audiences that are constantly being measured—the writers,
actors, directors and producers—and complaints come not just
from those whose productions rank low or middling in the lists.
Norman Lear, perhaps the single most successful creative TV
entrepreneur in the world, has harsh things to say about the
perpetual scramble for numbers:

> Network insistence on instant success ... and the industry's
> obsession with ratings and profits [is] squeezing the joy out of
> our efforts. ... the pressure to do one's very best has been
> forced to take a back seat to the need for high ratings.[1]

Aaron Spelling, another prosperous commercial producer (*Fantasy Island, Charlie's Angels*) scorns the practice of listing the top
ten programs in the press:

> What really bothers me [is] the space and publicity that TV
> critics and columnists give this stupid game. These are the
> same critics and columnists who tell us TV is terrible and we
> should be doing programs of more depth. Well, you can't have
> it both ways. If you want better programming, then stop adding
> fuel to the ratings fire. Stop glorifying the meaning of ratings.[2]

Not only the emphasis given but the techniques used, are
nettling to Lear and Spelling and hundreds of their cohorts.
Neilsen's audimeter is placed in 1,170 homes; it is a little black
box attached to a TV receiver. It is activated when the set is

---

[1]Speech to the Hollywood Radio and Television Society, Sept. 9, 1981.
[2]Speech to The Academy of Television Arts and Sciences, August 20, 1981.

turned on, and it records on tape each channel tuned in, and for how long it is watched. Its readings serve as base samples for from 68.5 to 70 million television homes throughout the country, a percentage of around .0017 at most. The trouble is, not all the sets are in working order all the time, not all the viewers stay in front of their sets while programs and commercials are on, and there is no precise way of interpreting the data.

Bob Shanks, TV director and producer, in his book *The Cool Fire* explains why ratings go on unchanged in spite of protests, congressional hearings, and frequent debates on the subject: "All who are serious about staying in television simply forget about how ludicrous the system is and accept it. After all, everyone is playing by the same rules. [The overnights are] an idiotic, meaningless and masochistic ritual and I participate in it every day."

The Nielsen system at least has a black box that processes tapes, but two other measuring techniques include sweat and switchable dials. In one, skin tests are made to record variations in the sweat of the viewer's hand; in the other, the subject is equipped with a control that may be switched to any of five positions: very dull, dull, normal, good, and very good. The procedure starts with a vintage *Mr. Magoo* short; thereafter the Magoo is used as the unit of acceptance. Thus a successful pilot is one that scores between 5.1 and 6.3 Magoos. Anything unfamiliar to a viewer runs low on the Magoo scale, whereas dogs, small children, and car chases rank high. Shanks tells of a time when he and Merv Griffin were called in by the research department:

> They showed us a graph of one of these pilot-type tests. The line was going along at a fairly regular frequency, with only minor variations, when suddenly it shot up to 100. "Quick," Merv said, "Tell me what I did there, so I can do it some more."
>
> The researcher, in deadly earnest, replied, "Florence Henderson punched you in the stomach."
>
> So much for research.

Of graver account than these fillips, are gimmicks for rating individuals. One of these is TVQ, which is used as a casting guide for networks and agencies. In this system, panels of viewers are polled as to the familiarity, popularity and "likeability" of actors and actresses. At the end of August, 1982, the highest TVQ in the land was that of Alan Alda, at 57; Carol Burnett rated 43, Bill Cosby stood at 36, Johnny Carson at 28, and Martin Balsam, an excellent actor, at 8. Any number of highly talented people who had not had the benefit of exposure on long-running programs, or on any programs at all, showed (or would have shown if rated by TVQ) a cold zero. Kathleen Nolan, two-term president of the Screen Actors Guild, condemned the system and sought legal action against it. "You can't get cast," she said, "unless you're on the list—but you can't get on the list unless you get cast." Ed Asner, who succeeded Nolan as president of SAG, called it McCarthyism. The Directors Guild, in a letter to its members, attacked the use of marketing surveys and statistical data as a basis for the acceptance or rejection of casting decisions, as "totally offensive to the creative process." In response, network and advertising agencies denied or soft-pedalled their dependence on these indexes—partly no doubt because they violate clauses in major guild contracts which bar interference with creative decisions. But workers in the trade have no illusions about any intention of the networks or agencies to abandon trivializing routines.

Still another shrinkage system is called Television Audience Program Evaluation (TAPE), which at one time served the research needs of CBS. It is part of an elaborate approach called "concept testing"—used by other networks as well—in which the key elements of a proposed TV movie are studied to determine whether the concept has enough audience appeal to justify production. "Factor analysis" is part of this offering, in which ingredients of movies that received high Neilsen ratings going back to 1960 are registered as positive factors, while those found in low-rated films are put down as negative factors. Nothing matters other than the rating; so that if a very well done *Hamlet* did poorly on the Neilsen chart, it was bad for the elements of regicide, a Danish locale, period dress, and duelling; conversely, if these same ingredients appeared in a ghastly horror film that played to big grosses in Peoria and elsewhere, they would be restored to good standing.

According to interpretations of TAPE data, America's mass audiences prefer to see a white person in a central role, and the themes they most favor are either "sensational or topical" with highest preference going to rape, hustling, under-age marriage, and incest, whereas stories dealing with serious political issues score low.

The industry's writers, no less than its actors and directors, are not enchanted by TAPE, TVQ, ARB, Trendex or Neilsen. Naomi Gurian, then executive director of the Writers Guild, issued a statement which held concept testing to be "the utmost in lunacy...an avoidance of responsibility...the network mentality is to say, 'My God, wouldn't it be nice not to have to make that decision? Wouldn't it be nice if that machine made it for me?'"

The bottom line, as they say at staff meetings, is that the chief day-to-day anxieties of the film and TV industries, and to an extent in publishing, are far less over questions of talent, quality of writing, production values, concept or style than over numbers of viewers, admissions, and paid circulation. The chief product of television, as pointed out by Clark and Blankenburg in *You and Media*, is aggregates of audiences:

> The networks are really in the business of manufacturing audiences, which are then advertised and sold to advertisers who wish to reach large numbers of people at relatively little cost.

Every now and then an opinion poll or marketing study blows up and scatters debris, to the distress of researchers and their customers, and to the glee of most of the rest of us. The *Literary Digest's* monumental blunder in 1936, when its poll predicted a landslide victory for Alf Landon over FDR,[3] is as hallowed in American memory as the famous wrong-way run in the Rose Bowl. Sampling techniques have greatly improved since that time, thanks to Gallup, Roper, Harris and others, so that today their projections are usually accurate to within 2 percent. Still, the meter-readers of the entertainment industry, whose authority was voluntarily conferred upon them by their clients, are capable of making extravagant and costly mistakes. The motion picture *E.T.*, which grossed $106,680,222 in the first 31 days of its release—the only film in history to take in that much money that fast—was passed up by Columbia Pictures on the basis of research, or so it was loudly rumored in the trade.[4] Frank Price, president of Columbia, downplayed the value (for which read accuracy) of movie marketing research. "If we paid that much attention to research, we never would have released *Kramer vs. Kramer* or *The Blue Lagoon* (both highly successful commercially and artistically)."

But there are still lower levels than any of these, at which research has been trivialized, and there is where the greatest damage has occurred. "Research" has been used politically to blacklist, harass, intimidate, exile, and morally to lynch dissidents, liberals, radicals, and "subversives." In the dessert days of Joseph McCarthy, to which more extensive allusion is made later, the FBI, the Army, police departments, the networks, the Catholic War Veterans, Jewish War Veterans, Veterans of Foreign Wars, the American Legion, advertising agencies, congressional committees, city and state governments, renegade Communists, labor unions, guilds, "American Business Consultants," a grocer in Syracuse, radio stations, watchdogs-for-hire like Aware, Inc., *Red Channels, Counterattack*, and various journalists all kept lists, most of them riddled with inaccuracies, many borrowed from other lists or duplicated—with misinformation intact—and all extremely prejudicial to people who were accused of no crime

---

[3]The electoral vote turned out to be 523 for FDR, 8 for Landon.
[4]Deborah Caulfield in *The Los Angeles Times*, 7.18.82.

and had no way to face their accusers. This mass of "research" placed in jeopardy, injured, and in some cases was fatal to people innocent of wrongdoing, living targets whose patriotism has since been abundantly established. In the 30 years since free-lance vigilantes like Ward Bond, George Sokolsky, Frederick Woltman and Roy M. Brewer all played policeman, the depth of degradation to which "truth" was put in the name of research has only begun to be explored.

But perhaps the most trivializing of all "research" in recent years has been at the hands of self-righteous amateurs like the grocery chain owner in Syracuse, N.Y., Laurence Johnson, who earned himself a few soiled pages in the history books by a combination of blackmailing and blacklisting in a period of multiple crusades to "ferret communists out of our entertainment industry," as it was put by the president of the General Ice Cream Corporation in a letter congratulating Johnson on his good work. This work involved what Erik Barnouw described as "a diabolical technique for bringing pressure on sponsors,"[5] a technique made effective by the cringing supineness of networks, sponsors and advertising agencies. Johnson, on the basis of his research into the activities of what he called "Stalin's little creatures," enjoyed many heady successes like getting Joseph Cotten, Judy Holliday, Jack Gilford and John Henry Faulk off the air, but he and his reign were brought to heel by Faulk in a dramatic law suit.[6]

Twenty years later the amateurs were still at it, although this time the victims were books, which are easier to blacklist because they cannot sue. In the town of Longview, Texas, a few counties northeast of Belton, sports capital for seventh-grade footballers, a man named Mel Gabler, formerly a clerk for Exxon, and his wife Norma, set up a clearinghouse for morals and patriotism which they called Educational Research Analysts. Their specialty was monitoring school texts and issuing, to more than 200 equally righteous groups around the country, lists of books they consid-

[5]*The Golden Web*, by Erik Barnouw, Oxford University Press, 1968, pp 273-7.
[6]Faulk was awarded $3.5 million in damages, later reduced by the court to $550,000.

ered likely to corrupt American youth. These included texts on sex and drug education, books in which psychology, sociology and anthropology were drawn upon in dealing with aspects of the human condition, and certain subjects apprehended by the Gablers to be dangerously suspect—internationalism, the United Nations, ecology, something called "values clarification," and the pet dragon of the TV fundamentalists, secular humanism. Also on their hit list were history books in which sainted historical figures were shown to be vulnerable in any way, and books in which the institutions of family, country, and good hard work were not properly celebrated.

Like the grocer in Syracuse, the Gablers in Texas had their triumphs. In 1978 the Texas Educational Commission rejected 18 texts that had been disapproved by the Gablers, and subsequently the power and influence of this Gothic couple grew to such proportions that they made the grade to a segment on 60 *Minutes*.

Edmund Fawcett and Tony Thomas, in their study called *The American Condition*, saw in the Gabler index

> a shocking glimpse of muddle and narrow-mindedness. ... It would be wrong to treat it as buffoonery that could easily be squelched. Local control remains a strong tradition and the Gablers are providing a service many school districts of state boards like. ... Academic freedom is usually thought of as protecting teachers from outside interference [but] many Americans subscribe to the upside-down definition offered by William F. Buckley, Jr., in *God and Man at Yale*: the freedom of men and women to supervise the educational activities and aims of the school they oversee and support.

Also, it might be added, the freedom, in research, to avoid looking for contradictory facts which could upset one's crusading hypotheses, to restrict the scope of inquiry by reducing it to the proportions of one's bias. Like Cerullo's shoes which fitted nicely into God's footprints, this fits into the broad pattern of trivialization.

20 ✐ Ready, Aim, Smile

> God, if I have to smile one more time, I think my teeth are
> going to fall out.
>
> —Donna K. Pitman
> Miss Florida, 1982

Man is the only animal that smiles, and Americans are the only
people who have made an industry of it. The smile has been
institutionalized by advertising: it gleams from coast to coast. Its
irreducible symbol is a circular yellow sticker, sold by the
millions: two black dots representing eyes, and a curving line for
the smile. It is even more ubiquitous than Robert Indiana's LOVE
design, in which the first two letters of the word rest on top of the
second pair. It was originally a painting, then a Christmas card,
then a postage stamp, and finally a massive sculpture in
Philadelphia's Penn Center.

The flights of United Airlines are through smiling, friendly
skies. A smile brightens every craft in the fleet of Pacific
Southwest Airlines. Fixed beneath a black dog's-nose radar-cone
at the tip of each ship is PSA's corporate smile. The company
takes this seriously, having adopted the motto, "The Airline That
Won the West . . . With a Smile." Its logo exhorts the traveller to
"Catch Our Smile." A full-page newspaper advertisement an-

nouncing terms of PSA's traffic between Los Angeles and Seattle devoted half its space to a legend, printed in large bold type, reading, "PSA. What a difference a smile makes." The words themselves form a smile.

"Say cheese," is the standard direction of the photographer who wants a subject to smile. The public-relations creed of banks, supermarkets and department stores, and of servitors looking for tips, is "Service with a smile."

God knows nobody but a misanthrope prefers a society of sullen scowlers. After all, the smile, unless it is sickly, sardonic, scornful, cynical or sneering, has the capacity to greet, disarm, embellish, brighten, engage or redeem. The trouble with the commercial smile is that it is forced: it illuminates, but by artificial light. The bonhomie of the mart is for hire no less than the grief of the professional mourner, and there is brisk trade in it—the smiling model, the chorine who grins as she pivots and kicks, the cigarette girl, the anchorman, the cheerleader, the vendor at the door, the man who parks your car—everyone, it seems, except the undertaker, who probably smiles to himself when he unloads a $5,000 coffin, and the tax collector, who presides over last rites for portions of our net worth.

Americans for a long time were sentimental about the smile, as evident from vintage song and verse. Ella Wheeler Wilcox wrote, "The man worthwhile is the man who will smile whenever everything goes dead wrong," and in another poem,

> Just the art of being kind
> Is all the sad world needs.

While the same sad world was racing toward still another of its periodic calamities, George Asaf counseled us that since worrying was of no use, we should just pack up our troubles in an old kit bag and smile, smile, smile. And there was Will Callahan's song, written in 1917 while armies were butchering each other in France:

> There are smiles that make us happy,
> There are smiles that make us blue,
> There are smiles that steal away the teardrops
> As the sunbeams steal away the dew...

But we had no smiling songs for World War II and subsequent Asiatic wars, because the condition of everything going dead wrong was no longer remediable by smiling about it. That sort of sentiment went out well before Pearl Harbor, and the social smile vanished along with the five-cent subway fare. Into the vacuum, however, came the selling smile of Madison Avenue, and with it, the political smile that is now requisite for all public figures. The presidential smile, invented by Franklin D. Roosevelt, was extended by Jimmy Carter to even toothier lineaments, and Ronald Reagan carried his photogenic smile with him wherever he went. At the very moment he was shot by Hinckley, he was smiling and waving.

In the service of advertisers and politicians, the institutional smile becomes an implement of trivialization, minimizing problems and difficulties, oversimplifying complexities that demand long and patient study, and promising, with generous resort to hyperbole, things that cannot be delivered. In this respect the smile, whether literal or figurative, is usually either a put-on or a put-off, a cover-up, a misrepresentation, or an outright lie. By suggesting that the good life is attainable with the choice of the right antacid, shampoo, stock broker, insurance company, beer, deodorant, jeans, soft drink or automobile, the professional smile becomes as cynical as it is empty. A singing commercial from Detroit, for example, tells us that

> Only Mustang makes it happen,
> Only Mustang makes life great...

Planters Peanuts assures us

> You don't need a party for the fun to begin, Let there be Planters, let the good times in...

A manufacturer of sodium bicarbonate manages both to divine and define the future in two lines:

> Don't think the future is something you can put off till
>   tomorrow, till tomorrow
> The future's Arm and Hammer.

Coca-Cola "classic" trumps even the *joie de vivre* of Browning's *Pippa Passes*:

> Coke's a thing that's eternally Spring
> And its taste is as honest as truth;
> It's as sparkling and bright as a star spangled night
> And as gay as the laughter of youth...

Freedom, like Coca-Cola's truth, finds itself inside a commercial jingle, this one for Gino's Heroburger:

> Come on everybody, let's rejoice, yeah,
> 'Cause Gino's gives you freedom of choice.

And the tobacco house of Chesterfield offers conjugates of pleasure:

> Make your pleasure true, pleasure long, pleasure filter free
> Don't just smoke from habit
> Get twenty wonderful smokes.[1]

The public not only puts up with such puffery, it rewards the product by buying it. To a great extent the American populace, like no other, has been conditioned—some say brainwashed—by years of relentless pushing, dogged exploitation of the smile, and advertising's imperfect sense of pitch. Barbara W. Tuchman, writing on *The Decline of Quality*, indicted Madison Avenue on several counts:

> From infancy to adulthood, advertising is the air Americans
> breathe, the information we absorb, almost without knowing
> it. It floods our minds with pictures of perfection and goals of
> happiness easy to attain. Face cream will banish age, decaffei-

[1]All these lyrics are from *Great Songs of Madison Avenue*, a collection of singing commercials by Peter and Craig Norback, Quadrangle, New York Times Books, 1976.

nated coffee will banish nerves, floor wax will bring in
neighbors for a cheery bridge game or gossip, grandchildren
will love you if your disposition improves with the right
laxative, storekeepers and pharmacists overflow with sound
avuncular advice, the right beer endows you with hearty
masculine identity, and almost everything from deodorants to
cigarettes, toothpaste, hair shampoo and lately even antacids
will bring on love affairs, usually on horseback or on a beach.
Moreover, all the people engaged in these delights are beautiful. Dare I suggest that this is not the true world? We are
feeding on foolery, of which a steady diet, for those who feed
on little else, cannot help but leave a certain fuzziness of
perceptions.[2]

The Good Life, as perceived by advertising in print and on the
air, has become synonymous with The American Way, and in
jingoist circles any challenge to this concept is considered near
treason. Social critics have inveighed against the forced feeding of
foolery over the years, some with regret or annoyance, others with
alarm and anger. Robert Osborne, in *The Vulgarians*, was fit to
be tied:

> The key to all is the *smile*. . . wide, youthful, brilliant . . . and
> everything is GOOD and GLAD day after endless day, hour
> after hour, page after page, program after program . . . and the
> fat and the fatuous are INTERCHANGEABLE and labelled
> the FULL life!

In a calmer vein, Norman Douglas, British writer, once said
that the ideals of a nation can be judged by its advertisements. If
he was right, Americans have less to smile about than ever.

[2]*The New York Times Magazine*, 11.2.80.

21 ✐ Simplifications

Is there a connection between simplification and trivialization? There are so many varieties of simplification that it is hardly ever simple to be simple. The family includes rustic simplicity, cunning simplicity, innocent, ostentatious, audacious, affected, and graceful simplicity. Simplicity of character may be the product of profound thought or of no thought at all; artful simplicity is achieved either instinctively or through trials of perception and discipline; scientific simplicity is expressed by stark formulations such as $E = MC^2$, a wisp of symbols extracted from vast complexities and calculations. And finally there is the simplicity of oversimplification, a close relative of trivialization and the most dangerous of the tribe.

Audacious oversimplification makes for trouble. When Marie-Antoinette, on being told her people were angry because they had no bread, replied, "Then let them eat cake," she trivialized a situation that ultimately cost her head.

George III had a simple solution for the pestiferousness of the Bay Colony: Send troops to occupy Boston.

Woodrow Wilson had a simple-sounding objective: Save the world for democracy.

Calvin Coolidge had a simple prescription for the good life: "Four-fifths of all our troubles in this life would disappear if we would only sit down and keep still."

Warren G. Harding found the presidency not at all baffling: "Government after all is a very simple thing."

Herbert Hoover had faith in the simple notion that prosperity was just around the corner of the Great Depression.

Neville Chamberlain made a simple prophecy to the world when he got back from Munich: "Peace in our time."

General LeMay proposed a simple strategy for ending the war in Vietnam: "Bomb them back to the stone age."

Max Rafferty, California educator, had an even simpler war program, not only for Vietnam, but all wars:

> Unleash the military. Congress and other civilians should get out of the business of running the war and let the military decide how to do the job.

Dixy Lee Ray, Chairman of the Atomic Energy Commission, disposed simply of the problem of handling nuclear garbage: "Waste disposal is the biggest contemporary *non*problem."

Dr. Edward Teller, when asked, "What are the problems involved with nuclear reactors?" replied, "The problems are called Ralph Nader."

T. K. Jones, a member of Reagan's National Security Council staff, had a simple program for surviving nuclear attack: "Dig a hole, cover it with a couple of doors, and then throw three feet of dirt on top. Everyone's going to make it if there are enough shovels to go around."

Reagan himself, perhaps the greatest simplifier of them all, always had easy solutions for complex problems. He began by simply *proclaiming* that the answers were simple:

> For many years you and I have been shushed like children and told there are no simple answers to the complex problems which are beyond our comprehension. Well, the truth is, there *are* simple answers.

And he had no hesitation about handing them out. On the
weighty problem of balancing the budget, for example:

> The best way to balance the budget is by all of us simply trying
> to live up to the Ten Commandments and the Golden Rule.

Of course Americans are not the only oversimplifiers, but we
are the most practiced, since we are constantly inspired to keep at
it by the examples of advertising and government. Awesome
aphorisms are stated in print, posturing as great simple truths:

"Tradition Is Something to Build On, Not Rest On" suggests a
moralistic exercise, but in fact it is the heading of an advertisement for the Chemical Bank of New York.

"We give you something you can't buy: Time" reads an ad for
an airline. Fine, except they are not giving but selling; and if they
are selling, then you are buying; and if your flight is delayed by
equipment problems or jammed runways or bad weather, the
value of what you are buying is lowered.

"The Man Who Reads Leads!" not only oversimplifies but is
simple-minded, considering the character of much that is
published and the quality of many past and present leaders who
may or may not be readers. The claim is made in an ad for the
Literary Guild of America.

"A Mild Sensation is what most people look for and almost
never find," sounds like a sentence in a book on pop psychology
written for high school freshmen. It appears in an ad for
Ambassador Scotch, and happens to be inaccurate: most people
are always seeking mild sensations, and finding them.

There is apparently no limit to the simplism of advertisers,
even when the product or service touted is relatively sophisti-
cated. One does not expect much from sales pitches for
delectably squeezable toilet papers or laxatives that generate
pleasure in the lives of soap-opera characters, these being
standard gothicisms in the TV marketplace. Yet they are hardly
less obnoxious than the self-congratulatory "messages" in which
sponsors thank themselves. After all, there are limits to the ways

in which a toilet paper may call attention to its qualities and uses. But a roll of paper is not a Rolls-Royce: one looks for finer style from a higher product. Usually the style improves with the expensiveness of the merchandise, but if the substance remains in essence as cushy-cushy as the toilet paper, where is the improvement?

Typical sponsor narcissism surfaced in the campaign for the Cordova automobile. Cordova suggests a romantic city on the banks of the Guadalquivir, where *bailadoras* whirl and stamp to throbs of flamenco. The protagonist for the product was Ricardo Montalban, a handsome actor with a natural and charming accent. You felt that you could trust him with your daughter in a Cordova, and you knew he would drive safely. But he spoilt it all by thanking the sponsor. *"Thank* you," he said to the product, though not to the ad agency which arranged for the commercial to be made, or to the casting director who arranged for hiring him. That would have been considered bad taste.

Another self-thanking sponsor is the brokerage house of Paine Webber Jackson & Curtis. "Thank you, Paine Webber!" goes the commercial, insistently, persistently, iterating thanksgiving from people of many walks, including long-running celebrities. One expects sponsors to admire, adore, revere and celebrate their own product—but to *thank* themselves—*themselves?*—before the masses?

The noisomeness of the principle was noted long before the time of the tube. Dr. Thomas Fuller, in his *Gnomologia* (1732) wrote, "He merits no thanks that does a kindness for his own end." In the case of sponsors, it is not even a kindness, it is cold business.

Auto-infatuation before a mirror gets in nobody's way, but self-admiration on a vast scale, before the world, trivializes both the product and the consumer, and in the end wearies us. "I'm nobody," wrote Emily Dickinson, who was somebody special, and she went on

How public, like a frog
To tell your name the livelong day
To an admiring bog!

Advertisers tell their names the livelong day—and night. Most of the time it is excusable, on grounds that their products perform needed or useful services. But to supplement name-plugging with manipulated feedback from the bog, to amplify and broadcast croaks of admiration from consumers, is to erode what little decorum there is left in our congratulocentric society.

Americans cherish "convenience," and use it as a selling point. Signs and legends reading, "For your convenience" appear all over the commercial landscape, sometimes in the most trifling contexts. If going to church is an inconvenience, simply dial a prayer; if it is inconvenient to study painting and strike off your own pictures, buy a paint-by-numbers canvas and fill in the colors; if inconvenient to read a novel, buy the digest; if inconvenient to question details, accept generalities.

Just as it is advisable to count the spoons after a guest brags of his honesty, it is well to mind particulars when generalities are flying loose. For though generalization is logically and justly in the service of simplification, it can also be ambiguous and damaging, as when manipulated by unethical advertisers. But on occasion, generalities which are perfectly benign, can trivialize by unwarranted expansion in matters such as the titles of movies or paintings. For example, *The Bible* is what Dino De Laurentiis thought fit to name a movie that dealt superficially with Adam and Eve, Cain and Abel, Noah, and a smattering of Scriptural headliners. It no more justified its title than a picture about Tobit, Judith and Susanna could properly be called *The Apocrypha*.

Only artists of the first magnitude can get away with titles like *The Creation* or *The Messiah* or *L'Enfance du Christ*. No doubt it is more feasible to approach grandeur musically than on film or canvas, but it takes unusual temerity to name 14 paintings collectively *The Stations of the Cross*, when 11 are executed in nearly solid black, three in nearly solid white, and all have vertical bands and stripes fixed in the same place. This series, by Barnett Newman, was accused by some critics of trivializing the Passion. Whether it does or not, it certainly simplifies.

Trivialization by simplification out of generalization is at its most dangerous when translated into personal influence and power. Hearst made the Spanish-American war his baby ("I'll furnish the war"); and Lyndon Johnson reduced the war in Vietnam to a personal affront. On March 16, 1968, he told his staff:

> Let's get one thing clear! I'm telling you now I am not going to stop the bombing. Now I don't want to hear any more about it. . . . I've heard every argument. I'm not going to stop it. Now is there anybody here who doesn't understand that?[1]

In *The Presidential Character*, James David Barber tells of Johnson's obsessive personalization of his role:

> His initial commitment to the war was taken in personal terms: "*I* am not going to lose Vietnam. *I* am not going to be the president who saw Southeast Asia go the way China went." By 1965 Johnson was speaking of "my Security Council," "my State Department," "my troops." With a sigh he would excuse himself from dinner saying, "I've got to go to Da Nang." It was *his* war, his struggle; when the Viet Cong attacked, they attacked him. After Pleiku, his response was "I've had enough of this. . . . By God, I'm going to Vietnam's aid." . . . He would say to startled visitors, "I could have bombed again last night, but I didn't," and "I don't want China to spit in my eye and I don't want to spit in China's eye." The Viet Cong, he said, "actually thought that pressure on an American president would be so great that he'd pull out of Vietnam. They don't know the president of the United States. He's not pulling out!"

The war to Johnson was a huge paint-by-numbers canvas, the numbers being his own hunches and convictions. Never mind the inextricably tangled weave of political and military considera-

---

[1] *The Presidential Character*, by James David Barber, Prentice-Hall, 1972, p. 86.

tions, logistics of men and material, historical and moral complications, deep divisions within his own country—never mind all that, Johnson had to go to Da Nang. He was a victim of the trivialization of oversimplification, and in turn he created thousands upon thousands of other victims.

If the Literary Guild was right in proposing that the Man Who Reads Leads, an adjustment would have to be made in the case of Lyndon Baines Johnson. He read only one book during his presidency, and by his own account did not read "six books all the way through" after leaving college.[2]

---

[2]The one book was *The Rich Nations and the Poor Nations*, by Barbara Ward.

22 ✍ Individualism

Next time you go to the market and return with a brown bag full of groceries, look at the bottom of the bag. You will see that along with the name of manufacturer is printed that of the worker who made or inspected the bag. Sometimes it is dated. An edition of April 12, 1982, bearing the imprimatur of the St. Regis Company ("Quality is our bag") bore the legend "Personally inspected by Vidal Yerena." Among Yerena's colleagues have been Carlos Muett, Sal Guzman, Paula Scheifels, John Turner, and Sally Boyle. Ms. Boyle even had her autograph duplicated on the bag bottom. For Crown Zellerbach there was a run of bags "Mfg. & Insp. by S. Delgato & Crew." For Trojan Kraft there was Henderson Holt and Manny Rivera.

You may be sure these workers get no fan mail, and few consumers notice. Yet the routine publication of their names represents pride of authorship, and no doubt makes for better and happier workers. There is no question of horn-blowing in this practice, since the credit is inconspicuous. Though it is a small matter, anything which honors an individual by recognition and affords the gratification of emerging, even a little way, from mass anonymity, does the opposite of trivializing: it symbolizes respect of employer for employee, and in so doing cannot fail to enhance self-esteem.

Credit for a few bag people does not advance the fame or fortune of St. Regis and Crown Zellerbach. The conceit pleases a few workers, inflicts no burden on the consumer, and passes unnoticed. But there is a form of credit-taking and name-naming which does just the reverse—it benefits companies, trivializes the consumer, and clamors for notice—always, be it said, with the cooperation of the consumer. This is the formulary of the fancy design label, the cachet in flowing script or chaste initials, imposed on jeans, belts, perfumes, wallets, leather bags, sheets, shirts, robes, scarves, automobiles, running shoes, eyeglasses, chocolates.

Bill Blass, whose monogram of two B's back-to-back has been impressed upon expensive apparel and affixed to large and small items of hardware, was commissioned by Godiva Chocolatier of Belgium, a house of sweets owned by the Campbell Soup Company, to design a line of chocolates. He did. They sold for $14 a pound late in 1981; maybe the price has gone up since. The centerpiece in each box bears the Blass insignia. But chocolates are not worn, just passed around and eaten, whereas Pierre Cardin belts *are* worn, and the name of the designer is embossed on the buckles. Dior lingerie-fabrics carry the name in the weave. A full-length T-shirt reads Givenchy-Givenchy-Givenchy in diagonal red stripes. The Dexter shoe ("American-made with your kind of style") bore the external logo "Dex" four times per pair. Both Jordache and Calvin Klein jeans place their names on the eye-catching rear.

Two cartoons embrace the subject: B. Tobey, in *The New Yorker*, has a smartly rigged woman emerging from an apartment building while an epauletted doorman holds the door open for her. She is wearing a scarf with "Hermes" in plain sight, a blouse with "Yves Saint Laurent" printed in large letters down its front, and a skirt on which the name of Bill Blass appears repeatedly in a checkered pattern; and she is carrying a handbag with GUCCI blazoned on it. "Good morning, Mrs. Kiley," says the doorman.

In *Playboy*, cartoonist H. Shoemaker shows a studio devoted to "Designer Tattoos." Bent forward across the back of a chair is a young woman whose buttocks are exposed to the tattooist's needle. On her nicely rounded bare right cheek is a design, nearly completed, faithfully replicating a Calvin Klein pocket patch.

Designers cannot be blamed—it's good business for them. At no cost to themselves or their manufacturers and distributors, they get free advertising on living mannikins—thousands of purchasers who express themselves through the identity of designers, and, in so doing, reduce themselves. Maybe the reduction is small, no bigger than the expanded identity of the bagmakers—but it is still an exercise in trivialization.

The difference between wearing a sandwich board and carrying an artifact on which GUCCI is prominently displayed is one only of degree. Yet so strong is the snob appeal of the chic label to consumers who buy and display it that they are willing to surrender tokens of individuality. And it adds up: a token here, a token there, an accumulation of tokens.

Fifty years ago, Herbert Hoover described "the American system" as one of rugged individualism. Since his time, the ruggedness has worn down. Nobody high in government today thinks of individuals in the way that Jefferson, Lincoln, Wilson and the Roosevelts did. The pushiness of fashion designers in fixing their signets on buckles and bows, is a mere feather-tickle compared to the blunderbussing by lobbies, cartels and conglomerates which hold the consumer in infinite contempt. A sordid example was the repeal by Congress in May, 1982, of a regulation of the Federal Trade Commission requiring used-car dealers to disclose known defects and warranty terms to prospective buyers. The used-car lobby had contributed prettily to the election campaigns of key senators and congressmen, and the investment paid off.

In the log of offenses to the dignity of the individual citizen, such an act as the used-car swindle is relatively small stuff. The record teems with major grabs, rip-offs, derelictions, accommodations, buy-outs and manipulations in which the public has been used as a punching bag, a bottomless quarry for taxes, a vast store of fodder wherewith to fight unpopular wars and pay for them as well. As a consequence of that kind of relentless attrition, the individualism of Hoover's system has become innocuous and inert.

Perhaps the most rugged individual of us all was Walt Whitman. He spoke to bag-makers and multitudes of men and women when he wrote

*The President is there in the White House for you, it is not you who
    are here for him.*
The Secretaries act in their bureaus for you, not you here for them,
*The Congress convenes every Twelfth-month for you, laws, courts . . .
    the going and coming of commerce and mails, are all for you . . .*
*The gist of histories and statistics as far back as the records reach is in
    you this hour. . .*
If you were not breathing and walking here, where would they all be?
I swear nothing is good to me now that ignores individuals,
The American compact is altogether with individuals. . . .

Alas, the American compact is no longer altogether with individuals, but with corporations, institutions and bureaucracies. The president is there in the White House for himself and his clique, the secretaries act in their bureaus for the president who appointed them, the Congress convenes every twelfth month for factions, influence peddlers, and regional interests. In the meantime, the governed have been melted down into a mass more lumpen than at any time in our history. We are at risk of becoming merely a statistical pool for censuses, audience ratings, political polls, market research, demographic studies and computer tanks.

There are always attempts to escape, some of them headlong, through movements known by catchwords such as beatnik, hippie, the Grim Generation, the Lost Generation, the Up-Tight Generation, the Hang-Loose Generation—all having in common a distrust of the values of their predecessors. Students especially have resented what Arthur M. Schlesinger, Jr., calls "the impersonal society that produced them."

> The world, as it roars down on them, seems about to suppress their individualities and computerize their futures. ... They see it as a conspiracy against ... identity in themselves. They have been given a sense of individual helplessness in the face of a social juggernaut. The highly organized modern state undermines their feelings of personal identity by threatening to turn them all into interchangeable numbers on IBM cards.

So hard is it to make a noticeable dent in the armor of our impersonal society, that occasionally parents try to do it for their children in the very names they give them. We find anomalies of spelling like Shirlee, Harrold, Fredd, Klaire, Iakob, Filis, Diahann, Patric—the object being to stand apart. Sometimes names are combined to form phrases or sentences, describe objects, make puns, play with alliteration or set up jokes. There actually are people in our midst named Ima Hogg, Shanda Lear, Mac Aroni, Preserved Fish, Ruby Bottoms, O. Hell, Fermin Gryp, Pearlie Gates, Sylvan Grove, Miles Hence, Gloria Mundy, Gladys Friday, Jack B. Quick, Tootsie Totty, Orange Marmalade Lemon, Nita Bath, Cigar Stubbs, Justin Time, Bigge Boozer, King David, Bud Rose, Blossom Plum, Golden West, Warren Peace.

These names could be smiled at and brushed off as Believe-it-or-Not trivialities save for their life-long consequence to the people who bear them. Whether the original object was to astonish, amuse or titillate seems questionable, since it does not take long for a novelty to wear off, and there is a limit to the number of times one can successfully repeat a joke. It would appear, then, that the basic intent is to be conspicuous. It may be the bearer's only chance.

But conspicuousness for its own sake, as in affectations of

name, speech or appearance, has nothing to do with the kind of individualism Whitman had in mind, nor is it to be confused with genuine eccentricity or dissent. The true eccentric is either oblivious to the opinions or conceit of the crowd, or disdains them. The phony eccentric uses oddity to conceal a lack of tone or talent, a pattern seen all too often in avant-gardists of small bore. The sincere dissenter, however, is a thing apart, and acts as a natural retardant or baffle to trivialization. By inclination the dissenter resists the settled comforts of dogma, scorns the complacency of the majority, disputes the arrogations of authority, and incites against the slackness of mediocrity.

The astringent values of dissent have been recognized in all free societies for a very long time, and the cost of denying dissension has been extremely heavy, in blood as well as treasure. Yet the lesson is one of the hardest to learn and retain. We enshrine Voltaire's generous offer to defend to the death the right of anyone to disagree with him, but when the chips are down, forget it.

We are pious about the right to dissent except where it crosses church or state, offends company management, is critical of the Pentagon, the presidency,[1] the two-party system, congressional committees, self-constituted guardians of morals and patriotism, cultural icons, Christmas carols,[2] and unconventional modes of speech, dress or manner.

The suppression of dissent has cost dearly in pain and life itself, in bloody labor strife, the murder of civil rights workers, the shooting of students, the hounding of real or fancied political

[1]Frequently newspaper readers write hot and angry letters to the editor about what they consider disrespect shown to the office of the president in some editorial or cartoon. Harold L. Ickes made a relevant comment from his perch as Secretary of the Interior under Roosevelt and Truman: "I would dare to dispute the integrity of the President on any occasion my country's welfare demanded it. . . . After all, the president of the United States is neither an absolute monarch nor a descendant of a sun goddess."

[2]George S. Kaufman lost a lucrative role in a network series when he let slip one night that he was tired of hearing "Silent Night" played relentlessly during the holiday season.

apostates. It may also have contributed to the most fruitless, exasperating and unpopular war in American history, because the purging of dissidents and critics of our foreign policy during the long dark night of Dulles, McCarthy, Cohn-Schine, McCarran and HUAC made us as prone to blundering as a person suddenly deprived of sight and hearing.

Playwright Arthur Miller, one of many important artists investigated by the House UnAmerican Activities Committee in the 50's, told a Vietnam Conference audience[3] in 1983 that starting in the mid-40's, "the left wing of the American eagle was cut off and it started flying around in circles." It became unAmerican and in come cases "almost illegal" to know anything about China.

> We are now repeating [in El Salvador] what we did in the case of China, which is to get rid of anybody in the [State] Department who understood anything about revolution,[4] so that everybody could come out of the club wearing the same striped tie and being comfortable with one another. I think the tragedy of Vietnam was the payoff for the 50's—that's when the blacklist was, that's when people were accused of being communists for any number of reasons, and the great patriots took over the country. And what they did was to knock the brains out [of the government] until finally we came to a Vietnam ... the people who might have remembered were in exile, they were gone, they were not permitted into the councils of government any more. Their viewpoint wasn't there. What we had instead was ignorance and self-interest.

"Every establishment," said Erik Barnouw, "needs the dissenter, to rescue it from its own foolishness." When majority opinion (often synonymous with the establishment) becomes tyrannical, as it tends to do under stress, it takes moral courage to oppose it. And in such a time, the danger to the community lies not in giving ear to dissent, but in denying it. The worst thing a State

[3]*Vietnam Reconsidered: Lessons from a War*, held at the University of Southern California February 6-9, 1983.
[4]A reference to the firing by the Reagan administration of Robert E. White, who had been U.S. Ambassador to El Salvador when Reagan took office.

Department or Foreign Office can do in any ideological conflict is to censor, forbid travel, or withhold passports and visas from dissenters against policies which are assumed (usually smugly and mistakenly) to be "not in the best interests" of the country.

"Say what you like about America," the English critic Kenneth Tynan wrote in 1968, "it can't be denied that you can say what you like."[5] Happily that has been true over most of the distance, but vicious exceptions have whittled away at our national stature. And there is no sign that we are ready to part with these exceptions, almost as though we need them as an addict needs a fix.

The tree of liberty need not, as Jefferson put it, be refreshed with the blood of patriots and tyrants from time to time. According to him, such blood is "the natural manure" of that precious tree. But today there are other, better fertilizers: reason, calm inquiry, and understanding. In applying them, it behooves us to instruct the groundkeeper that dissenters are not weeds to be pulled up.

[5]*The Observer*, London, 3.17.68.

23 ✍ General Alarm

Every age, if and when viewed with alarm, comforts itself by citing how awful things were some time back. A favorite ploy, by now a cliché, is to quote some bitter indictment which exactly describes all the things that are currently going to hell, and then, after the reader gathers that it was written only yesterday, disclose that it was actually said by some despairing Greek or Roman 2000 years ago.

This works nicely when comparing real or fancied wantonness of generations of youth, and occasionally there are striking political or military parallels such as that between the divide-and-conquer stratagems of Philip of Macedonia and Adolf Hitler. But it is risky to assume that because a country once went through a bad time similar to what it now faces and made a good recovery, it will automatically get over the perturbations of the present.

What makes the present different from all previous eras is a series of irreversible changes in the conditions and quality of life. First, the electronic revolution. It has speeded up the metabolism of commerce and industry, brought media literally into the home, altered the political process to the point where the shade of a candidate's makeup on television is a factor in campaigns, and advised us of the outcome of elections before half the

country was through voting. It has also invaded the last precincts
of privacy through systems of national data banks which hoard
our credit ratings and various other parcels of information,
possibly including how we think and with whom we associate.

Another thing that will not go away is the population
explosion; it will only get worse. Too many workers for jobs, too
many children for teachers, too many sick for health services, too
many renters for apartments, too many cars for freeways.

And the crowning irreversible change is the unprecedented
threat—constant, Damoclean, ugly—of nuclear disaster. Dr.
Teller's favorite genie will never go back inside the bottle. The
best we can hope for is a mutual agreement to desist from mutual
annihilation, and in an unstable world notorious for the unre-
liability of its agreements, that would be cold assurance.

So viewers-with-alarm in the autumn of our century have
plenty to be alarmed about. A canvass of warnings and denuncia-
tions of the drift of our society by thinking people who are
respected by other thinking people, and of items in the news,
would run longer than this book, but a quick look at typical
samplings will give an idea of the intensity of the alarm:

Robert Osborne, in *The Vulgarians*:

> ... a culture of foaming nonsense now engulfs us all with its
> banal, cute, odorless, dainty, sudsy message ... jingles,
> coupons ... pseudo-art, sung recruitments, sung everything
> ... we founder in a pudge fudge ... our conviction and
> resolution dwindle away and we begin to pay the neurotic price
> for our affluence in apathy, despair, or physical violence.

Anthony Lewis, editorial writer for *The New York Times* (May 12,
1981), concerning our defense of military aid to the right-wing
government of Argentina on the grounds that we "share values"
with that country, specifically a belief in God:

> The question is one of our own soul. ... Are things at such a
> point that we Americans must enlist torturers and murderers as
> our allies and proclaim their values, their God, as ours? ...

How must we appear to our most important Latin neighbors, Mexico and Venezuela? How must we appear to ourselves? What kind of country are we?

Robert Nozick, philosopher, in *Philosophical Explanations*:

If our lives cannot have meaning, if we are no more than puppets of causes, if we have no worth that the actions of others are bound to respect, then we are devoid of value.

Henry Skornia, critic:

The nation's brain power has been criminally trivialized and "kitschified." The quantification of quality prevails. There is no large talk; all is, indeed, small talk and small thought—about celebrities, money and "things."[1]

Don Bresnahan, documentary producer:

We are in the headline business. ... Sometimes we entertain more than we perform. ... We are guilty of giving you too little because we are desperately afraid you really don't want any more. And you probably don't.[2]

Edward Albee, playwright, speaking at UCLA in 1981:

... our economy fallen, an entire generation of students turned off from the democratic process, television turning the minds of young people into cornmeal...

Barbara W. Tuchman, historian:

In culture the tides of trash rise a little higher by the week: in fast foods and junky clothes and cute greeting cards, in films devoted nowadays either to sadism or teen-agers and consequently either nasty or boring ... in endless paperbacks of sex and slaughter, Gothics and westerns; in the advertising of sensation-fiction which presents each book as the ultimate in horror, catastrophe, political plot or world crime....

Arthur Herzog, in The *B.S. Factor*:

We are barbarians in business suits.

[1]In *Chicago Journalism Review.*
[2]*Newsweek*, 4.19.82, p. 23.

Anthony Burgess, novelist and essayist, in *The New York Times*:

> Everything seems to be going wrong. Hence the neurosis, despair, the Kafka feeling that the whole marvelous fabric of American life is coming apart at the seams. . . .[3]

Agnes de Mille, choreographer:

> We are prepared to buy a war, but we spend a pittance for our spiritual well-being—or even education. What is the Pentagon saving us for?—People feel alone and sealed off. They want to scream, "Is there anybody who can hear me?" How do we break through?

Paul Goodman, in *The Community of Scholars*:

> American society is an interlocking system of semi-monopolies notoriously venal, an electorate notoriously unenlightened, misled by mass media notoriously phony.

Henry Miller, in *The Air-Conditioned Nightmare*:

> I . . . look upon America . . . as a fruit which rotted before it had a chance to ripen.

Archibald MacLeish:

> . . . churchly hooligans and flag-waving corporations and all the rest of the small but bloody despots . . . have made the word Americanism a synonym for coercion and legal crime.[4]

Norman Thomas:

> If you want a symbolic gesture, don't burn the flag, wash it.[5]

Dean W. R. Inge:

> Americans are not a thoughtful people; they are too busy to stop and question their values.[6]

Norman Cousins:

> . . . Sleaziness has infected the national culture in recent years.

[3]*"Is America Falling Apart?"* 11.7.71.
[4]In *The Nation*, 12.4.73.
[5]Quoted in *Johns Hopkins Magazine*, November, 1973.
[6]Quoted in *Wit and Wisdom of Dean Inge*, Ed. by James Merchant, Arno, 1927.

There seems to be a fierce competition, especially in the worlds of entertainment and publishing, to find ever lower rungs on the ladder of taste. ... to suppose that a nation could detach itself from moral dictates and yet remain free of violence was as irrational as imagining that an individual could live in anarchy and yet be secure.[7]

Betty Friedan, feminist leader:

Many of us feel stuck on a plateau of disgust and despair at the irrelevance of current American politics, of left and right, to the real problems.

David S. Broder, syndicated columnist:

Today, this vast, rich and powerful nation is governed by people who, reducing their status to clerkships, (are) prepared, against their better judgment—to forward ... any kind of simple-minded scheme that they think will command a popular majority.

John Gardner, ex-Secretary of Health, Education and Welfare:

We are plunging headlong into an unknown future, dragging with us the outgrown slogans, attitudes and institutional apparatus of a world that is vanishing.[8]

Harris Poll released in December, 1973:

Fifty-three per cent of Americans interviewed feel there is "something deeply wrong with America."[9]

Alan Wolfe, sociologist:

One of the crucial questions of the next decade will be how America will respond to its decline. (June, 1982)

Leon A. Arkus, director emeritus of the Carnegie Institute Museum of Art:

What is at stake is America's cultural value system. The revival

---

[7]"An Epitaph for the Saturday Review—and Culture, too," *The Los Angeles Times*, 8.23.82.
[8]*In Common Cause*, by John Gardner, W.W. Norton, 1972, p. 250.
[9]"What America Thinks of Itself," *Newsweek*, 12.10.73, p. 4.

of and hullabaloo over junk leads to a debasement of taste and stimulates the creation of further junk.

New Yorker editorial, 7.15.85:

> Once, it was considered disappointing if an artist "sold out" for commercial reasons; now the disappointment comes if a businessman compromises his profits for artistic reasons... The public, turning to our culture to find out about the world, discovers there nothing but its own reflection.

Henry Fairlie, in *The Spoiled Child of the Western World*:

> America is today the only nation in the West that has the opportunity, and, above all, the capacity to create a public philosophy which has meaning and is compelling in the private lives of its citizens. At least, since the beginning of this century, it has not done so. As the public estate of America has grown ... the mind and imagination of the country have increasingly disengaged from it, and left it without a public philosophy.

Mortimer J. Adler, philosopher, in an interview:

> Think of the paperbacks in the grocery store, the drug store. Lousy! They're just as much mind-killing as the bad TV is mind-killing. What's the difference?

Sander Vanocur, TV journalist:

> Television news programming has made us all, on both sides of the tube, spectacle-weary, sensation-weary, information-weary. Our senses have become numbed, our imaginations have become obsolete.

Herbert Kohl, teacher and author, on the effect of TV on children who watch it "attentively and regularly":

> What results ... is the impoverishment of personality and the trivialization of life. ... We must find ways (in TV) for the development of serious drama and non-shrieking comedy and to provide time for the consideration of people and events in depth. If we do not, we may end training another generation of TV adults who know what kind of toilet paper to buy, who

know how to argue and humiliate others ... but who are thoroughly incapable of discussing, much less dealing with, the major social and economic problems that are tearing our society apart.

Raymond Chandler, author, in a letter to a friend:

... (T)elevision's perfect. You turn a few knobs ... and lean back and drain your mind of all thought. And there you are watching the bubbles in primeval ooze. You don't have to concentrate. You don't have to react. You don't have to remember. You don't miss your brain because you don't need it.

Associated Press dispatch from Washington, January 22, 1982:

The National Association of Broadcasters (has) dissolved the organization's Radio and Television Codes of Good Practice.

Tom Shales, columnist, *The Washington Post*:

Kids control the TV sets in most homes during the first hour of prime time, and if you look at the shows that succeed in this period each week, you get the impression American kids are the biggest bunch of dummies on the planet Earth, and are determined to stay that way.

Ramsey Clark, former Attorney General:

We need to realize that when we talk about crime in America, we're not talking about "them"; we're talking about the character of America.

Sheila Benson, critic, reviewing Francis Ford Coppola's *One From the Heart*:

(The film) revels in ... surfaces. We've lived among surfaces so long that we'd better find them exhilarating; they're what we have.

"Aristedes," on the magazine *People,* in *The American Scholar*:

The appetite for such an extortionate amount of trivia is unslakeable, as is, apparently, the appetite for celebrity.

William Faulkner, in *Essays, Speeches and Public Letters*:

Bad taste has been converted into a marketable and therefore taxable and therefore lobbyable commodity.

Anne Strick, in *Injustice For All*:

A society that relentlessly presents violence as entertainment will increasingly find violence entertaining—and its courts overflowing.

Andrew Hacker, in *The End of the American Era*:

There is a growing suspicion that the American nation has lost its credentials as a teacher of moral lessons; that our presence abroad is evidence only of power, carrying no enlightenment in its wake.

Frederic Wertham, psychiatrist:

If democracy does not do away with violence, violence will do away with democracy.

Howard T. Senzel, in *Cases*, a book on criminal justice in New York City, published in 1982:

What comes to court is the behavior of the society around it, its political weight and moral values intact. It's the same old system of justice, but it now fails because America is now a failure.

Kevin McAuliffe, reviewing Theodore H. White's book, *America in Search of Itself*, in *The Progressive*, Oct., 1982:

White now believes America is (self-destructing, like the Roman republic) and for the same reason: We have debased our currency, dissipated our authority, trivialized our politics, become cynical about our own values, and extended our global reach beyond the capacity of any democracy to sustain.

Christopher Lasch, in *The Culture of Narcissism*:

American confidence has fallen to a low ebb. Those who

recently dreamed of world power now despair of governing the city of New York.

T. Obinkaram Exhewa, Nigerian about to return to his home-land after 20 years in America:

Americans simplify and abbreviate everything they come across ... (their) social and intellectual life is so bathed in clichés that it is nearly impossible to think a fresh or original thought ... your head swarms with ready-made phrases, stock expressions and instant, prepackaged ideas. America blunts one's finer sensibilities by insisting that life is a grabfest, a jungle, a dog-eat-dog fight.[10]

Paul Walters, in a speech seconding the nomination of Harold Stassen for president, at a Republican convention:

We are turning from a democracy to a hypocrisy.

William K. Zinsser, in *Pop Goes America*:

The whole country is under sedation ... complacent ... self-righteous....

George Stigler, economist:

The trouble is that hardly anybody in America goes to bed angry at night.

Each of these censures invites amplification, but the last two cut close to the quick of our subject. There is a chronic state of national inertia except when it comes to selective irritations. Arrival at moral outrage requires first of all moral discrimination, and then the capacity to be indignant. For example, at the height of the healthy clamor by the Carter administration and the press over the Scharansky and Ginzburg trials in Moscow, there appeared a news story that went relatively unnoticed: the slaughter by a Guatemalan army unit of 114 unarmed, poverty-stricken Neckchi Indians—men, women and children—in a village only 80 miles from the capital city. While it was proper for our president and Congress to protest and to impose sanctions against

[10] "A Nigerian Looks at America," *Newsweek*, 7.5.82, p. 13.

the persecution of dissidents in a far-off fringe of Asia, where were the same exalted agencies of indignation when it came to the murder of unsuspecting and peace-abiding Indian serfs in one of our own Americas, only six hours by air from LAX? Was not this massacre, too, a violation of human rights?[11]

One of the difficulties about outrage is that its object is not uniformly perceived to be outrageous. Only in the arts is the capacity for indignation generally accepted, refined, transformed, charged with feeling and significance, and ultimately presented to the world. The sins of the media in America are many, but they do not include persistent and wilful indifference to crimes against humanity, whereas government, in its clumsiness, and when it suits it, not only turns deaf ears and stony eyes to atrocities, it perpetrates them.

There is more conscience in the average weekly showing of *60 Minutes* than in the fallout of a year's activity by the average government bureau. It took a book and a motion picture, *The Voyage of the Damned*, to expose to a wide public the callousness of President Roosevelt and his State Department when Hitler sent a shipload of stateless Jewish refugees to a programmed doom. Their lives could have been saved by the utterance of a single word: Yes.

Roots and *Holocaust*, both jackpots of television, drew some, if not all of their strength from a simmering sense of outrage in the hearts of their authors. The underlying passion of *Hearts and Minds*, the film on Vietnam which won for Peter Davis an Academy Award, seethed with barely controlled outrage.

The origins of such works are usually clear: somebody in the *60 Minutes* crew was outraged by corruption in Chicago;

[11]Apparently counting on the U.S. government to take no notice of its vicious violations of human rights, Guatemala kept right on torturing and murdering not only dissidents but friends and relatives who inquired about them after they disappeared. Throughout a period spanning several years into Reagan's second term, the U.S. sent millions of dollars in military and other support for a Guatemalan dictatorship that ranked as one of the world's worst. For a marrow-chilling account of the terror in Guatemala, see the leading "Talk of the Town" article in *The New Yorker* of July 29, 1985.

someone at ABC, or in a production company associated with it, was outraged by what happened to the Nez Percé Indians 120 years ago: someone in network radio was outraged by Vittorio Mussolini's boast, on blowing up a troop of Ethiopian cavalrymen, that it looked from the air "like a budding rose unfolding ... it was beautiful." Each of these people became, in a sense, an activist for decency, for rights, for justice; all created dramas or documentaries that were seen and heard by audiences to which the flame of indignation—or at least a pilot light—was passed on.

Indignation and moral outrage are not to be confused with anger and hot temper. The latter have short fuses and short duration; they burn themselves out quickly. When one is angry enough to break furniture, smash windows or chew the rug, the excursion is self-limiting; crockery quickly gets used up, a few wrecked chairs or broken windows are usually enough, and who can chew a whole rug? Of all the human emotions, anger is perhaps the most easily slaked, as suggested by the proverb that a soft answer turneth away wrath.

Indignation, on the other hand, is not eruptive: it may grab suddenly, but it does not soon let go. Unlike the forces at work upon what Hamlet called the native hue of resolution, indignation's effect is not "sicklied o'er with the pale cast of thought"; rather, it strips away native caution, tends to embolden thought, and leads, in its best sessions, to constructive resolution.

Once you start looking for them, works of outrage and indignation pile up quickly: Goya's *The Disasters of War*; poetry from Shelley to Ferlinghetti; plays of protest out of Ibsen, Hauptmann, Toller, Brecht, Miller, Fugard; great thrusts for reform against cruelty to children and the poor, in Dickens's *Bleak House, Little Dorrit, Oliver Twist*; Gian-Carlo Menotti's devastating opera, *The Consul*; Picasso's *Guernica*; the fiery canvases of Orozco; the murals of Rivera; the caricatures of Daumier (one of them, whose target was King Louis Philippe, landed Daumier in prison for six months); the scathing art of George Grosz, which so nettled the authorities that he was heavily fined for "corrupting the inborn sense of virtue innate in the German people"; the social art of Shahn and Gropper; the political cartoons of Thomas Nast and Rollin Kirby of our American past; the cartoons of Conrad, Herblock, Auth and Oliphant of the American present; and *writers*—the list would run on for pages.

So we are not necessarily helpless and hopeless against the heavy forces of trivialization. There have been, and are, heartening models of counteraction everywhere, even though widely scattered and perpetually embattled.

24 ✐ Summit Trivialization

"The president," said Woodrow Wilson, "is at liberty both in law and in conscience, to be as big a man as he can."

Unfortunately he is also at liberty to be a small man, and the last five presidents—Johnson, Nixon, Ford, Carter and Reagan—have exercised that privilege. Not in every last word and act of their incumbencies, but often enough, and in sufficiently telling ways, to contribute to the steady spread of trivialization, and to loosen the tone of the presidency itself.

Not one of these men was well read or deeply informed in national or world history; not one had notable command of language or felicity of style; none had native wisdom or philosophic sense; none seemed to project his thinking beyond exigencies of the moment, to the figure that he might present to the future; not one rose above jockeying for the most exploitative "image" of himself and his administration; not one brought dignity or magisterial stature to his commission.

Although some worthy and signal things were achieved in most of these presidencies (at the time of writing the last was little more than halfway through), in every case they were overshadowed by failures of petty-mindedness, provincialism, arrogance, pique, and, in one instance, criminality. A fine domestic program was eclipsed by an unnecessary and vicious war; detente with two chronic adversaries was overwhelmed by Watergate; the solid accomplishments of Camp David were followed by stupid blunders relating to the Shah of Iran and our embassy hostages; the same president who had wanted to impeach an innocent Supreme Court Justice quickly pardoned a guilty predecessor who faced certain indictment and probable impeachment.

A few earlier presidents were also trivia-prone in their own right, but no great stakes were involved in their time. The five lumped here demonstrate that trivialization is not the copyright of any party; it belongs to us all.

The requirements of a president include worldliness, sophistication in dealing with foreign and domestic leaders and issues, a dignity proper to the first citizen of the oldest and most powerful democracy, and a functioning sense of tact. Yet from these five have come strokes of poor judgment and bad taste that would not be expected from a reasonably well-educated head waiter. Such as alluding publicly to "Montezuma's revenge" (diarrhea attributed to unsanitary food or drinking water in Mexico) during a state visit to that country; ordering White House guards to be accoutered in the kind of uniforms that went out with operettas set in Transylvania; permitting secret service functionaries to ask to inspect food served in Buckingham Palace while a guest of Queen Elizabeth; falling asleep on the Pope; quoting an 11-year-old child (his own) during a televised debate on the gravity of nuclear war.

The so-called Great Debates—Nixon vs. Kennedy in 1960 and Carter vs. Reagan in 1980—were themselves trivializing. Daniel J. Boorstin, Librarian of Congress and editor of a 20-volume history of American civilization, wrote that the four campaign programs in 1960

> were remarkably successful in reducing great national issues to trivial dimensions....[1]

[1]Daniel J. Boorstin, *The Image, or What Happened to The American Dream*, Atheneum, 1962, p. 42.

The Carter-Reagan debate was, if anything, a few notches lower, considering that its most remembered line was, "There he goes again"—on a point, incidentally, in which Reagan turned out to be wrong.

Of the five recent presidents—indeed of all 40—Reagan is in a class by himself. By the time he had been in office for half a term, he had destroyed or dismantled 50 years of painstaking social legislation, and in the process successfully trivialized entire segments of American society through nullification, liquidation, denigration, quantification, and oversimplification.

Little of what Reagan stood for and did as president came as a surprise to those who knew him, travelled with him on campaigns, or were familiar with his choice of advisers and confidants. His antagonism toward welfare programs was such that at the time of the Patty Hearst kidnapping, when the Hearst family agreed to a demand of the kidnappers to provide food to the poor as a partial ransom, Reagan said, "It's just too bad we can't have an epidemic of botulism." Death to the poor, he was saying, for accepting ransom food; and death also to demonstrators on college campuses: "If it's to be a blood bath, let it be now." Said as Governor of California. Trivialization by liquidation.

Facts never bothered Reagan—they could be trifled with in the same way he trifled with the poor, with education, with the environment, with the disabled, with public health. Robert Scheer, in an article published three months before Reagan was elected president, wrote that throughout the campaign

he would continue to use erroneous information that worked with crowds, even after he had been told it was wrong. For example, his claim that a government study showed that Alaska had greater oil potential than the known reserves of Saudi Arabia. Those of us travelling with him soon discovered that he had gotten the report wrong, and [his] press aide Jim Lake conceded it. But Reagan had grown too fond of the line to drop it and claimed to his aides that it was based on a newspaper clipping that he had picked up somewhere but could no longer find.

One of Reagan's most outrageous misstatements, contradicted by every newspaper file in the country, by several volumes of encyclopedic weight, and by plays and movies on the subject, was that there existed no blacklist in Hollywood. He made the statement several times. Apparently no amount of evidence could change his belief, just as nothing can persuade those who deny the existence of the holocaust.

If ever there were a pygmy in giant shoes, it is this man, who has no apparent grace or talent beyond being able to read a script with the competence of a professional actor, the glibness of a prosperous businessman discussing politics at a dinner party, an all-purpose utilitarian smile, a nicely groomed smartness at saluting military persons, and an air of confidence that he cuts an admirable figure in his entrances and exits. He is endowed with neither a keen wit nor a gift of language, and he has only the vaguest sense of history. He is unlettered in art and science and waddles like a stegosaur in economics, but worst of all, he is a man without the slightest humility or compassion, whose every gesture of interest in the working class, in blacks, in the elderly, and especially in the poor, was contrived for show and ratings.

In Reagan the twin defects of arrogance and ignorance, which often go together, are well met. Only a country reduced by the value-shrinking of endless mindless entertainment, its judgment numbed by commercials, disgusted by Vietnam and Watergate, confused and frustrated by the bungling of two lackluster presidents before him, could have elected him— unthrilling as was the prospect of returning his opponent, Jimmy Carter.

The deep disappointment and concern of anti-Reaganites was not so much that he quickly trivialized the presidency to the size of a breadbox compared to its dimensions under some of his predecessors, but that the country trivialized itself. Anyone familiar with Reagan's political career before 1980 fully expected him to perform as he did. What was not anticipated was the nakedness of his toadying to the rich, his sadism toward the poor, the cynicism of his appointments, the shamelessness of his gaffes and self-reversals, and his crass attempts to shift responsibility for the early reverses of Reagonomics onto prior Democratic administrations.[2]

Instead of immediate and widespread alarm and revulsion when Reagan began to show his hand in Washington, the media and the country went along with him. TV commentators, including the usually reliable regulars on *Washington Week in Review*, joined legions in rating Reagan a "Great Communicator," and a figure of wondrous affability, when all the time he was communicating mostly dismay to millions of Americans. His hearty geniality only made the picture worse, like a warm sun, blue sky, and gentle breeze over a bloody battleground.

Almost with the dumb, blinkered vision of a bull attacking a red cape rather than the spangled toreador waving it, even those objecting to Reagan's persistent appointment of foxes to take care of chickens focused on the foxes instead of the foreman running the ranch. These critics, like the public in general, had been so reduced by the trivializing process that they railed against James G. Watt, Secretary of the Interior, as though *he* were ultimately responsible for what he said and did; they berated Caspar Weinberger as though Reagan's defense budget was *his* fixation; they fumed about Anne Gorsuch and her defiance of a Congressional committee as though she, not Reagan, had at first ordered subpoenaed files not to be given up; they grumbled about a lumber company lobbyist being picked to head up the forest service, a nuclear proponent to head the Department of Energy, and a Secretary of Labor opposed by organized labor. Obviously

[2]Scheer, writing in *Playboy* before Reagan was nominated, recognized the pattern: "The brilliance of Reagan is that he can absolve his own politics of any responsibility while fixing blame on all past steps taken to solve any of the problems."

Reagan approved of these functionaries and how they functioned, or he would have fired them as he did his first Secretary of State and various other officers who had the temerity to resist the mold.

Paradoxically, the only element of the population whose judgment had not been impaired by trivializing forces—perhaps because least directly exposed to them—was the blacks, whose disapproval of Reagan's performance early in 1983 was indexed at more than 90 percent. Part of that result was because they were the hardest hit in all areas of social service, but there may also have been their intuitive sense of wrong, sharpened by many years of having borne so many wrongs.

The degree to which the electorate had been narcotized by mediocritization was reflected in the way the country at large tolerated the astounding effrontery, and at times opacity, of their president. Any people who could remain passive while Reagan mused aloud about taxing unemployment benefits while cutting corporate taxes, hounding the disabled for "overpayment" while engaging a $50,000-a-year government communications officer to cut wood and clear brush on his (Reagan's) Santa Barbara ranch;[3] crippling child and maternal health programs,[4] while Nancy Reagan renovated the White House beauty salon (called by her The Cosmetology Room) with thousands of dollars of furnishings, fabrics and cosmetics donated by America's beauty industry; taxing health insurance premiums while adding billions to an already monstrously inflated military budget, with no controls on waste, inefficiency or outright profiteering; lowering the minimum wage for teen-agers and extending the legally permissible working hours for 14- and 15-year-olds; delaying enforcement of rules to govern diesel emissions; lowering impact standards for car bumpers ("a victory for automobile manufacturers"—*Los Angeles Times*); opposing sanitation standards that would require farm owners to provide toilets and

[3]UPI dispatch, 12.20.82.
[4]Mariam Edelman, President of the Children's Defense fund, stated in January of 1983, "Many thousands of poor mothers and children are being denied services vital to life and health as a result of federal budget cutbacks."

drinking water for their workers; excusing manufacturers of weapons systems from having to give warranties to the Defense Department; hacking away at federal food programs; relaxing prosecution of Food and Drug Act violators;[5] limiting enforcement of rules against job bias; easing up on antitrust enforcement; downgrading human rights in foreign policy; declaring that affirmative action is not a high government priority; sharply reducing the number of health and safety inspectors to check conditions in the country's mills and factories; pardoning a Watergate burglar (even Gerald Ford, who pardoned Nixon, did not try that); equating legal abortion with slavery as a moral issue (in those very words); awarding a high honor posthumously to Whittaker Chambers, a Barnumesque figure at best—and so on and on. Any people who could read about all this in newspapers and hear it reported on the air, without clamoring for repudiation, had to be in a kind of trance, in a daze of ethical apathy.

It became a question of morale. Robert Hatch, film critic, reviewing Mel Brooks' *History of the World, Part I* (in which, among other things, the Last Supper is treated as a subject for buffoonery, and there are jokes about genitals and homosexuals), confessed that the success of Brooks at the box office frightened him:

> I cannot avoid bracketing it with the success of Ronald Reagan, as evidence that Americans can now be counted on to rally behind anyone who offers them a debased performance expensively staged and aggressively promoted ... it is a little hard to rejoice in the morale of a country which, having been shown excellence by Jefferson and Buster Keaton, is now dancing attendance on the likes of Reagan and Brooks.[6]

Nor did it enchant those who hoped their Chief Communicator would show qualities of taste and discretion, to hear him say,

---

[5]Described by John G. Dingell, Chairman of the House Committee on Energy and Commerce, as "an open invitation to drug [and] food companies to violate federal law, thus risking the lives of 230 million Americans."—*New York Times*, 8.9.82
[6]*The Nation*, 6.27.81.

"When we get to heaven we'll find the streets are guarded by U.S. Marines."

Nobody expects a president to be unfailingly error-proof, well spoken, and considerate of all of the people all of the time. There have been several presidents who lacked some of those qualifications on occasion, without trivializing the office. But not until Reagan has there been so grand a display of inadequacy on so many fronts. He took the lead in sheer abundance of gaffes, a modest sampling of which might include his announcement that the Pope approved of his Nicaragua policy (promptly denied by the Vatican); his assurance that a nuclear missile, once launched from a submarine, can be recalled (it cannot); his claim that the Canal Zone is American soil (it never was); his pronouncement that he was "not trying to do anything to try to overthrow the Nicaraguan government" (he was); his statement, in 1985, that no German adults from World War II were still alive (thousands were); his allusion to the invention of Rubik's Cube as a product of American free enterprise (Rubik lives in Communist Hungary); his expressed belief that there is in the United States today as much forest as there was when Washington was at Valley Forge (way off); his assessment of the Contras in Nicaragua as "the moral equal of our Founding Fathers" (no Founding Father was a rapist, a felon or supported a tyrannical dictator); his charity toward Nazi soldiers, whom he called "victims, just as surely as the victims in the concentration camps" (obviously he knew little or nothing about either the Nazi military or the concentration camps); his contempt of the World Court (the only president to defy it—even Calvin Coolidge, his hero, urged adherence to the Court); his venture into science with the declaration that atmospheric pollution is caused not by automobile exhausts and industrial emissions, but by vegetation[7] (strangely, smog was unknown in the forest

---

[7]To which he added, "So let's not go overboard about setting and enforcing tough emission standards from man-made sources."

primeval); his insistence upon laying a wreath in a German military cemetery that included among its dead SS troopers who had executed American prisoners of war.

And then there is what has been called the fun side of Reagan. Joking and joshing are not exceptionable in a president, assuming that they engage wit and point, as in Lincoln's case. But even humor can be trivializing when it denigrates, or reduces serious issues to one-liners, as in Reagan's notorious ad-lib:

> My fellow Americans, I am pleased to tell you I just signed legislation which outlaws Russia forever. The bombing begins in five minutes.

"If this kind of remark could spring from him on the spur of a moment, what kind of reaction could be expected of him in a real crisis, where decisions affecting the survival of the world might have to be made in a matter of minutes?" asked John B. Oakes, editor emeritus of *The New York Times*.

Nor was there much comfort to ethnic sensibilities in Reagan's joke about a cockfight:

> How do you tell who the Polish fellow is at a cockfight? He's the one with the duck. How do you tell who the Italian fellow is at the cockfight? He's the one who bets on the duck. How do you know the Mafia was there? The duck wins.[8]

That trivialization should attach itself to the modern presidency is particularly worrisome, not only because of the enormous visibility of the office, but because the process of reduction is inverse to the steady aggrandizement of the powers, responsibilities and even physical circumstances of our presidents. Increasingly we have given them the perquisites of royalty, coddling them with servitors and appurtenances of luxury, seeing to it that, once they leave the White House, they may live like kings without ever having to do a

---

[8]The following day, Reagan said a reporter had misinterpreted the story, and called its publication "a cheap shot."

lick of work, since taxpayers underwrite a quarter of a million dollars each year to cover "expenses," plus an allowance of $40,000 for phone bills alone, and other benefits not generally assigned to the unemployed. Hence if one of these uncrowned monarchs, in or out of office, misspeaks, or lies, or makes tasteless jokes, or mangles the language, it cannot possibly escape wide notice, or fail to trickle down to the many who are influenced by almost everything done, said and worn by a super-celebrity.

Because of its conspicuousness if nothing else, the presidency is the last office in the world where mumbling and bumbling should be accommodated. Unfortunately Reagan, notwithstanding episodes of glibness, seems often mystified both by common syntax, and by the geography of where he's at. Out of the public record come such embarrassments as:

On a question of whether he was still for official relations with Taiwan:

Um, I guess it's a yes.

On being asked about a recent statement:

You don't really want to get into the mistakes that you said I made the last time, do you?

On returning from a trip to Latin America:

Well, I learned a lot... I went down to find out from them and their views. You'd be surprised. They're all individual countries.

Again, on being asked about a previous statement:

I don't know whether I said that or not, ah, I really don't.

On a question of whether he had paid his state income tax:

You know something. I don't actually know whether I did or not.

On the issue of segregated schools:

> I didn't know there were any. Maybe I should have, but I didn't. I was under the impression that the problem of segregated schools had been settled.[9]

The fumbling represented by these fragments was neither deliberate nor intended to trivialize, but nonetheless it slighted both U.S.-Taiwan relations and the issue of school segregation. However, Reagan, thanks to what legions of countrymen and pockets of media perceived as non-stop charm, mastered the art of consciously trivializing his own shortcomings, and on at least one occasion was able to make jelly out of as tough a journalist as Roger Mudd. In *The Columbia Journalism Review* of May-June, 1980, C. T. Hanson gave an example of how Reagan "managed, mostly through his amiability, to take a polite but critical question from Mudd and turn it to mush:"

> MUDD: The most generally circulated picture of you is as a strong, very likeable, optimistic, generous, secure, gracious man, not much interested in the detail of governing. A powerful but well rehearsed communicator, whose appearances before the press are limited for fear that your lack of knowledge about specifics will get you in trouble. Do you have some comment for me?
> REAGAN: Yes, I do. That's not... *(laughing)* ... not true at all.
> MUDD: None of it is?
> REAGAN: Oh, I like some of those other things you said. *(Laughing)* They may not be true, but I just did enjoy hearing them.
> MUDD: *(seeming nonplussed)* Well, they... you're... I'll... I'm glad you did. But... people... say that you are not much for detail. My question is why not?
> REAGAN: Well, it's true that I have never regulated who should play tennis on the court down here... a good executive delegates... but I make the decisions *(chuckling)*....

Mudd's projection of "the most generally circulated picture" of

[9]These and more, are documented in *There He Goes Again: Ronald Reagan's Reign of Error,* by Mark Green and Gail MacColl, Pantheon, New York, 1983.

Reagan as "strong, very likeable, optimistic, secure and gracious," was at variance with other pictures of him as weak in judgment, hateful to millions of victims of his policies, foolishly optimistic (in 1980 he said he believed the budget could be balanced by 1982 or 1983) and ungracious whenever crossed or annoyed. Among commentators of national rank, Anthony Lewis found him "rigid, ignorant and irresponsible;"[10] Colman McCarthy accused him of having "crassly pandered to unctuousness" on religious issues;[11] Arthur Schlesinger, Jr., said he "hardly knows what is going on" and that his "triumph over anomaly, fantasy and failure is due in great part to the serene and contagious optimism with which he walks away from car crashes";[12] Edwin M. Yoder, Jr., saw in him "simply an old actor who thinks that what counts is a good script to read";[13] Seymour Hersh termed him "without question the most ignorant president we've ever had, but he's terribly bright and terribly manipulative";[14] John B. Oakes classed him as a man of "shallow, rash, and superficial judgment"; William Styron, after an evening at the White House, called the president "frightening. There's nothing there. He spent the whole night telling showbiz stories about the old days in Hollywood. It went on forever." Styron and Arthur Miller, who was also present, shared the feeling that Reagan was "oblivious, sealed off from any serious discussion by his own affability.... 'You can't get near him,' Miller insisted, 'He wouldn't know what you were talking about.'"[15]

Yet no number of published opinions, and none of Reagan's blunders seriatim, seemed to have the slightest effect on his popularity in either the polls or the polling booths, which may be one of the chief indicators of the extent to which trivialization has numbed the American people. Jules Feiffer summed

[10]*The New York Times*, 2.9.84.
[11]*The Washington Post*, 2.12.84.
[12]*The Wall Street Journal*, 4.20.84.
[13]*The Washington Post*, 1.27.84.
[14]*The Honolulu Advertiser*, 11.11.83.
[15]Cited by James Atlas, in "The Connecticut Axis," *Vanity Fair*, July, 1985.

up this phenomenon during the 1984 election campaign, in a strip whose text read

> If Reagan had a Ferraro problem, he'd deny that there was a problem...then he'd make a joke about the problem...then he'd say the media invented the problem...then he'd take a vacation to get away from the problem...then Nancy would have to remind him that there was a problem...then the polls would show that 87% of the American people approved of his handling of the problem.

"Politics," wrote George Jean Nathan, "is the diversion of trivial men who, when they succeed at it, become important in the eyes of more trivial men." Though this would be too sweeping and cynical if applied to the likes of Jefferson and Lincoln, who were also politicians, the focus sharpens on approaching the super-mediocrities of the recent past. Reagan, like the four presidents who preceded him, was encouraged, supported and advised by men in whose eyes he was extremely important. One of these was Justin Dart, the California millionaire who first persuaded him to enter politics, and who in 1982 announced that he and Reagan agreed on everything relating to government. In an article on Dart that spread over seven pages of *The Los Angeles Times* (February 6, 1982), Bella Stumbo reported

> In Ronald Reagan, says Dart, he has more than a close friend. He has an ideological soulmate as well. According to Dart, his views reflect Reagan's on everything from economic policy to foreign affairs.

Because Dart's views encompassed not only issues and attitudes on which Reagan had been explicit but several on which he had not, Dart's comments to Stumbo may be read as reflecting the tastes and proclivities of his president. Not least among inferences to be drawn was the kind of man to whom Reagan listened and to whom he was spiritually close.

On the subject of redwood trees, they indeed saw eye to eye.

"I'm for preservation. I say we should preserve the redwoods, sure, maybe 100 acres of them, just the way God made them, to show the kids," Dart said earnestly.

On protecting the environment:

"There's too goddamned much selfishness in this world. These environmentalists who talk about preserving the wilderness in Alaska—how many bloody goddamned people will end up going there in the next 100 years to suck their thumbs and write poetry?"

On degrees of privilege:

Dart, whose personal worth has been variously estimated at $20 million to $200 million, does not regard himself as "overprivileged." ... The "underprivileged," Dart said, "are mainly victims of their own laziness and/or 50 years of this socialist government we've got" (begun by "that sonofabitch FDR"...).

On Reaganomics:

Dart agrees that Reagan's economic program is designed to more immediately benefit the rich than the poor.

On the philosophical base of Reagan's program:

"Ron has arrived at this philosophy because he thinks it is right."

On altruism:

"I have never looked for a business that's going to render a service to mankind. ... Greed is involved in everything we do. I find no fault in that...."

On human rights:

At the mention of human rights he turns belligerent. "It's none of our goddamned business," he snapped.

On priorities in national affairs:

"I'm interested in the national economy and our defense ability, not all those crappy little issues like equal rights and abortion...."

Also classed as crappy little issues were school segregation, school prayer and the Equal Rights Amendment.

On women's rights, he ran into a *non sequitur*:

> "In the old days, when a man wanted to relieve himself, he just pulled up at the nearest redwood and peed. Now, we gotta put up a bunch of women's johns—just so they can get to be waitresses!" His voice reeked with contempt. "All these crazy ideas do is cost *money*," he exploded.

But then public convenience was never a concern for Dart. When he was a young man managing his father-in-law's chain of drug stores,

> he realized he could double the profits in a basement soda fountain, merely by installing an escalator. . . . "One escalator was all I wanted—the escalator *down*," he explained slyly. "Hell, I figured people could *walk* back up."

Exactly. Let them walk up. Let them eat cake. Feed them botulin. Serves them right. Crappy, trivial little people.

25 ✒ Reduction by Greed

One of the ironies among the uncoded prescripts of moral justice is that greed, which constantly seeks increase and is rarely content with abundance, ends up by decreasing the greedy. Both men and nations trivialize themselves by lusting so hard for power, gold, possessions or advantage, that their intellect and spirit become blunted, there is no longer joy in the game, and ultimately they have nowhere to go but down.

America has been generous many times in the past, with help to the hungry and poor of other nations, and by quick response to the insults of catastrophe. But in recent times that help has been politicized, and our charity made strategic. We proffer help to the starving and indigent so long as the starving is done under a government friendly to ITT or Anaconda or the accommodation of some of the military hardware on its territory. In other words, the kind of benefit that sticks to the fingers. We tend to inquire less of a country's needs than of its attitude toward a third party whom we may not like. Oftener than not, as a result of this test, we find ourselves showering bounty on despots and scoundrels who are detested by their own people.

One of the hardest tasks which any society can assign to itself is to check pandemic greed, especially when it is on the rise. Of course we can no more hope to eliminate greed than to wipe out pests with pesticides, but at least in the wars of entomology, greedy insects are confronted and controlled. Bugs, unlike conglomerates, do not hybridize with other species, whereas ITT, whose study is the telephone and telegraph business, and which prospered mightily at it, rapidly acquired 250 other companies, including 83 hotels, 420 airport parking facilities, 42 bakeries, 333 finance offices in 24 states, and two million acres of timberland. It operates two Distant Early Warning systems, as well as the Space and Missile Center at Vandenberg Air Force Base, and from time to time it has manufactured and/or sold potato chips, corn chips, Wonder bread, Smithfield hams, lawn seed, fertilizers, weed and insect poisons, chemical cellulose, six kinds of insurance, surety bonds, magazines, books (Bobbs-Merrill) and navigation systems for laser-guided bombs used by two types of bombers. The combine's greed long ago exceeded national bounds, sometimes with dramatic effect. Conspicuous among its foreign operations was its involvement in the overthrow of the Allende regime in Chile.[1]

Corporate and individual Gimme-ism, while by no means exclusively American, has lately advanced like a runaway infestation and affected all classes, not stopping at the upper levels. Very few who are able to rake in far more than what they need to be rich or very rich, pay the slightest honor to the old maxim

If you have a good-sized bone
Let the other dog alone.

Frank Yablans, Hollywood producer, commenting in February, 1983, on the unprecedented commercial success of the movie *E.T.*, said

Our American system is such that you can only enjoy that success for a moment. Already the corporate pressure is on . . .

[1]Nowhere is there a more stark and succinct precis of ITT's substance and style than in an article by Herb Borock in *The People's Almanac*, by David Wallechinsky and Irving Wallace, Doubleday, 1975, pp. 407-9.

to top that success. The banks in this country say things like, "Last summer you did $380 million at the box office; this summer you did only $300 million. What's wrong?!" It's madness, but it's America's way of corporate life.

It was also a corporate way of life for the inconceivably flush oil industry, which was not above double-dipping (collecting for the same sale twice, by canny bookkeeping), cheating on oil pumped from Indian Reservation wells, and charging motorists for road maps which were once given to them for the asking. (It was to benefit the already superwealthy oil industry that the Reagan administration proposed a bill to reduce taxes by $40 billion over a ten-year period.)

Everybody wants more, more, more. Conglomerates, banks, ball clubs, players, doctors, lawyers, dentists, plumbers, networks, studios, actors. In May, 1982, Marlon Brando filed a suit seeking damages of $48 million because up to then he had received only $2.7 million, in addition to a million dollars paid up front, for his role in *Apocalypse Now*, claiming his agreement entitled him to millions more.

The public is encouraged by the advertising media to be greedy in a hundred ways, because, what the hell, we *deserve* everything we can get, just like Brando, the ball players, the owners, the conglomerates of insurance, telephone and oil, the manufacturers who make wrenches and pliers that cost taxpayers as much as though made by Faberge. Henry Skornia is in despair about it: "Greed has become our fetish. 'Throw it away,' 'Spoil yourself,' 'You deserve it,' ... our Bible texts of this insane religion [which], bred and spread by broadcasting, is now bringing our nation to its knees and to shame."

The cupidity of the medical profession is so notorious and unregenerate that it constantly keeps alive the question of how long it will be before some kind of national health insurance is imposed. Ripoffs in the art of Hippocrates today range all the way from the case, documented by *60 Minutes*, in which a patient who died after 23 days in a Florida hospital, left for his widow a legacy of a hospital bill amounting to $77,167—from this, to the fees routinely charged by an internist of my acquaintance who runs up a levy of $500 for an office checkup, but will not validate the patient's parking ticket, and demands $75 merely to drop into a hospital room and ask his client, "How are you feeling this morning?"

Recently cataract surgery has become simplified through the use of the intraocular lens implant. It is done in the surgeon's office under local anesthetic, and the procedure takes about 15 minutes. Sometimes five or six such operations are performed by a single team in a single day. The breakdown of costs for this service, by one of the leading ophthalmic centers in the country, is as follows:

Measurement of eye or implant lens (an earlier 10-minute procedure)	$200.00
Implant lens (actual cost, $50)	450.00
Surgeon's fee	3,000.00
Assistant Surgeon's fee	600.00
Anesthesiologist's fee	550.00
Use of operating room (in surgeon's own suite of offices)	1,000.00
Healon (introduced in eye during operation)	65.00
Local anesthesia	13.24

Since cataracts are a disease of age, the affected population is the likeliest of all adult groups to be handicapped by diminished income, but this counts nothing to cataract specialists. Their attitude resembles that of the OPEC nations when things were rosiest for them—they have something the world needs, and by God the world is going to pay for it.

What is remarkable about this shade of greed, is the small detail. Though they are big earners, these operators are not big spenders when it comes to their venerable patients. One might think that for what they demand, the ophthalmology cartelists might throw in a dab of healon instead of charging more for it than its weight in gold ($65 for a squirt in the eye). Or the anesthesiologist, since he is charging over a dollar for every two seconds of his time, might be sporting enough to furnish the $13.24 worth of anesthetic at a wholesale rate; say, $8.67. To students of greed, it is the $50 of the $550 that seems so exquisite—to say nothing of the 24 cents of the $13.24.

Apologists for the outrageousness of medical fees argue that the life of the patient is in the hands of the surgeon and anaesthesiologist, and that this responsibility carries a high price. But the same can be said of the airplane pilot who carries even greater responsibilities, and who is exposed to the same risks as his passengers. Surgeons walk away from mistakes, for which they are paid the same as for success, but the pilot can do no such thing. The best pilot in this world does not earn $3000 for each 15 minutes at his controls. Indeed at least two of the major American airlines in the mid-80s tried to haggle pilots' salaries down.

Lawyers, among other pragmatists, share with the medical profession the same robust spirit of enterprise. It is not uncommon for an attorney to charge for a phone conversation from the time he picks up the client's call. Just as in the electronic clockwork of the telephone company, the cash register starts spinning from Word One. Normal amenities, like:

"Hello, Harry, how are you this morning?"

"I'm fine, Bert, just back from a weekend at Vegas."

"I hope you did all right."

"Not too bad. —What's on your mind?"

"About the deposition, I was wondering if—"

Already this exchange has cost the client money, as though he were leasing a satellite communications circuit to Mozambique.

While not all grabbers are as approving of greed as Justin Dart ("Greed is involved in everything we do. I find no fault in that"), even economists like Milton Friedman acknowledge

that it is basic: "What kind of society isn't structured on greed?"
But the writer Paul Erdman is more sweeping and, at the same
time, specific: "The entire essence of America is the hope to
first make money—then make money with money—then
make lots of money with lots of money."

The credo is sock-it-to-'em, and the 'em is invariably,
everlastingly, the consumer. The telephone monopolies,
richer than some of the nations of the world, are forever
finding novel ways to boost the bills of their subscribers. No
longer may a local emergency call be made without fee; most
companies charge for dialing information.[2]

Certain parking violations draw heavier fines than speeding
tickets used to cost a few years ago.

A man going to a downtown theater may pay twice as much
to a parking lot as he pays for the movie.

A repair shop charges a minimum of $27.50 (plus the cost
of materials) to handle an appliance whether the item needs
only a soldered wire or a replaced belt—a two-minute job.

Whenever anything goes amiss with a commodity—
whether too much rain spoils the raisin crop, or a freeze
destroys oranges, or a small war cuts off an oil supply, or a
strike cripples transportation of goods—the subsequent rise in
prices is not, as a rule, even partially absorbed at the source by
the distributor or by the retailer, but is passed directly on to the
consumer. The profits of utilities, corporations, middlemen
and merchants in any emergency are sacrosanct; only the
profit of the consumer may be reduced with impunity, and as a
matter of course.

The effect of all this is to contribute to the average person's
sense of being lowest on the totem pole, a status tantamount to

[2]One of the choicer rip-offs. There is no charge for Americans to call a foreign
country for information, but to get a number in the next county in most states, a
fee is charged, with 50 cents per query the average toll. It is like being fined for not
having 5000 sectional phone directories in one's home, or for asking an airline
about its flight schedules. One pays for the privilege of *preparing* to do business
with a phone company.

being trivialized. If out of the exaltation of greed by the Darts and the acceptance of it by the Friedmans; if the net result of institutionalized grabbing were a stronger, happier, more confident society, one might look less askance at our condition. But apathy, despair, disgust, neurosis, sleaziness, insecurity, dwindling resolution, diminished expectation, receding hopes—all terms used by social critics to describe our present state—suggest the opposite.

Alas, there is no easy way to loosen the grip of greed, and none guaranteed to work; but one approach is to make it less attractive by limiting the rewards of avarice. This is the unstated but obvious intent of anti-ripoff bodies like Common Cause, the Better Business Bureau, Consumer Advocates, and various other monitoring organizations. Theoretically the same intent is also at the core of the government's antitrust operation, and, ultimately, of relevant civic and criminal law. But greed is not illegal *per se* except where it grossly overreaches; and its exercise, as well as the resistance it provokes, are largely moral matters. Nevertheless things have changed since Samuel Johnson wrote 200 years ago that remorseless and unfeeling lust for gold represented "the last corruption of degenerate man," and Carl Sandburg, 150 years later, agreed with him:

> . . . *too much money has killed men*
> *and left them dead years before burial:*
> *the quest of lucre beyond a few easy needs*
> *has twisted good enough men*
> *sometimes into dry thwarted worms.*

What has changed since Sandburg wrote that in 1936 is that today there are watchdogs like Ralph Nader, John Gardner, Archibald Cox, Senator William Proxmire, Congressman Henry Waxman, and radio and TV consumer-defense programs, as well as sentinel posts like the General Accounting Office and the Securities Exchange Commission, all trying to make sure that greed does not run hog wild. However, at this writing the SEC under Reagan was getting ready to lower its standards on disclosure of illegality, arguing that "information about illegal conduct by management is not necessarily crucial to an informed investment decision by the public. ... Expectations of profit, rather than ethical issues, are the SEC's concern...."[3]

All the more reason to give honor and support to the vigilant.

[3]Article headed, "SEC to Reverse Policy on Disclosure of Illegal Conduct by Companies", in *The Los Angeles Times*, 11.19.82.

26 ✣ Effects

For the first time we live in constant awareness of the frailty of vast forces and amplitudes. We have poisoned rivers, sickened bays, and killed one of our Great Lakes. The oceans are endangered. Our rains turn acid. The earth itself could be burned to ash in less time than it takes to roast a pig.

If the planet is no longer secure, how much less so a nation, even a strong one. Since nothing anywhere can any longer be taken for granted, from the viability of Eskimos in their struggle against alcoholism to the survival of Amazon Indians in their struggle against Brazilian ranchers, from the durability of economic systems to the capacity of the globe to feed its jostling billions, from the integrity of the atmosphere to the neutrality of outer space—how can one possibly assume that the American condition is sound enough to get us through this century, let alone the next, without social, cultural and political dislocations worse than the recurring depressions, repressions and nasty little wars that have characterized our recent past? How can we muddle through if our culture is as shaky as serious thinkers think it is?

Trivialization has brought us down in many measurable ways, and it could bring us down still further. The bleak truth is that uninspired and uninspiring people are in the ascendancy; one of them, at this writing, is in the White House.

If the premises put forward up to now are correct—if we are indeed suffering from a trivialization syndrome—if what Adlai Stevenson called "America's exalted purpose" is of little interest to us, if what he called our potentially inspiring way of life is of less account than sports and games; if education matters less than sensation; if respect for human rights, for property, for equity, for law, for justice, for simple honesty, are smaller than respect for the need to have a good time and the right to use guns; if life itself has diminished in importance; if the moralist La Rochefoucauld was correct when he wrote, "Those who give too much attention to trifling things become generally incapable of great ones"—if all of this is operating in our country, then what are the effects? I venture to suggest some, which I believe are all too readily recognizable:

Half the electorate stays away from the polls.

The inverse proportions between quality and popularity keep widening.

Social and educational programs are cut back, and repressions are recycled to put back into service.

Honesty is more and more considered square and old-fashioned, as in the case of the California janitor who found and returned a quarter of a million dollars in ten- and twenty-dollar bills, and for so doing was ridiculed and abused by his neighbors to the point of having to move his family from the neighborhood.

Criminals in government, after being convicted and sentenced, are published profitably, and movies are made of their books.

Security has become so vulnerable that few places are safe. People are shot and killed in markets, bars, banks, on street corners, riding on freeways, in their homes. One cannot even feel wholly secure about eyedrops and headache remedies in the medicine cabinet.

The bonds of family, of matrimony, of faith become increasingly frazzled; people turn more and more to panaceas, to cults, to anodyne; they insulate their lives with trivia in order not to think or to feel too much; they do anything to escape anxiety, which often only increases anxiety.

The list goes on, but it is relatively simple to take inventory and point with alarm. What is harder is to propose remedies, the first requirement being to direct our thinking to the converse of La Rochefoucauld's axiom—to give attention to great things, not trifling ones. That is a heavy abstraction, a stiff order, much easier proposed than disposed, yet over the years there have been countless attempts to do just that—to isolate and attack societal ills through recommendations, hunches, hypotheses, projections, inspirations and apprehensions ventured by no end of utopians, visionaries, reformists, educators, social scientists, analysts, critics, and deputed commissions. Most of their propositions have been either ignored, dismissed as unfeasible, or attacked by factions that would stand to lose stock or advantage if the ideas took hold. Even when remedies have worked, like the nexus of economic and social reforms under the New Deal, they have subsequently been eroded, and at times, especially under Reagan, obliterated. None of which is any reason why hope should be abandoned and no new platforms drawn.

An exercise sometimes performed in creative writing courses, party games or transactional analysis is to write out what one would wish for his or her epitaph, or to sum up one's philosophy in few enough words to fit legibly on a sweatshirt. Such compression is not easy, as anybody knows who has tried to close an overstuffed suitcase. But if articles of faith are hard to set down, there are always articles of hope, and a hundred partygoers, creative writers and analysands, put to the task of coming up with ideas which might help to reverse the drift toward trivialization, would probably deliver a hundred different theories. There is always a stubbornly constant ferment of prospectuses—good, bad, indifferent—in the form of books and articles, symposia, studies undertaken by think tanks, universities and the press, and special projects. In the following pages, still more notions are ventilated, some modest and others ambitious, but none with much hope of success unless the dangers of persistent trivialization become apparent even to the audiences of *Blood Orgy* and *Laverne and Shirley*, to the congregations of Falwell, Cerullo and Moon, and (so long as we're dreaming) to state and national legislators. Most of these platforms will get nowhere without education, but some cannot wait for edification of the masses. There are occasions when dramatic action is taken *pro bono publico*, or to "serve the national interest," without the consent or foreknowledge of the public. Such, good or bad, were the Louisiana Purchase in 1803, the Bay of Pigs invasion in 1961, and various strokes of statecraft involving the breaking or repair of diplomatic relations.

Obviously, the main targets for reform are government, politics, education, law, religion, the press, broadcasting, advertising, sports, and, to a lesser extent, the arts. Government and politics are of course foremost among these because they directly affect us all. Both are intimate, not pageants in a remote capital; they have to do with the lives and safety of your family and yourself; and whether you can afford to marry; or, if you're married, whether you can afford to have children. Politics is the instrument which determines not only whether there is offshore drilling, free abortions for the poor, wholesale deregulation, coddled shahs and fresh witch hunts, but whether your son or daughter may be expended on a battlefield, or whether you yourself, surrounded by the conveniences and comforts of home, will be cremated in a blast of thermonuclear fission.

Whatever chance there will be for us to reverse the dangerous trends indicated by the observers and commentators in these pages, it rests on no magic prescriptions, no panaceas, no single, no dozen, no hundred specific reforms, but rather on broad, basic and very old principles. The only new aspect is the scope of their application, and the seriousness with which they are put to work.

Three hundred years ago, La Rochefoucauld recognized that there is such a thing as "a general revolution which changes the taste of men as it changes the fortunes of the world." He was not speaking of armed revolt, but of altered goals. Again and again, thinkers whose works have best stood the test of seasonal changes in thought and the general moodiness of history have spoken to the feasibility and attainability of solutions and cures—assuming always that, as earlier noted in the maxim of Petrarch, the invalid wants to be cured. Thoreau was encouraged by "the unquestionable ability of man to elevate his life by a conscious endeavor," and certainly his disciple Gandhi put that premise to work.

Christopher Lasch, at the very end of *The Culture of Narcissism,* having shaken his head over existing social patterns, including general erosion of competence, allowed that "the will to build a better society" has managed to survive, and, with the support of traditional localism, self-help and community action, requires "only the vision of the new society, a decent society," to be reinvigorated. If this was being unrealistically wishful, Lasch himself is not without support. Norman Cousins, in his moving though premature epitaph for the *Saturday Review,* concluded among other things, that

> Humanity's greatest problem has never been the absence of answers to complex situations. Its greatest problem has been the absence of will to attack problems. . . . Progress begins with the belief that what is necessary is possible. Hope is a practical reality because it supplies the energy for converting intangibles into tangibles.

Clearly the need is to generate moral energy, to command the times rather than merely to go along with them, to discover what our man in Walden called "continuous employment of our nobler faculties." A thousand employments seek to recruit these faculties; the big question is whether the hopers and believers will find enough help from the rest of America to sustain them in their work of rescue—whether, to begin with, anyone will listen to them. Unfortunately the task is made harder by the default of media. When press and broadcasting parody themselves by placing the taste of Coca-Cola higher than the legitimate hard news of the entire world, there is imposed on millions of consumers, the responsibility of sorting out their own values and priorities with no help from established organs of information. Every time this happens, it adds to the vast store of superficial and inconsequential trash which forms a kind of toxic dump in our common neighborhood, and it makes the labor of resisting and neutralizing trivialization, that much more difficult.

27 ✐ Bodies Politic

No priesthood ever initiates its own reform. That's our trouble.
—George H. Gallup

It must be acknowledged that the process by which we elect presidents has nothing to do with finding the best man in the country for the office. The two-party system, state primaries, nominating conventions, the electoral college, all have come under scrutiny and criticism, yet they have continued unaltered with all their flaws intact, as though there were something sacred about them. An historian of the University of Leyden, Johan Huizinga, observing us from the tranquility of The Netherlands, wrote, "Long before the two-party system had reduced itself to two gigantic teams whose political differences were hardly discernible to an outsider, electioneering in America had developed into a kind of national sport."[1]

Most of the Founding Fathers, were they able to tune in from the spirit world, would probably come to the conclusion that American democracy, as practiced today, is a failure. The majority of our elected representatives have higher loyalties than to the people they represent—to their parties, to lobbies, to a

[1]*Homo Ludens: A Study of the Play Element in Culture*, by Johan Huizinga, Routledge & Kegan Paul, 1980.

234

persuasive president who rings them up on the telephone, serves them breakfast, invites them to Camp David for the weekend. Not only during campaigns but in the routine performance of office, in press conferences and media interviews, most of the officers we elect are groomed by speech coaches, briefing drills, party strategists, kingmakers and princemakers. They are processed as surely as packaged goods in a supermarket.

Our political conventions are in many ways a national disgrace—noisy, rowdy, sprawling, cliché-ridden, saturated with provincialism, reduced at times to horse-trading and thimblerigging by delegates "meeting in an atmosphere of colossal clowning and high-pressure methods, wholly unregulated by Federal law."[2] Audiences at the scene and at home are subjected to a succession of spielers, ballyhooers, manipulators and party hacks. When once in a great while someone makes a telling speech or searching comment, nobody listens. The throng quiets down and pays attention only when the headliners come on. The same Paul Walters who, in nominating Harold Stassen, told a Republican convention that we were turning from a democracy to a hypocrisy, said later in the speech:

> No one is for air or water pollution, and yet they surround us. The 13th Amendment ... prohibits involuntary servitude ... yet young men who cannot even vote are drafted to kill and die in a war that is never explained.
>
> We are taught, thou shalt not kill, do unto others as you would have them do unto you, and love thy neighbor. And yet 10 percent of our gross national product is spent on war every year, while hunger and poverty abound both at home and abroad.
>
> The fault lies not in the black man aspiring for what is rightly his, or in Communist stars, but in ourselves. For the true tragedy is, we are not even *trying* to reach our ideals.
>
> And those few who do put principle above personal ambition are threatened with prison, such as Dr. Spock ... or ridiculed, like Governor Stassen, the modern Don Quixote.

[2]John H. Ferguson and Dean E. McHenry, in *The American System of Government*, McGraw-Hill, 1959, p. 222.

As Sancho Panza told Quixote, "Don't die, Don Quixote, don't die." For the greatest guilt in this life is to die without good reason.

And then, aware that the auditorium's powerful amplifying system had not been able to override the uproarious din of delegates walking up and down the aisles, chatting or arguing about everything except what was being said from the rostrum, Walters ended his speech with a comment that expressed the convention as accurately as its carnival atmosphere of balloons, bunting and confetti: "Thank you for your inattention."

But the electorate as a whole suffers from inattention. Less than 60 percent of America's voting age population turned out in the 1976 general election (31 percent in the nation's capital, 40 percent in South Carolina, 52 percent in discriminating New York state). Things have changed radically since the day Alexander Hamilton, speaking to the New York ratification convention in 1788, rejoiced in the democratic good sense and discernment of the populace: "It is the fortunate situation in our country, that the minds of the people are exceedingly enlightened and refined." Almost two centuries later, notwithstanding an endless bombardment of information by the media, a third of all Americans seem not to be able to tell a democratic aspiration from a comic strip. A survey made by professors at the University of California circa the war in Vietnam, disclosed that 39 percent of the general electorate sounded "happily fascistic" when asked questions such as whether the majority has the right to "abolish" minorities (28.4 percent yes); whether a politician's methods should be overlooked "if he manages to get the right things done" (42.4 yes); whether "almost any unfairness or brutality" is justified in carrying out "some great purpose" (32.8 yes); whether Congressional committees under certain circumstances should be allowed to waive rules and deny witnesses their rights (47.4 yes). Professor Herbert McClosky, who coordinated the survey, commented:

The findings furnish little comfort for those who wish to believe that a passion for freedom, tolerance, justice and other democratic values springs spontaneously from the lower depths of the society, and that the plain, homespun, uninitiated yeoman, worker and farmer are the natural hosts of democratic ideology.[3]

That was in the late 60's. But the trend has been apparent for at least half a century, and it continues. Back in 1944, Gunnar Myrdal, Swedish economist and sociologist, noted that political participation of the ordinary citizen in America was pretty much restricted to intermittent elections, and concluded that our politics "are not organized to be a daily concern and responsibility of the common citizen."[4]

The electorate had not advanced much in its sense of responsibility by the early 80's. John V. Lindsay, former mayor of New York City, blamed television, which he believed had delivered both candidates and voters to the manipulations of shrewd consultants and pollsters. Public participation in the electoral process, he feared, had made the process itself seem extraneous.[5]

At an "Elections '82" seminar in Washington, D.C., John Deardourff, a consultant who labored in campaigns of President Gerald R. Ford, Senator Howard H. Baker, and 11 Republican governors, corroborated the views of Myrdal and Lindsay:

> For most people the electoral process is a once-a-year event. That's politics to them. ... The threshold of interest in politics and elective office is not very high. ... Voters don't want to know very much. Don't overload their circuits.[6]

Deardourff need not have cautioned about overloading circuits. The question is whether the circuits carry enough

---

[3]Cited in "Instant Electorate," by Robert Sherrill, *Playboy*, November 1968, p. 176.
[4]*The American Dilemma*, by Gunnar Myrdal; Harper, 1944, p. 214
[5]*Channels* magazine, August/September, 1981.
[6]Cited by William Endicott in an article, "More TV in Political Picture," in *The Los Angeles Times*, 11.1.81.

voltage to keep voters politically awake from day to day and week to week. But it is quite probable that the electoral process would become more than a once-a-year event if only voters believed they could do something about anything between elections. If they become disillusioned, impatient or outraged by the way things are going, they have no resort except to grumble and write letters. Even the biennial elections do not let off enough steam for the seriously disaffected; they must wait two more years to purge an entire slate.

In the intervals between elections, voters have no incentive to make politics a daily concern and responsibility. Perhaps they *might* have if incumbents accountable for the state of each state and of the nation, those who have the power to initiate, advise, consent, appropriate, enact laws and override vetoes, were severally and conspicuously identified with each issue on which they cast a vote—or whether they vote at all. The vast majority of voters knows only a minority of its representatives at any level of government. This gross defect might be remedied by making available to voters a kind of running box score of performances. It is the sort of thing done routinely in keeping tabs on athletes. Throughout the baseball season, practically every sports page in the land carries a statistical summary of each game played, as well as cumulative averages, league standings, and much more. Daily and Sunday. Great care is taken by the press, and expense run up, to keep the public advised on the daily motions of the stock market; on weather reports from as many stations at home and abroad as can be crowded into the allotted space; on racing results; on ship arrivals and departures; on corporate earnings and pollution levels. Some newspapers run weekly synopses of a dozen or more current soap operas ("Sean was arrested when Daisy revealed he killed Sybil. . . . After Alex informed Stuart he remembered Stuart's butler shot him, Stuart arranged to botch Alex's surgery . . . Vanessa plunged to her death after staging a brouhaha with Lorie...").

The question presents itself, whether the performance records of public officials are not of greater consequence than the track records of horses; whether the level of political pollution is not as important as the level of smog; whether box scores of city councils, state legislatures and Congress would not convey information of more significance than those of baseball, basketball, and other statistics-bearing sports.

While a daily grid of voting records would no more guarantee remedy than any of the socio-political nostrums that have already been (and are constantly being) proposed, it suggests distinct advantages; it would be non-partisan, easy to carry out, would entail no added expense to the reporting media, and could not possibly harm the electorate. Mere publication of the standings would not itself illuminate issues upon which legislative voting records are based, but the public generally has a fair sense of what the issues are. Much less clear to the voters is just who is supporting or opposing what bills, and why, and who stays away from the divisions.

The long-term effect of posting such daily tallies would be to habituate the electorate to expect them; to stimulate curiosity and inquiry concerning tabulations; to help familiarize voters with issues, and, through improved understanding, to brake one of the worst tendencies of landslide elections—the defeat of exceptional incumbents who deserve re-election (the throwing out of babies with the bathwater) and, conversely, the retention of incompetents who would otherwise be brushed away in a sweep.

Along the way, such practices as pairing off in voting by legislators might come under a scrutiny not hitherto given. Supporters of pairing do not, by the way, number among their friends Ralph Waldo Emerson, who in *Conduct of Life* wrote:

> What a vicious practice is this of our politicians at Washington pairing off! As if one man who votes wrong, going away, could excuse you, who mean to vote right, for going away; or as if your presence did not tell in more ways than in your vote.

Suppose the three hundred heroes at Thermopylae had paired
off with three hundred Persians; would it have been all the
same to Greece, and to history?

The same Emerson alluded to the antiseptic effect of "pitiless
publicity," and the phrase was picked up by Woodrow Wilson
decades later as a prescription against the ills of government. In
the case of the modest proposal made here, which is not a reform
but a service, the publicity would not be pitiless but persistent,
and, by that token, educative. Some papers already carry such a
feature, but only sporadically, and most of them are small,
including throwaways like *The Marina News* of the Belmont
Shore district near Long Beach, California.

Wilson's opponent in the presidential election of 1916, Charles
Evans Hughes, did not agree with him on many things, but they
shared belief in the sterilizing powers of publicity. "Publicity is a
great purifier," said Hughes,

> because it sets in action the forces of public opinion, and in
> this country public opinion controls the courses of the nation.[7]

That may well be, but publicity is not always a purifier, nor, as
Tennyson saw it, "a fierce light," nor as Joseph Pulitzer believed,
"the greatest moral factor in our public life." It can be dirty, mean
and destructive. By 1951 the art of publicity had, in the opinion
of Learned Hand, become a black art which was here to stay,
with every year adding to its potency.[8]

Publicity was responsible for creating, among other excrescences on the body politic, such super celebrities as Senators
Joseph McCarthy and Patrick McCarran. Though McCarthy's
political power ended in the ignominy of censure by the Senate,
he nevertheless gave his name to an era and an ism, and
demonstrated more vividly than any other public man in our
history that pitiless publicity can damage, ruin and even kill
innocent victims.

[7] Address, Manufacturer's Association, May, 1908.
[8] Address, Elizabethan Club, May, 1951.

The media helped out in this. Press, radio and television treated McCarthy with the respect and space usually accorded heads of state; they flocked to his press conferences and public appearances, eager to circulate still more accusations of communist taint and influence. And when the senator's charges failed to hold up, as they almost always did fail, they accepted his word that investigation was continuing and that there would be, never fear, proof positive forthcoming. McCarthy's personal ambition, wrote Jack Anderson and Roland W. May in *McCarthy, the Man, the Senator and the Ism*, may have started him rolling, but

> it was the press that kept the wheel turning. You can discount his native cunning; had it not been for the Fourth Estate he'd have used this talent in a vacuum. Any way you slice it, it adds up to the same thing: If Joe McCarthy is a political monster, then the press has been his Dr. Frankenstein.

"For years," wrote Paul Hoch in *The Newspaper Game*, "every little drool from McCarthy's mouth was sure to wind up on page 1 ... a symbiosis developed—the witch-hunters lived off the media and the media lived off the witch-hunters." Richard Rovere found reporters responding to McCarthy's summonses "like Pavlov's dogs to the clang of a bell." Victor Navasky, in *Naming Names*, noted that reporters did more than respond— they initiated. He quoted William Wheeler, an investigator for the House Unamerican Activities Committee, as saying that "journalists like Howard Rushmore and Ed Nellor and Willard Edwards would write an [accusatory] article and then give it to [witch-hunters] like McCarthy—who would put it in *The Congressional Record*, and therefore you couldn't sue."[9] Alan Barth, one of the editors of *The Washington Post*, condemned "punishment by publicity":

> Allegations which would otherwise be ignored because they would be recognized as groundless and libelous are blown up on front pages and given a significance out of all relation to

[9]*Naming Names*, by Victor Navasky, Viking, 1980, p.151.

their intrinsic merit after they have been made before a committee of Congress. Thus, what is one day properly regarded as unpublishable gossip is treated the next day as news of great moment because it has been uttered under official auspices. ... Refutation, no matter how compelling, never catches up with the charges. ... In addition, many newspapers welcome such charges and inflate them for political reasons or for their commercial value in stimulating street sales.[10]

While it is too much to expect that the press and broadcasters, whose publicity created and reared skulks of monsters in this period, would spontaneously refrain from doing so again if the history of heresy-hounding were to be repeated in a second McCarthiad, it is perhaps not too much to ask that during any interregnum they institute a simple non-partisan procedure like a daily tabulation of voting records. Then maybe there would be smaller chance of reruns of that dark age.

Whenever the media are remiss or recreant in political matters, they are like a policeman breaking the law, or an Attorney General committing a felony. For ideally the media, as journalist Gladwin Hill wrote, function as a shadow government

bird-dogging the activities of the formally constituted government, creating its public image and operating as a somewhat unplanned element in the general system of checks and balances.[11]

The only trouble is, the bird-dog needs to be bird-dogged, lest it forget its mission and go rooting through garbage as it did in the time of McCarthy. And the responsibility of watching the watchers rests, God help us, with the public at large. What is needed, wrote William L. Rivers, is a public that understands how each medium works

and is prepared to criticize it, challenge it, and to require that it live up to its best possibilities. ... We must be wary of our

[10]*The Loyalty of Free Men*, by Alan Barth, Viking, 1951, p. 11.
[11]*The Los Angeles Times Book Section*, 8.29.82.

tendency to respond to the image on the 6 o'clock news.[12]

It is not as though either media or citizenry lack for high models. They are constantly around us. All of the great documents of freedom—the Declaration of Independence, the Bill of Rights, the Universal Declaration of Human Rights—reach for better possibilities. The latest of these instruments, created by a United Nations Commission chaired by Eleanor Roosevelt, contains among its many articles one which deals with accusation and detraction by slanderers. It provides that no one shall be subjected to attacks upon his honor and reputation, and proposes that everyone has the right to protection against such attacks.

The preamble to that Declaration consists of just a few sentences linked by whereases, but it alone would be enough to neutralize regiments of trivialists, except that very few people bother to read it, and fewer act upon it:

> Whereas recognition of the inherent dignity and of the equal and inalienable rights of all members of the human family is the foundation of freedom, justice and peace in the world; Whereas disregard and contempt for human rights have resulted in barbarous acts...

The United States was a signatory to the Declaration when it was adopted in Paris on December 10, 1948, which means that we ratified propositions we helped to frame. If we had stood by our professed principles and supported that document with the kind of energy and resources we poured into shoring up recurringly bankrupt policies of containment, then much of the crud that has descended on us from wars, social upheavals and political eruptions would have been dissipated, and we would long ago have begun to lighten our consciences and spirits.

We may still be able to get out from under, but we don't have all the time in the world to do it.

[12]*The Other Government: Power and the Washington Media*, Universe, 1982.

28 ✒ Bugbears

In 1949, writing for an anthology called *Years of the Modern*, Henry Steele Commager concluded a collective portrait of his fellow countrymen with this paragraph:

> In large measure, the destinies of mankind are, for the moment, committed to this people. Not ambitious for power, they have achieved power. Not eager for responsibility, they have been unable to escape responsibility. Inclined to parochialism, they have been thrust into world leadership. Fundamentally peaceable, they have been led by circumstances to become the arsenal of the western world. Only the future will reveal whether they will find, in their heritage, their history and their character the resources to quicken their minds, embolden their spirits, fire their imagination, lift up their hearts, and fit them for their duties and their destiny.

It is getting on toward a half century since that was written, and we may well ask whether our minds have been quickened. By what? Television? By the acts and sayings of Johnson, Nixon, Carter, Ford and Reagan?

Have our spirits been emboldened? By misadventures in Asia? By a continuing tug-of-war over civil rights and segregation (busing is in, then out; school desegration is achieved, then all but nullified; the University of Alabama admits blacks, but blacks are oppressed in South Boston). Emboldened by Watergate? Attica? Abscam? DeLorean?

Has our imagination been fired? Yes, briefly, by moon shots and space probes, but these were largely boons to NASA, the aerospace industry, and the hundreds of thousands of spectators who jammed the highways leading to Cape Kennedy and Edwards Air Force Base. Then the excitement died down, and we went back to the sports page and Disneyland. Have our hearts been lifted? By inflation? By a recession variously known as a depression? By a whole series of grubby episodes involving government officials and vicuña coats, crooked deals, bribery, perjury? By the spectacle of a president unconditionally pardoning his predecessor for all federal crimes which he had "committed or may have committed while president"? By massacres, including the work of the Manson cult, the Jonestown calamity, various police shootouts (six Simbianese Liberation corpses in Los Angeles, eight religious zealots in Memphis), and the shooting of the Kennedy brothers, Martin Luther King, George Wallace, Reagan, union officials, assorted blacks—and through all this slaughter and mayhem, persistent national lobbying against gun control?

By disclosure in the Senate's Committee on Intelligence hearings that our CIA had instigated death plots against foreign leaders in Asia, Africa, Central and South America and the Caribbean?

If after all that has happened since 1949, Commager's hope that our resources of heritage, history and character might fit us for what he calls our duties and destiny—if that hope is still alive, and its lease is extensible to the end of this century, then a few things will have to be done.

1. First, we must take pains to grow up as people. Not grow rich—we are already rich. Not grow powerful—we are already powerful, though we have learned that power is not enough to win wars in Asia or spring hostages in Iran and Lebanon. Not grow proficient—we are already the sharpest and most inge-

nious technicians in the world, except for isolated enclaves like the Swiss with their watches, the British with their Rollses and the Japanese with their chips. Instead we need to grow up in our attitudes toward fixations that have plagued us for decades, so many disquietudes that it would take a volume heavier than this to begin to document them all. Among the exhibits are three bugbears so conspicuous that it would be derelict not to bring them up in relation to the forces of trivialization.

We must get over the notions that (1) social programs are a swindle and public welfare a racket; (2) anything, including security, can be bought if there is enough money; (3) everything left of center, including liberalism and what the right calls "secular humanism," is antagonistic to God, country, and our most cherished values.

Taking these misgivings in sequence, (1) the paroxysms of rue and rage expressed over welfare assistance for the poor usually come from people so snugly insulated by affluence that they do not know at first hand a single person actually on relief, they have never spent a day in the company of one, or an hour in one's home. The odds are overwhelming that such complainants have never read any substantial literature on the subject, or been educated by exposure to a single documentary film like Frederick Wiseman's *Welfare*.

Nancy Reagan, in an interview with Mike Wallace shortly after she had bought a quarter-million dollars' worth of china place-settings for the White House, suggested that the way to take care of deserving indigents was through voluntary contributions, and she cited a needy case whose circumstances, described on a local TV program, so moved viewers that several of them volunteered to help. A stunned Wallace pointed out that this involved a single, isolated instance and could in no way apply to the millions out there. Mrs. Reagan did not respond; she smiled, and the interview went on to other matters.

Actually the worst extravagances in welfare are by and for the rich and powerful. The president of the United States does not pay for domestic help out of his government salary, nor does he pay rent, or any of his family's medical, utility or telephone bills. He gets free transportation, free entertainment, vacations with pay any time he likes for as long as he likes—all at taxpayers' expense. In Nixon's years as president his family and staff enjoyed 75 maids, butlers, cooks and technicians, as well as a fleet of cars, planes and boats, 16 helicopters, 11 Lockheed Jetstars, five Boeing 707 jetliners. Also several million dollars worth of renovations to his Florida and California homes. This was the same Nixon who said, "We are faced with a choice between the work ethic which built this nation's character, and the new welfare ethic that could cause the American character to weaken."

In contrast to Nixon, Thomas Jefferson had to fork over $10,000 of his own money to pay for wine consumed at the White House during his eight years in residence.[1] The cost of Ronald Reagan's frequent excursions to his ranch home in Santa Barbara, and his holidays in the Bahamas and elsewhere, also came out of the national till.[2] During which period school lunches were being cut back, and services to the poor trimmed or cut.

The assumption that welfare recipients are mostly idlers, malingerers, lazy slobs, moochers or bums who scrupulously avoid getting a job, is a cruel libel on a class that cannot reply through press conferences, planted releases, lobbies or P.R. men. According to two government agencies, the commonly held suppositions about cheating and freeloading are upside down. The Department of Health, Education and Welfare reports that the incidence of fraud among welfare recipients averages around

[1]See *Milestones! 200 Years of American Law*, by Jethro K. Lieberman, West Publishing Co., St. Paul, 1976, p. 372. Lieberman also cites the fact that when, in 1825, John Quincy Adams spent $61 of federal money to buy billiard equipment for the White House, he was denounced for turning the executive mansion into a gaming establishment. He paid the government back out of his own pocket.

[2]Associated Press dispatch from Washington, mid-1982: "President Reagan, while proposing more deep cuts in welfare and social programs, wants to increase the White House operating budget by 17%."

four-tenths of one percent, whereas the IRS estimates that 34 percent of private income nationally goes unreported. And— crowning touch—*Time* discovered that the U.S. spends less on social welfare than any other big industrial country.

The idea that most workers would rather collect unemployment or welfare benefits than earn money at a job, is punctured every time a thousand people queue up for five jobs, as happened outside a state office building in Los Angeles on November 8, 1982, and in many other places before and since; but the fiction persists among people who have never missed a meal for lack of a meal ticket, or had to go into hock to pay their rent.

A good many people who unprotestingly pay taxes to procure wrenches for the Pentagon at $9,609.00 each (cost to manufacturer, 12 cents), who underwrite Congressional junkets of dubious value, shore up venal and corrupt foreign governments, bail out ailing corporations, and fund assorted extravagances in space, cannot stand the idea of poor and hungry Americans receiving food, clothing and rent money simply because they are poor, hungry and have had no luck finding jobs. "Every time someone gets into the check line with a basketful of generic beans and day-old bread and then hands the cashier food stamps," wrote Nancy Amidei, head of the Food and Research Center in Washington, D.C.,

> everyone else in the line thinks, "Hey, that's where my tax dollars are going!" And heaven help the poor old lady if she has dared to buy doughnuts too. This helps explain why there isn't more resentment over tax giveaways to people who already have lots of money. It is hard to see your taxes at work in the money that slips, untaxed, into somebody's wallet, so I propose giving rich people their tax benefits in the form of "luxury stamps." That way, whenever somebody gets into the checkout line with lobster and winter asparagus and pays with luxury stamps, everybody else in the line can say, "Hey! That's where my tax dollars are going!"

A sardonic suggestion, but it does not exaggerate the attitude of many otherwise reasonable people who are implacably hostile to the notion of giving a 45-cent meal to a 12-year-old, or to an unsupported 80-year-old. Their view is vividly presented in a letter to the editor of the *Los Angeles Times* from one Mrs. Ellis, on 2.24.85:

> From whence comes this recurring theme that we "owe" something to the unemployed, unsheltered, unwell, etc.?...[they are] the leeches of our culture...It is a well-worn and true adage that "God helps those who help themselves."...If we don't leave well enough alone, a handful of hard-working conservatives will have to shoulder the burden of providing shelter and food for thousands of bums....How did people survive in the days before welfare, free shelter, free meals, Medicare, Medicaid, ad nauseum? It turns my stomach.

Small wonder the poor, ill, undernourished and unemployed are thought of by hard-working conservatives as bums and leeches, when the nation's conservative leader has been setting the tone for years. In a 1964 television speech, Reagan made a joke about hunger:

> We were told four years ago that 17 million people went to bed hungry every night. Well, that was probably true. They were all on a diet.

In 1966 he defined unemployment insurance as "a prepaid vacation for freeloaders," and when he became president he proposed a 19.1 percent cut in such insurance. Congress, to its disgrace, gave him all but 1.7 percent of what he called for. In 1984, nettled because the media were carrying news of unemployment, he posed the much-quoted question, "Is it news that some fellow out in South Succotash someplace has been laid off?"

Reagan is certainly not the first president under whose administration there have been poor and unemployed, but he is the first to trivialize the situation, crack jokes about it, and aggravate the problem by making the poor poorer.[3] The trivializing mode is clearest in his South Succotash remark, which not only reduces the background of the subject to a four-corners hamlet, so remote one doesn't even know where it is ("someplace"), but implies that a jobless person in Succotash is of less account than one in, say, Cleveland.

Again, it all comes together as a vast pattern of reduction. Disapproved or "inferior" people become leeches, bums, Schoen-bugs, hillbillies, numbers, expendables, unemployables, right elbows, or even ciphers, as in the case of the victims of the holocaust whose very existence was later denied. The needs and concerns of people become prepaid vacations for freeloaders, matters of small moment, crappy little issues.

(2) Not even the farthest-out ascetic mystic would ask or expect a flush American to give up his cherished materialism in exchange for vows of poverty and Gandhi loin cloths. But curbs on conspicuous greed have always been tolerated so long as they do not deprive the Hunts and Forbeses of their hobbies and mansions. Measures such as the blue-sky laws starting in 1911, the Securities Exchange Act of 1934 and the Federal Regulation of Lobbying Act of 1948 were passed without letting of blood, and their objectives were for the most part met. The act of 1946 required legislation, and quarterly reports of activities. The procedure worked, up to a point; but then, as usual, loopholes were found and exploited, and it became necessary to investigate fresh violations.

[3]This was substantiated repeatedly, one of the most exhaustive analyses appearing in a series headed "Numbers Worsen—Poverty: Toll Grows Amid Aid Cutbacks" by Richard B. Meyer and Barry Bearak in the *Los Angeles Times*, July 28, 1985. A breakdown of anti-poverty programs slashed by Reagan, and the percentages of cuts he demanded, contained the following: Social Security, 10.4 percent; food stamps, 51.7; housing assistance, 19.5; aid for families with dependent children, 28.6; supplemental security income, 2.5; general employment and training, 43.9; compensatory education for disadvantaged students, 61; nutrition for children, 46; low income energy assistance, 37.5; vocational education, 37.5; Job Corps, 42.9; work incentive program 100 percent; public service employment—entire program cancelled at the president's request.

Lobbying *per se* is legal and often benign, as in most ethnic, racial, consumer, citizen, farm, labor and professional groups. But when it comes to commercial, industrial, military and foreign interests, benignity leaves quietly.

Franklin D. Roosevelt's Secretary of the Interior, Harold L. Ickes, complained in 1937 that the most powerful lobby in Washington was the Forest Service—no deadly menace, as we look back. But 24 years later, the power of lobbies had grown to such an extent that President Eisenhower, in his last address to the nation, warned that the greatest danger to our future subsumed, in effect, a massive lobby. It was the famous military-industrial complex speech, in which the President, who had been Chief of Staff of the U.S. Army, said that the conjunction of an immense military establishment and a huge arms industry was something new in American government, and that its total influence—economic, political and spiritual—

> is felt in every city, every state house, every office of the federal government. We recognize the imperative need for this development, yet we must not fail to comprehend its grave implications.
>
> Our toil, resources and livelihood are all involved; so is the very structure of our society. ... We must guard against the acquisition of unwarranted influence, whether sought or unsought, by the military-industrial complex. The potential for the disastrous rise of misplaced power exists and will persist. We must never let the weight of this combination endanger our liberties or democratic processes. We should take nothing for granted.

Nor, he could have added, should we take anything for granted in contexts of *less* than war-and-peace and life-and-death issues, where instead of a military-industrial complex, there are industrial-commercial complexes seeking to buy legislation.

Twice in California alone, referendum initiatives to mandate separate smoking and non-smoking areas in public places ran far ahead in the polls until the tobacco industry poured millions of dollars into campaigns to discredit and defeat the measures. The

National Association of Used Car Dealers contributed funds to the campaigns of strategically useful congressmen, and won a relaxation of ethical standards, translatable, naturally, into profits. The beverage industry outspent, by a ratio of 60 to 1, advocates of a bottle-deposit law aimed at recycling glass and metal containers, and was successful in seven states. When the initiative came up in California for the first time in 1982, the industry was there again, to the extent of about $8 million, and once again big bucks won out.

Marvin Barrett, in *Broadcast Journalism*, cites a study by the Media Access Project in 1980 which found a "strong correlation" between broadcast expenditures and the number of votes received in three Colorado initiatives; in some contests, business interests outspent their opponents by as much as 100 to 1. In June, 1981, a California proposition to tax big oil profits was defeated when oil companies in and out of the state put up $5 million against $314,000 raised by opponents. An even worse disparity showed up shortly after the Three Mile Island accident, when the nuclear industry laid out $4 million to fight anti-nuclear advocates armed with a budget of only $22,500. Guess who won.

It is up to the electorate to control the exercise of what Eisenhower called "misplaced power," by mandating far stricter discipline over lobbying activity. "Only an alert and knowledge-able citizenry," Eisenhower said in that same speech, "can compel the proper meshing of the huge industrial and military machinery . . . so that security and liberty may prosper together." It follows that if a citizenry can compel the proper meshing of huge machines, it can also control smaller ones.

Under a law signed in 1962, any person who offers a congressman a bribe in order to influence his actions, and any congressman who accepts such a bribe, could be fined $20,000 and imprisoned for 15 years. Yet campaign contributions by interests—any interests—which stand to profit from the passage or defeat of pending legislation constitute a form of persuasion that is only one degree removed from bribery itself. The second meaning of bribery in both the Random House and Heritage dictionaries is, "anything serving to persuade or induce."

According to the language of Statute 18 USC 201, a campaign contribution, or even a fee for a speech to an organization

would be punishable as bribery if it could be proved that the offer was really a direct attempt to buy the legislator's vote or otherwise influence his official actions.[4]

We are kidding ourselves if we think that corporations or unions or any interests situated hundreds or thousands of miles distant from the bailiwicks of a particular state are *not* trying to buy votes or influence political action when they contribute funds to campaigns in that state.

Lobbyists have the right legally to lobby their heads off directly to the public—through media, barnstorming speeches, and all channels open to free speech—but corporation contributions to candidates who vote on issues affecting them should no more be countenanced than should a professional baseball club's sending presents to selected umpires.

And it might not be amiss if former congressmen and senators were enjoined from becoming licensed lobbyists, in which capacity they use their experience as officeholders, paid for at public expense, to benefit private interests in legislative matters. Among well-known graduates of the Senate who have done this are Joseph H. Ball of Minnesota, who lobbied for ship owners; Scott Lucas of Illinois, who represented manufacturers, insurance companies, an association of chain drug stores, a lumber company, a telephone company, a sugar company, Texaco, and the Republic of Panama; Joseph C. Mahoney of Wyoming, an airline; Burton K. Wheeler of Montana, oil. Richard S. Schweiker of Pennsylvania, who resigned from the Reagan cabinet, became an insurance lobbyist.

Denying lobby licenses to former congressmen may sound

[4]"Review of Lobby Laws," in *Legislators and Lobbyists*, Congressional Quarterly Service, 1965, p.48.

excessive and impossible to achieve, but there was a time when nobody believed that commercial TV, which once enjoyed nine-figure incomes from cigarette advertising, would ever exclude those products from the tube, or that the powerful tobacco industry would submit to a mandatory warning in its advertising and on its packages of cigarettes that the Surgeon General had determined cigarette smoking to be dangerous to health.

If reformers ever get so far as to enjoin certain types of lobbying, they might go further and interdict incumbent presidents from going around the country in election years to promote pet candidates of their parties. It places the opposition at an unfair disadvantage because of the intense media coverage of a president's every move. Moreover, if we insist on exalting the office of president by piling on royal perquisites, then presidents should respond regally by staying above the fray. Genuine kings and queens do not run around their kingdoms huckstering for parliamentary candidates.

(3) The one national attitude which has been passed down from administration to administration, crossing party lines and invading almost every area of American society for the last sixty years, has been a reflexive antagonism toward anything construed as menacing, abrasive or even uncomplimentary to capitalism. Paranoia is unseemly in a prosperous giant, and the effect of our psychosis has been to alienate us from much of the world, spill blood in ghastly, unwanted wars, drive us into awkward and embarrassing diplomatic gaffes like demanding that Europeans violate their Soviet pipeline contracts because we did not like what was going on in Poland.

If suddenly we got over our chronic angst, the Pentagon would be deprived of its biggest fund-raiser, which is the Soviet threat to pulverize us at any moment. The big tocsin sounds punctually at appropriations time, when inevitably we are found lagging behind the Russians in this or that category of arms, and we must scramble to catch up. Mort Sahl offered us some comfort with the suggestion that if the Russians steal our secrets, then *they'll* be two years behind. The need to draw even with our adversary, and then go him one or two better, is always presented as extremely urgent,[5] notwithstanding universal awareness that both sides long ago arrived at an absurdly redundant overkill capacity, each bristling with a nuclear arsenal that could wipe out the other several times over.

This exorbitant charade belittles the architects and engineers of our still unrivalled war machine. For to propose that we must constantly fidget and fret behind our defenses is to imply that our system is in momentary danger of being corrupted by Soviet infiltration of all kinds, political, economic and everything else. Just how trivializing this menace is was considered by William Winter, journalist, in the summer of 1982:

> How many people in the world clamor to emulate Soviet popular art, music, clothing—even Soviet ideology? ... Nobody anywhere calls for copying anything Soviet today. But everyone everywhere witnesses the adoration of US culture (with all its sad faults!). It is America's rock music, American blue jeans, longhair and discos that are popular ... even, you may be astounded to learn, in the Soviet Union!! Walk down the streets of Moscow and you may be approached by young Russians wanting to buy your blue jeans and T-shirts ... Ever hear of anybody trying to buy Soviet clothes? ... Oh come on, let's be sensible.
>
> Do you really think anybody wants to copy Soviet economics? [It] does not attract anybody, has no worrisome influence. Yet from the way our policy designers have been talking all these years, we are in mortal danger because there's an international communist conspiracy and the goblins'll get you if you don't watch out.[6]

Red goblins have long been by far the favorite chimeras of political opportunists and demagogues. The procession began with A. Mitchell Palmer, third of Woodrow Wilson's Attorneys

---

[5] On March 4, 1983, in a dispatch from Washington, Robert C. Toth reported to *The Los Angeles Times* that the United States overestimated the growth rate of Soviet military spending in each of five years from 1976 to 1981—an "embarrassing revision." According to Toth, "the CIA and Defense Intelligence Agency have agreed that Soviet defense spending is growing at a slower rate than previously believed."

[6] *William Winter Comments*, July, 1982.

General. He was shrewd enough, as early as 1919, to sense that an easy way to fame and power lay in inventing and exploiting a Red Scare. The Russian Bolsheviks were then conveniently novel, ultraradical, and noisy enough to serve as model dragons. Americans had hardly learned how to spell Communism when Mitchell ordered a series of raids, all illegal, on homes and labor headquarters. On a single night in January, 1920, he caused to be arrested more than 4000 alleged communists in 33 different cities. Historian Samuel Eliot Morison recalls the episode:

> In New England, hundreds of people were arrested who had no connection with radicalism of any kind. In Detroit, 300 men were arrested on false charges, held for a week in jail and denied food for 24 hours, only to be found innocent of any involvement in radical movements. ... Palmer emerged from the episode a national hero. ... In New York the anti-radical campaign reached its climax when the state legislature expelled five Socialist members of the assembly, although the Socialist party was legally recognized and the members were innocent of any offense.[7]

At a cabinet meeting a few weeks later President Wilson cautioned Palmer, "Do not let this country see red," but red is exactly what the country was exhorted to see many times since then, by many persons and agencies. The goblins were back in force throughout a disgraceful epoch of loyalty oaths, informers, blacklists and a roster of "subversive" organizations drawn up by a succession of Attorneys General under Harry S. Truman, plus a Supreme Court which served as "a compliant instrument of administrative persecution and congressional inquisition,"[8] prosecutions under the Smith Act, deportation terror among aliens, censorship of foreign mail, and denial of the right to travel. Government agencies worked with vigilante groups whose very names suggest the hysteria fomented by hyper-patriotism: House Committee on UnAmerican Activities (HUAC), Senate Internal

---

[7]*The Oxford History of the American People*, by Samuel Eliot Morison, Oxford, 1965, p.883.
[8]*The Great Fear*, by David Caute, Simon & Schuster, 1978, p.144.

Security Subcommittee, Subversive Activities Control Board, Alliance For the Preservation of American Ideals, Federal Loyalty-Security Boards, Americans Battling Communism, The Anti-Communist Christian Crusade, Red Channels, State Un-american Activities Committees (notably in Washington and California), Red Squads—local police detachments set up to spy on and harass suspected subversives in seven major cities.[9] The leaders of this orchestrated campaign included some of the least admirable characters in our political history, like J. Parnell Thomas, Chairman of HUAC, who went to prison for taking kickbacks from his staff; Joseph McCarthy, whose sleaziness was finally too much for his fellow senators; John Rankin of Mississippi, who never bothered to conceal a virulent anti-semitism (on Capitol Hill one day he called Walter Winchell "a little slime-mongering kike"); John N. Mitchell, Nixon's Attorney General, who went to prison for his part in the Watergate coverup, but not before having menaced conservationists who wanted to preserve our forests, lakes, rivers, coastlines and national parks ("the conservation movement is a breeding ground of communists and other subversives. We intend to clean them out, even if it means rounding up every birdwatcher in the country") and sundry congressmen who took bribes, or, on occasion, accepted honors from Generalissimo Francisco Franco and other active friends of our active enemies.

What was trivialized in all this, was the character of America. Other countries have had, and some continue to have, repressions far worse than the excesses of our extremest infatuates. Disgraceful as were our undulant Red scares, nobody was tortured—physically, at least—there was no equivalent of the harsh gulags of the Soviet Union, or Chile's infamous soccer-stadium prison and wholesale murders, including that of Allende; there was no brutalization and execution of opposition, as happened under both Shah and Ayatollah in Iran; no unexplained disappearances, as in Argentina; no mad butcher, as in

[9]Detroit, Cleveland, Dayton, Toledo, Cincinnati, Los Angeles and New York City.

Uganda; no Soweto, or covert liquidation of political prisoners as in South Africa; no Auschwitzes and Belsens, as in Nazi Germany. But America cannot be judged, nor does she judge herself, by the same gauge as those countries. A standard of measurement—one of many—is that no other country in the world, not even the freest and most enlightened among them, has so extensive a literature of rights, justice, and liberty in its many forms. West Germany, notwithstanding its regeneration, has yet to produce a book comparable to *The Great Fear*,[10] by David Caute, for example. Publication and distribution of a book comparable to Caute's in the Soviet Union, documenting the many gross abuses of freedom in any period of that country's recent past, would at the very least guarantee prison or exile for its author, editor, publisher, and, possibly, bookdealers who sold it. Caute, incidentally, makes the sharp point that "when official America sins, she sins doubly: against her victims, and against her own traditions, ideals and rhetoric." Once again we come down to essences of quantity and scale. A small, wry, redemptive consolation rests in the thought that, perhaps there is more of good substance to *be* trivialized in America than anywhere else.

[10] Nor little that is comparable, in other countries, to such works as Bert Andrews' *Washington Witch Hunt*, Henry Steele Commager's *Freedom, Loyalty, Dissent*, Lillian Hellman's *Scoundrel Time*, Owen Lattimore's *Ordeal by Slander*, Merle Miller's *The Judges and the Judged*, Philip Dunne's *Take Two*, or Telford Taylor's *Grand Inquest: The Story of Congressional Investigations*.

29 ✑ TV Repairs and Muckrakers

Among domains damaged by trivialization, that of electronic news is the most likely to repair itself. With radio, TV, cable, satellite and other technologies in a state of constant turbidity, like the Red Spot of Jupiter, it is entirely possible that as hours of newscasting are extended and specialization increases, many of the present abuses such as banter, distortion, hypercompression and showmanship will diminish. When a station or network transmits news 24 hours a day, the pressure is off; not even inveterate comedians can keep up small talk all day long; and there will be fewer occasions for Dan Rather to complain, as he did before a meeting of radio and TV directors in late 1980:

> Time—we need time. The evening news ought to be an hour. And I'm not talking about an hour to play with. I don't mean "give us (an extra) half hour and we'll do nice, soft mood pieces and entertain you." I mean, we need that time to tell the American public the important things that are going on in the world.

Given the time needed, there would still be stretches of soft news, of amiable nudges and fatuous giggling on local newscasts, but the ratio of twaddle against hard news and straightforward delivery is bound to shrink.

Pending the millenium, when all news will be delivered in a balanced, objective way, hewing to the principles of Murrow, Friendly, Cronkite and Koppel, certain reforms have been suggested. ABC News's president, Roone Arledge, in February, 1981, challenged rival networks to exclude news specials and major documentary programs from prime-time ratings competition:

> Serious news programs are a public service that rarely attract a large audience, and they shouldn't have to compete with light-entertainment programming. Right now, each network is penalized in the weekly averages if it puts on a serious news program.

NBC briefly toyed with the notion, CBS rejected it outright. Only ABC went through with it.

Bob Teague, New York anchorman who was shrilly critical of TV news practices in his part of the forest, seconded Arledge's suggestion for a moratorium on news ratings and went further, proposing that TV executives nationwide agree among themselves to drop the rating system and instead compete for qualitative ratings by an independent monitoring board of former journalists, educators and "a representative cross-section of the population in that particular broadcasting area." Criteria would include accuracy, clarity, scope, sensitivity, initiative, even grammar, and the results would be codified in a monthly breakdown. The performance of each broadcaster would be graded each month (excellent, good, fair, poor) and the current rating posted at the top of each broadcast, the way movies carry G, PG, R or X ratings before credits come on. The result, Teague thinks,

> would be heightened competition for journalistic excellence instead of numbers. Viewers who want to know what's going on could then make intelligent choices as to which station's news

programs to watch, instead of blindly tuning to the one that Nielsen or Arbitron say more people are watching, perhaps for the wrong reason.

A worthy goal, but it has far less chance of succeeding than Arledge's moratorium, because not one station would entertain for a moment the idea of flashing RATED POOR or RATED FAIR ahead of its own news. It might not even post a GOOD rating if a local rival had a grade of EXCELLENT. Even more of a problem would be the makeup of Teague's blue-ribbon monitoring board. "Former journalists" might include a Pegler; "educators" might embrace the founder of Oral Roberts University; "a representative cross-section of the population" might in some situations include a Klansman, a lobbyist, a union organizer, a union buster, a numbers man, a militant, a pacifist, or the head of a cartel. Life is tough enough as it is.

Teague found support for some of his advocacies from two of the most respected old hands, Cronkite and David Brinkley. Cronkite was worried about the future "a couple of generations or so" down the line:

> I'm not sure what you are going to end up with. It would be disastrous if [network television news] started using the local formula of funny talk, pretty-boy-pretty-girl news, trivialization of the news.

Brinkley attacked both the cosmetic approach and the race for ratings. He told Teague that if he were running a news program, either local or network,

> I certainly wouldn't be looking for the handsome[st] men and best-looking women I could find. I would look for the most talented and experienced. ... No question about it, a lot of this [the airing of inconsequential news and general fluff, is caused by] the pressure of trying to build up an audience. ... The better way to do it is to put on an interesting program about the things that matter. ... Trivia is trivia, whether it's on the street or on the air. If you want to develop an audience and have it

stay with you over a period of time, I think the way to do it is to
put on a program of news that has some meaning.

Perhaps a more workable reform is a Teague suggestion that
competing flagship stations in every city agree among themselves
not to broadcast essentially the same news simultaneously at 6
and 11 in the evening. He proposes that each station take a
different time segment, arguing that not everyone's lifestyle is
attuned to watching the tube at the same time each day. In New
York City, for example, ABC could put on its local news from 6
to 7, WNBC from 7 to 8 and WCBS from 8 to 9. On successive
years, the times would be rotated. To the objection that stations
would be unlikely to surrender an hour of prime time at which
they normally carry high profit-making entertainment, in order
to run less lucrative local news commercials, Teague replies that
his idea calls for giving up only one hour per day per year on a
rotating basis; thus each station would make the same sacrifice
the same number of times.

But this proposal is essentially quantitative, whereas Brinkley's
prescription for attracting audiences by putting on programs
about "things that matter," and Rather's insistence that the public
be told "the important things," and Arledge's repeated references
to "serious news," and Cronkite's warning against trivialization of
news, all go to the core of the matter—substance.

Another core-targeted proposal, this one going into the
ethics of the in-depth interview, is made by Joe Saltzman,
award-winning documentarian and chairman of broadcasting
at USC's School of Journalism.[1] Saltzman believes that the
standard approach to the electronic interview is faulty, and
because of it, a number of broadcasts, including the West-
moreland-CBS documentary, have brought parties to litigation. The electronic interviewer in cases like this, Saltzman
argues, is in an untenable position, being forced to go out and
catch information on the fly, to tape material that is often

[1]"CBS and Westmoreland: Want Fairness? Break the Rules," by Joe Saltzman,
Emmy Magazine, May-June, 1985.

rambling, incoherent, or not carefully reasoned, and then try to give it shape and clarity in the editing room. With the best intentions, he may distort or misrepresent.

To avoid this, Saltzman proposes a procedural overhaul that is long on both probity and studio time. Before doing an interview, he suggests, the reporter should spend hours with the person

> talking about everything and anything. Get to know each other. Go over the material that must be covered on camera. Know what you want to ask. Find out what the person wants to say and considers important. Take notes. Work with the person to ensure that statements are presented in the clearest way possible.
>
> Then do the video interview... if necessary let them ramble, saying whatever they want on the subject. Then re-ask specific questions if the answers are not clear or brief enough.... It is never necessary to entrap or embarrass anyone.
>
> This technique assures everyone—no matter how difficult it is for an individual to speak on camera—a fair shake.

Saltzman feels that the spontaneous interview is unfair to the person unaccustomed to making concise 30-second statements before a camera, and because of this, much of what is said is doomed to be cut, or fragmented and strung together in a way that distorts its intention. What does this do, he asks, to the

> inarticulate, reflective, or just plain people who cannot speak spontaneously about anything, but who have much to say if broadcast journalists take the time to listen and help them express themselves in an alien medium? Why not accommodate television's unique demands by allowing the individual the dignity to think over something before saying it in front of a camera, to have time to reflect on a question without looking guilty or stupid?... and why shouldn't the [interviewer] be given the leeway to make sure the information is being offered in a way that it can be used... without chopping it to bits?

Saltzman's approach would make tougher demands on the

reporter's time,[2] but on the other hand it might save time in the editing room, and, more importantly, save both time and expense by keeping parties out of court.

Endorsement from on high—they don't come higher—was expressed by Bill Moyers, who wrote Saltzman:

> The purpose of extended conversations which I used to conduct on public television to the benefit of an audience exposed for the first time to a Henry Steele Commager or Samuel Eliot Morison or Dame Rebecca West, was always to get the essence of what the subject thought. I spent days—sometimes weeks—preparing by reading what the guests had written and what had been written about them, and I conducted the interviews for as many as three or four hours in order to get the one hour that best reflected their thinking. I do this for the interviews on documentaries, too, which of course reduces the heat of the experience but compensates with the light that is shed upon the person's ideas. What a beastly myth that one does his or her best thinking on the spot, under pressure, sweating at the hands of a prosecutorial interrogator. Theater, perhaps; thought, no.[3]

As for substance on TV, it is not accidental that an investigative news program, *60 Minutes*, topped the ratings several times and has been close to the top consistently. With few exceptions these programs, and those of ABC's *20/20* and PBS's *Frontline*, have dealt with matters that matter, with serious concerns. In an era when violence is a marketable commodity, when execution and massacre are revived as instruments of redress, when assassination turns out to be a secret form of diplomacy, when anger, greed, rip-offs, kickbacks, bribes, bared

---

[2]Very often the time of the interviewee is more valuable than that of the reporter. In Warsaw once, in the course of a series of radio broadcasts I did for CBS (*One World Flight*), I interviewed the first post-war President of Poland, Boleslaw Beirut. The meeting was in the presidential palace, and several people were waiting to see him. Though he was head of state with many pressing concerns on a heavy agenda, he insisted on conversing with me for two hours before we started recording, and carefully went over all of my prepared questions. It was Saltzman's principle in action.

[3]Letter to Joe Saltzman, 5.30.85.

fang and flung dung are commonplace, investigative journalism performs powerful services as an astringent and antiseptic. Much of what it reveals may be disturbing and unwelcome, but then so are bad-news medical diagnoses. They are *necessary*; and if occasionally there are abuses of the investigative process— entrapment, the ambush interview, the hidden camera, misrepresentation, invasions of privacy—these, though not to be condoned, are perhaps a small price to pay in return for the "pitiless publicity" and "fierce light" that Emerson and Tennyson recommended so highly. Abuses committed in pursuit of truth and justice are to be avoided, and we call on the Bill of Rights and the American Civil Liberties Union when they are not, but occasional transgressions of this order are no reason to curb or banish Seymour Hersh, Mike Wallace, Morley Safer, Bill Kurtis, Harry Reasoner, Robert Scheer, Ed Bradley, Geraldo Rivera, Peter Lance, I. F. Stone, Peter Davis, Jessica Mitford, and all other good ferrets.

The muckraker represents an antidote to trivialization. To an expert, piddling transgressions are hardly worth revving up for. The term muckraker itself does not begin to suggest the honor due, for to describe a crack investigative journalist as a muckraker is a little like calling Heinrich Schliemann, who discovered and excavated ancient Troy, a ditch-digger. The word was first given wide circulation by Theodore Roosevelt, to whom we do not generally look for felicity of speech, and when he used the word he was nervous about it, saying that muckrakers were valuable, but only if they know when to stop raking. Any journalist could have told him that it is much more important to know when to *start* raking—and second most important is how the rake is handled; and third is whether anybody is going to have the courage to publish what turns up in the teeth of the rake.

Emile Zola was a lot more than a muckraker when he exploded the Dreyfus case; Woodward and Bernstein were much more than muckrakers on the trail of Watergate; and Jessica Mitford, although apparently at peace with the symbols of muck and rake (she titled one of her books *The Gentle Art of Muckraking*), is so far above that term she is practically in orbit.

Time and again effective muckrakers have inspired in all of us—except their targets, naturally—the same feelings of relief and vindication that we enjoy when Gary Cooper disposes of the three thugs in *High Noon*, when the town bully gets flattened by the town librarian, when Idi Amin's hostages are snatched away from Entebbe in the dead of night.

They are a comfort to have around.

30 ✐ Remedies at Law

Justice being depicted traditionally as a goddess, she invites metaphors of gender. In the temperate zones of abstraction, she is vestal and serene, like her sorority sisters Ceres and Minerva, but in practice she can be passive, indifferent, cold, flighty, maverick, cruel, or as negotiable as a whore. For laws are insular, and, to the extent that they express the will of whatever element of a society prevails for the moment, they are as subject to change as everything else.

"Law," said one of America's best lawyers, Aaron Burr, "is whatever is boldly asserted and plausibly maintained." Sometimes implausibly maintained, as Burr himself was to find out before he was through with the courts. Nor is law a straight-line evolutionary process, like so many progressions in the arts and sciences. It has a history of meanders, tergiversations and reversals. At one time the United States Supreme Court ruled that blacks were so far inferior to the white race that they had no rights which the white man was bound to respect, and that they might "justly and lawfully be reduced to slavery for their benefit." That judgment, like other gross codifications before and since (including the silliest of all constitutional events, the Prohibition Amendment) was eventually reversed, the point here being that

267

massively trivializing legislation, such as reducing human beings
to parcels of property, and mandating temperance, creates its own
reforms by backlash, revolution, or war.

But in areas where the need for revision ˙is subtler, where
grievances are not fulminating but chronic and of low voltage,
where resistance to offensive restraints is dulled by long acceptance, reform does not occur spontaneously; it requires bold
advocacy, broad support, proselytizing, and persistence.

The faults in the adversary system, the scandal of overcrowded
court dockets, incompetent judges, inequities in sentencing of
the poor, blind spots and misdirection in legal education—few of
these are confronted by political candidates, deans of law schools,
the A.C.L.U., or factions of the judiciary. It took a scrappy
nonprofessional like Anne Strick (see page 101), a rare lawyer like
Wayne Brazil (page 104), and scattered jurists like Judge Macklin
Fleming (page 100), even to call the roll of wrongs in the
intrenched win-system of American jurisprudence.

When it comes to solutions, there have long been, and are
constantly being generated, earnest opinions. Judge Fleming
feels that the critical problems of modern society cannot readily
be solved by the judicial process under the adversary system, and
that attempts to do so will only make matters worse by increasing
and accentuating the problems. Wayne Brazil, on the other
hand, is hopeful—yet his hope is on the order of a pale petition,
and does not go very far:

> My hope is that practitioners, legal educators, and profession-
> als in the fields of mental and social health will ... commit
> some resources at least to determining whether or not a
> problem exists that warrants further study. ... Legal education
> should draw upon the results of such efforts to help prepare
> young lawyers to cope with the pressure they will experience in
> practice. ...

Strick has not the slightest question that the problem exists, and is
as prolific in suggesting reforms as in ticking off indictments. But
first she cites a wide range of remedies proposed by others: Jerome

Frank, political liberal, advocates special education for trial judges, and school courses in jury service; John Frank, conservative, recommends eliminating all automobile cases from the court system; former U.S. Attorney Whitney Seymour, Jr., would like to see an end to plea bargaining, and expansion of the court's role in areas of social problems such as consumer protection, welfare and health services, and public school funding; Professor of Law Fred Rodell wants to sweep the board clean—get rid of all lawyers, make it a crime to practice law for money, abolish all legal language and principles "which confuse instead of clarify the real issues that arise between men," and substitute arbitration boards or panels of experts in each field of dispute; Edgar and Jean Cahn, co-Deans of Antioch Law School, propose a Neighborhood Court System which would accentuate local accountability and resolution of disputes "to provide the aggrieved with a source of remedy that does not subject him unnecessarily to the perils of foreign jurisdiction."

Strick, while respectful of these and other ideas put forward prescriptively, is impatient with their proponents for leaving unchallenged the adversary system itself, which she feels is beyond repair or salvage.

> The most sophisticated legal mechanisms and benign remedies cannot surmount an ethic that makes them artillery. Nor can the most constructive laws imaginable rise above ... a method structured to produce ... only victors and vanquished. ... Our adversary procedure, together with its idiosyncratic concepts of lawyer, judge, petit and grand juries, is no longer tolerable. All must go. We must start over.

Since none of her select attestants except Rodell agrees with her about throwing out the whole adversary apparatus, and no one including Rodell offers substitutes that satisfy her, Strick herself stakes out a program built on a series of premises that are logical and theoretically feasible, but which, given the steel-ribbed fixity of our legal procedures, have little chance of being consummated this side of Utopia. Still, that is no reason not to accommodate them in our thinking, just as we accept the plausibility of the Ten Commandments knowing full well that they are broken all the time and will go on being broken.

The salient features of Strick's concept are establishment of a new legal system "for society's health and welfare, rather than as predominantly punitive"; it must be "multireferant rather than bipolar ... neither accusatory nor litigious, but preventive, ameliorative, information-seeking; not argumentative, but discussional; not punitive, but constructive"; archaic laws must be dropped from the books; traditional trappings such as bench and robe, arcane language and ceremonial behavior must be replaced by an atmosphere that encourages ease, openness, natural response and understanding; the system must employ "at levels of prevention, mediation, evaluation and treatment," experts from a broad spectrum of human-behavior disciplines, including mental health, anthropology, sociology, economics, penology, education and vocational guidance. The entire system must be positioned at the greatest possible remove from Authority's thumb.

How to achieve all this? Start by summoning a Special Assembly that would "optimally include the least culture-bound, most free-flying minds from all fields of human behavior and welfare." Members of the Assembly would be chosen

> by nationwide vote of matriculating students, teachers and practitioners in each field. There must also be lay persons ... and representatives of the major disadvantaged subgroups of our society; among them, Indian, Chicano, black, poor, women; the 18-25 group and the over-65; as well as those who have been imprisoned and have since led productive lives. ... [The] Assembly must be directed by Congress not merely to design, but specifically to make operative at the federal level, a new legal system [which] we must then, through local legislatures, direct our states to emulate.

Lawyers would not be locked out of this plan, but kept down to a sub-group. "The single fixed condition is that legal professionals, drilled in polarity, must comprise only a small minority of the membership." Strick cannot quite bring herself even to call them lawyers in this context, but neither does she want to exclude them.

It is easy to smile at this grand proletarian concept, and many legal professionals have done that and more—they have laughed at it. But the democracy of Anne Strick, like that of Ralph Nader, is profound, and at times it embodies religious principles without it ever being called that—as when it demands that our legal system *exemplify* the ethic that it claims to value, that it "eulogize reason and human dignity," that it seek truth and understanding, that it place compromise and conciliation above vindictiveness and punishment, and that it stop directing each man "to be his brother's competitor in pursuit of his own selfish interest."

There is something touching—depending on one's philosophy—about the idea of rehabilitated former prisoners sitting as members of a vital Assembly. And why not? As a body, they might well have deeper insights into criminal behavior and penology, and translate them into more human terms, than the average judge.

Traditionalists may be outraged by Strick's idea of dispensing with judicial black robes, the cries of "Oyez," and other ceremonial hogwash left over from a time when the Church, which lives by pomp, and the State, which indulges it, were one. But the sad truth is that a scandalously large number of judges are unfit to be sitting where they are. "Whores become madams," Lawyer Martin Erdman called them, and got into trouble for it; Judge Samuel Rosenman, aide to President Franklin D. Roosevelt, believed that in far too many instances

> the benches of our courts in the United States are occupied by mediocrities—men of small talent, undistinguished in performance, technically deficient and inept.

Judge Tim Murphy scotched the impression, held by some critics of the court system, that alcoholism is the occupational disease of the bench. "It is not alcoholism," he corrects, "[but] laziness. It is terribly difficult to make some judges work."

While there are of course many fine judges, and some who may be great, our jurisprudence is crowded with biased, mercurial, idiosyncratic, arrogant and egocentric types. Lewis M. Isaacs, Jr., who for 27 years was director of the Federal Bureau of Prisons, testified in a hearing that judges too often are persons "whose ignorance, intolerance and impatience are such as to sicken anyone who stops to think about them ... some judges are arbitrary and even sadistic ... [it] is notoriously a matter of record."

The standard honorific, "Your Honor," is as anachronistic in the late 20th Century as Your Majesty, Your Lordship, Your Excellency, or Your Holiness. There was nothing in the slightest degree honorable, for example, about Judge Webster Thayer, whose opinion in the Sacco-Vanzetti case was denounced by Supreme Court Justice Felix Frankfurter as

> unmatched ... for discrepancies between what the record discloses and what the opinion conveys ... a farrago of misquotations, misrepresentations, suppressions and mutilations ... honeycombed with demonstrable errors, and infused by a spirit alien to judicial utterance.

To address as "Your Honor" this malevolent, strutting, bigoted judge, must have been difficult for anyone of decent sensibilities.[1]

If I seem here to deal at disproportionate length with a single treatise marshalled by a woman who never spent a day in law school, it is because I concur with Leonard Boudin of Harvard, that "it required a non-lawyer to see that the emperor has no clothes," and also because nobody before or since Strick has, to my knowledge, gone so far in two directions—attacking the adversary system and proposing ways and means to supplant it. Hers is by no means an antic performance, if we are to believe Former Justice of the U.S. Supreme Court Tom C. Clark, who,

[1]Charles Curtis, in his book *It's Your Law*, tells of being in Thayer's chambers many years after Sacco and Vanzetti were executed, when suddenly Thayer started "strutting up and down boasting that he had been fortunate enough to be on the bench when those sons of bitches were convicted."

while disagreeing with the book's criticisms and recommendations, urged that

> Every lawyer should read it—and after recovering from his
> initial anger—start to work helping in the modernization of
> legal techniques and procedures. Perhaps *Injustice for All* may
> unwittingly become a judicial innovator, arousing the public
> as well as the lawyers to action and thus initiate a second
> renaissance in judicial administration.

The innovation needed for such a renaissance would probably
not have to be all that innovative. As pointed out by Strick, other,
older countries long ago sized up the adversary system for what it
is—a massive trivializing power—and have established programs
that resemble in spirit, if not detail, the Special Assembly she
calls for.. The Chinese consider litigation disreputable; in Japan
lawsuits are deplored even by the plaintiff, with the practical
result that there is a paucity of litigation. In France, Norway,
Italy, Switzerland, Denmark, and, in all probability, other
countries, lay persons are involved in the administration of
justice, and there is special education for assistant judges, and
curricula in the humanities to which every law school should
address itself.

In 1982, the widely disseminated *Odyssey* series on public TV
presented a documentary entitled *Little Injustices*, which took
viewers inside a simple rural court in the Mexican boondocks,
and showed lay jurisprudence in action. The hearing was
uncomplicated, straightforward and fair, and quickly resolved the
issue—recovery of damages sustained when two young men,
having put away too much tequila, ran their truck into a house.
The decision left all parties to the suit satisfied, the young men
anxious to make restitution, the plaintiff content. The whole
thing was wrapped up in no time, yet it was the sort of matter that
in American courts might have dragged on for months or years.

Not that Americans have to go abroad for models. In Des
Moines, a Community Corrections Program has shown what
can be done by way of community-based alternatives to a variety

of standard criminal procedures, including new approaches to pre-trial confinement of those who cannot afford bail and post-trial lockup, and who are disadvantaged under certain circumstances by traditional approaches to probation. In place of these, the Des Moines agenda offers "supervised release within the community," of convicted persons who meet certain criteria. Such release, it is argued, permits

> the maintenance of family and community ties crucial in rehabilitation ... avoids the jailing that dehumanizes and scars, and that ultimately escalates the community's endangerment. Allowing the released person to hold a job outside prison walls promotes continuity with positive aspects of his past life and thus helps create the self-esteem basic both to rehabilitation and prevention. Supervised release avoids the family indigence generally attendant upon a chief wage-earner's imprisonment. Finally, such release saves society money: the cost of supporting the individual's nonremunerative prison confinement, together with the loss of wage-earned tax dollars consequent upon jailing.[2]

Through programs such as this, says Strick, any community can enfranchise itself. Positive thinking, that's what it takes. "No one need give us power over our own lives. We possess it already. We need only join in its use." To accept helplessness, she goes on, can be fatal. Societies whose citizens find themselves getting nowhere when they protest, or plead, or vote for changes that are not made, and who cannot find ways of overcoming their powerlessness, stand in peril of demoralization and of ultimately falling prey to a false "rescuer" who, like Hitler, may spread disintegration and death all about him by way of seeking and finding a "solution."

The case for dismantling the adversary system and reforming the administration of justice, as seen by Strick and her seconds, omits from purview any mention of the law becoming *tougher*

[2]*Community Based Corrections in Des Moines*, U.S. Department of Justice, Law Enforcement Assistance Administration, 1973, cited in *Injustice For All*, p. 210.

against certain malefactions, especially those of broad social consequence. Also omitted, no doubt for reasons of dubious pertinence rather than oversight, is mention of the most recent phenomenon in American mores, the celebrity of prominent convicted criminals, and their reward by publishing deals, TV-movie contracts, and fat lecture fees.

The Des Moines program is admirably workable when it comes to supervising release of a car thief, forger or rapist, but what is to be done when a wealthy corporation illegally dumps dangerously toxic wastes? Ira Reiner, City Attorney for Los Angeles, is contemptuous of fines for company executives guilty of what he calls "life-threatening activity." He believes imprisonment must be mandatory: "If it is only a fine, it would just be considered part of the cost of doing business."[3]

Since the goal of fitting punishment to crime has long been sought, reformers whose aim is to make rehabilitation fit both crime *and* punishment are understandably upset when rank miscarriages of justice go unredressed. There is no comparison between the destructiveness of a reckless driver and that of a manufacturer whose smokestacks pour carcinogens into air breathed by millions of people. Violative generation of smog is not a trifling misdemeanor, nor can it claim any of the meager discounts we tend to lay off against crimes induced by anger, jealousy, passion, poverty or hunger. Scattering poisons on the ground, to the winds, and into streams and oceans, betrays a callousness and greed for profit that in its anti-social warp is worse than arson, if only for the reason that pollution, unlike fire, cannot be contained or localized.

And then there is that subtler form of pollution, the contamination of standards which permits convicted felons who have disgraced their country to bask in acclaim and wallow in fees and royalties. The alumni of Watergate emerged from prison to find themselves sought after by publishers, producers and lecture

[3]A law proposed by Art Buchwald provides that "Any company executive who overcharges the government more than $5 million will be fined $50 or have to go to traffic court three nights a week."

agents. G. Gordon Liddy, E. Howard Hunt, Jr., John Dean, John Ehrlichman, and Charles E. Colson vaulted to a celebrity they would never have achieved had they not been caught in a conspiracy. The true heroes of that sequence, on the other hand, were of little or no interest to publishing houses, networks and agencies. There were no lavish movies about Archibald Cox, Elliott Richardson, Donald Ruckelshaus, or others among the good guys in Washington. The reader may have trouble remembering the names of the decent few, but none whatever in recalling the heavies. For this the media are chiefly to blame, but there are plenty who share their guilt.

A certain amount of public curiosity is natural: there are people who will go far to see a 500-pound bearded lady who can do the split and whistle bird calls at the same time. But endorsement and advancement of political freaks by responsible entrepreneurs is another matter. When in 1977, Howard Hunt, strategist of the Watergate break-in, addressed 500 secretaries at the Holiday Inn in Harvey, Illinois, during National Secretary Week, he was introduced by a desk manager who cautioned members of the audience not to leave while Hunt was speaking. The gist of Hunt's message was that the American press was altogether too nosey about "clandestine affairs" in government; that his 32-month prison sentence was "political" and "pure harassment," and that if Richard Nixon was pardoned, he, Hunt, should have been pardoned also. The manager of the Inn, asked by a journalist how much Hunt was paid to speak to the secretaries, replied, "None of your business. We wanted some type of speaker that the secretaries would really go wow over. With Hunt they got their wow."[4]

Five years after Hunt's stand in Harvey, the lecture business was still in full throttle for ex-convicts of Watergate. In the fall of 1982, G. Gordon Liddy appeared at the University of Southern California, where he spoke to a packed auditorium of students

---

[4]As reported by Roger Simon, syndicated columnist of the *Chicago Sun-Times*; Hunt was paid $2000 for his 53-minute talk.

and got a standing ovation. The following week, members of a class on communications on the same campus were asked what person in all history—arts, letters, science, sports, government, the humanities—they most admired. Selections included Newton, Shakespeare, Michaelangelo, Einstein, Martin Luther King, Franklin D. Roosevelt and others of high account, but one young man, an architecture major, picked for his all-time hero ... G. Gordon Liddy. He was not joking. Nobody in the class challenged him.

Hardly anybody anywhere in any way challenges the unrepentant, self-righteous, boasting felons who operate in the shadows of government. There obviously should be a limit to the extent to which crime pays dividends. Such a limit was imposed not in the U.S., but in Australia, whose Broadcasting Tribunal in 1982 banned a TV commercial for a Brazilian coffee because it showed Ronald Biggs, one of 15 men convicted of a $7.2 million theft from a British train in 1963, sipping coffee on an apartment balcony in Rio de Janeiro. Between sips he said, "When you're on the run all the time like me, you really appreciate a good cup of coffee." Biggs had escaped from prison in England and made his way to Brazil, where the government had no interest in extraditing him. Far from downplaying his credits as a robber, Biggs went on to say, smiling, that at the price this coffee was being sold in Australia, it was a "real steal."

Biggs was paid $10,500 for his services to Brazilian coffee; Hunt was paid $2000 for his services to himself. In both of these transactions, a proposition was broached, the substance of what each had to offer was made known to the parties, a contract or agreement was drawn, and a presentation delivered. The broadcasters of Australia were above accepting revenue from a commercial whose production enriched a criminal vaunting his crime. No such scruples obtain in analogous situations here,[5]

[5]On February 23, 1983, Biggs was treated as a celebrity in an interview with Melody Rogers on the program *Two on the Town*, over Channel 2, CBS, in Los Angeles. The segment, taped in Rio, included a replay of the coffee commercial. The tone of the interview was one of mutual amusement, warm and friendly.

although thus far no one has yet proposed that any of the Watergate prison class go on the air to push a product. That, at least, would be interdicted by sponsors as well as networks, chiefly, I suspect, because it would be construed as "controversial"—the same standard by which political mavericks and liberals like the actor Ed Asner are denied access to, or dropped from, program listings. Yet book and magazine publishers, radio and television news executives, movie producers and high-powered interviewers think nothing of paying handsome fees to graduate felons whose celebrity is a by-product of the courts and prisons of America.

No fair-minded person would deny former convicts the right to make a living. There is no moral limit to how much Hunt, Liddy, Ehrlichman, Haldeman, Dean, *et al.*, may acquire in the way of riches through real estate, insurance, industry, the arts, the professions—any of a thousand capacities—so long as none of them exploits his own crimes against the people of the United States. The spirit of the Des Moines program does not apply here. Rehabilitation is a process of repair, but instead of repairing, the Hunts and Liddys do further damage by wowing secretaries, students and sympathizers with their justification of clandestine affairs and elevation of dirty tricks to the status of patriotic acts.

Congress, maker of laws, might well consider a simple formula whereby, without denying freedom of speech and press, these unregenerates would be obliged to repay all or a substantial part of the bonanzas they enjoy from lectures, books, articles or broadcasts, whenever those productions draw or touch upon their careers as conspirators, or their views on foreign affairs or domestic security—in other words, whenever they profit from exploiting their crimes. They simply do not come into the court of public opinion with clean hands; and while they should be permitted to have their say on crime and punishment, they should not be compensated for it. Their earnings under this arrangement could be divided in interesting ways, including a percentage to the court system to help make up the costs to taxpayers of trials, convictions and imprisonment; and another percentage to various schools for having perverted the uses of the higher education to which they, unlike the run of ordinary criminals, had access.

This, minuscule as it would be in the range of potential legal reforms, might help to restore to the country a little of the dignity that was stripped from it in full view of the watching world by the steady trivialization of values which contributed to Watergate in the first place.

31 ❧ Curricular Notes

All vast abstractions like religion, law and education, seek codification as inexorably as running water seeks channels. Always the flow is downward—theism to church to priest to congregant; jurisprudence to court to judge to lawyer to litigant; education to institution to teacher to student. The course of each is through a dense growth of systems, rituals, rules and procedures, and these undergo changes from time to time. Movement in religion can be glacially slow, as in massive orthodoxies; changes in law may be convulsive when brought about by mandate, public pressure, revolution or war. But education, unlike religion and law, is constantly fidgeting with its codes, studying itself, fending off critics, seeking new modes, experimenting, scrounging for funds, wrestling with questions of academic standards, curricula, ethics, freedom, faculty mix, minorities, accountability, accreditation, research, collective bargaining, industrial and government relations, the military, the church, politics.

Approaches and systems go back to Plato and Aristotle, Quintilian's *Institutio Oratoria*, Erasmus, Locke, Spencer, Eliot of Harvard, the Binet Scale, pauper schools, monitorial schools, state schools, land-grant colleges, progressivism, the ladder system, the Montessori system, and now, lately, the Paideia Proposal.

One might think that, having gone through so much and tried so many different tacks, education can be trusted to find its way and resolve its problems by applying the very powers of scholarship that it uses, teaches and deals with all the time. For example, on the single issue of faculty tenure—a hot question in colleges and universities—an eleven-man Commission of Academic Tenure in Higher Education worked up a report that explored every imaginable angle of the subject—the history of tenure, pros and cons, institutional responsibility, need for research, legal ramifications, recommendations. The bibliography ran to 161 items, including treatises bearing on "The Protection of the Inept," "Bulwark of Academic Freedom and Brake on Change," and "Tenure, Or Seven Years to Life in an Institution."

Yet notwithstanding heavy accumulations of experience, manpower, and expertise, there is less assurance now than ever that the scrutinizers, wardens and commissioners of Learning will be able to keep American education from sinking into the same mire of mediocrity that has swallowed so many other components of our culture.

The fact is that schools have *always* been influenced, if not controlled, by the best or worst ideals of national character, a process that conveys to pupils and indoctrinates in them the elements which form those ideals. German scholarship, once among the proudest ornaments of civilization, almost overnight took on the arrogance and vileness of Nazism; professors, provosts and chancellors turned into toads just as readily as the farmers, laborers, clerks and everybody else who rallied around Hitler. Educational idealism shifted so violently into reverse, that dissenting or racially unwelcome teachers, savants, philosophers and scientists were discredited, disenfranchised, expelled or destroyed.

In contrast to the supineness of the German students who offered little or no resistance to the rise of the Third Reich, impressive spine was shown on American campuses in opposition to the war in Vietnam and Cambodia. The hope of liberals in the early 80's was that the successors to these activists would be equally alert and vocal against creeping philistinism and trivialization, even if only in the form of classroom discussions, student editorials, teacher evaluations, or question-and-answer exchanges when lecturers like J. Gordon Liddy showed up. But no, Liddy was given an ovation; best-selling books on campuses were the same bland ones favored by the rest of the country (in mid-'82 the top five books were on preppies, Rubik's cube, and cats); students, like the rest of the movie-going public, stood in long lines for *The Exorcist, Star Wars,* and *Raiders of the Lost Ark;* they also contributed to the high ratings of TV trash, and were as avid about sports as any other segment of the population. Having been given no encouragement from the larger society to pursue liberal education and its goals, they went on their way perpetuating clichés and carrying forward the delusions and compromises of their elders.

The wonder is that education is not in total shambles. Beset from time to time by political administrations hostile to the humanities in general and education in particular, the institution suffers fools like Governor James "Pa" Ferguson of Texas, who vetoed a bill to support the teaching of foreign languages because, he said, "If English was good enough for Jesus, it's good enough for the schoolchildren of Texas." It struggles against a perpetual anti-intellectualism which is as American as hot dogs and Coca Cola; it is plagued intermittently by epidemics of falling test scores, grade inflation, frivolous courses, multiple-question exams (which not only reward partial guesswork but discourage originality); it is hobbled by budget-cutting, political jobbery, pressures from alumni, power cliques and lobbies, and is rigidified by boards of regents made up mostly of satraps of law, business and industry.

Reforms will continue to be studied and proposed, documentation will keep coming from presses and mimeo drums, experiments noble and otherwise will be undertaken, and a quarter of all Americans will continue to consume education. But nothing basic will change until the character of the country changes, until we get over the conviction that the be-all and end-all of education is practicality; until Homer is given equal time with Home Economics; until we reverse the tendency to assign higher and higher scientific and technical sophistication to baser and baser uses; until schooling becomes a stimulant rather than a narcotic; until the priorities and goals of teaching are shifted from the mechanics of turning out diplomas and degrees to the art of thinking for one's self and arriving at a state where the best is no longer looked on as alien and exotic, but as a part of daily life.

One could fill a library shelf with suggestions for modes and means of achieving objectives on which qualified panels might agree. This is not the place for large projections, but there are two matters, one express and the other extensive, which ask to be ventilated briefly.

The first involves the study of etymology as one of the earliest courses in primary and secondary education. I cannot begin to understand the universal neglect of this subject in basic curricula, where it belongs alongside grammar, syntax and spelling. The origins of words are often so colorful, poetic, romantic, amusing, or charged with history that they arouse wonder and curiosity in children. It is no idle exercise to acquaint students with the fact that the names of five days of our week, three months of our year, and a rich array of words like cereal, morphine, harmony, cupidity, psychology, uranium, hygiene, comedy, lamp, ogre, volcano, panic, and that adjectives like jovial, martial and venereal, all derive from gods and goddesses; that the modest little daisy was originally, and poetically, named for the greatest body in our solar system (it was called "day's eye" because the golden center of the blossom resembled the sun, and the petals, rays of light); that the vehicle *coach* was named for a town in Hungary; that *cigar* comes from a locust whose shape it resembles; *sardine* from Sardinia; *cravat* from Croatia; *damask* from Damascus; *tangerine* from Tangiers; *suede* from Sweden; *turquoise* from Turkey; *milliner* from Milan; that the words blanket, silhouette, shrapnel, martinet, diddle, loganberry, marcel, maudlin, sandwich, all come from actual persons; that cobalt and nickel are named after goblins, and mean ones at that.

There are many hundreds of derivations which could enchant children, and help them to appreciate the color, flexibility, playfulness, power and beauty of language. Most important of all, exposure to etymology would tilt them toward inquiry, especially if they were assigned to bring in two or three fresh word origins every day for a week or month; it would give them a sense of shared proprietorship in language, tune up their spelling, open them up to the relationship of history, myth, legend, foreign cultures, trades, professions, sports, arts, sciences and slang to living speech.

There is no respectable doctrine which holds that, assuming proper ends are met, learning should not be fun; and in the teaching of languages there are more opportunities for games and sport than are afforded by just about any other subject. The enjoyment of words for themselves has a staying power well beyond formal schooling, as is apparent from the universal popularity of crossword puzzles, anagrams, crostics, Scrabble, and punning. So there is every reason to suggest that along with the standard texts used in the teaching of English, there might well be ancillary materials, edited to suit particular age groups, out of books like those of Willard R. Espy,[1] Ivor Brown, Eric Partridge, and Joseph T. Shipley.[2] Then perhaps students might approach reading and writing with something resembling relish instead of weariness or wariness; they might be interested enough to look up words instead of taking a stab at them, hoping they guess right; they might experience pleasure rather than boredom

[1]Especially Espy's *The Game of Words* and *An Almanac of Words at Play.*
[2]Especially Shipley's *Dictionary of Word Origins,* Philosophical Library, 1949.

in distinguishing between gamut and gambit, idol and idyll, pique and piquant, flaunt and flout, imply and infer.

The other matter relates to a discipline that is relatively new—the teaching of the performing arts, chiefly film and television. To begin with, writing, acting and directing are not now, never have been, and never will be exact sciences. If they were, a cadre of experts would have developed, just as there are master physicists and engineers and men who specialize in cryogenics and putting out fires in oil wells. And there would never be such a thing as a flop. But sometimes one gets the feeling, on college campuses, that TV and film and theater *are* treated as exact sciences, and this may be the reason why so much emphasis is put on machinery, on construction in the spirit of the erector set.

Concern for technique is proper and necessary, but in the teaching of the performing arts, too many instructors are sacrificing soul for console, getting lost in lenses and apertures, dissolves and interlocks, balop projectors, multiple-image prisms, chroma-keys, and the rest of the marvelous hardware that is part playroom and part factory.

Technique has a mystique of its own, and is not to be denigrated by comparison with other elements in the arch; but it belongs, like everything else, within a sensible perspective. Basically, technique is the most controllable ingredient of any collaborative process in or out of drama. It is more amenable to manipulation, and much less stubborn and balky than content, by which is meant story, character, theme, motivation, development and the other components by which audiences are made to suspend disbelief.

Unlike talent, skill can be acquired. One need think only of the impeccable brushwork and faithful detail of the copyist who sits before a masterpiece in an art museum, and sets down everything smoothly, flawlessly, photographically. It is an exquisite form of unoriginality: in extreme manifestations it is occasionally morbid, as in the art of the successful forger.

No disrespect is implied toward that most faithful of all reproducing machines, the camera, in calling it a beautiful but dumb instrument. It goes only where directed, and sees only what the artist wants it to see. It is in the *vision* of the artist that the art lies.

Pauline Kael, reviewing a work by an eminent film school graduate, Francis Ford Coppola, wrote about *One From The Heart*:

> This movie isn't from the heart or from the head, either; it's from the lab. It's all tricked out with dissolves and scrim effects and superimpositions and even aural superimpositions.
>
> Some artists become Jesus freaks; movie artists are more likely to become technology freaks. ... The artist has been consumed by technology. T.S. Eliot's "I can connect nothing with nothing" has become a boast.[3]

It is incumbent upon the teaching of the fine arts, that the curriculum be aimed more toward the mind than the meter, more toward the heart than the hand, and altogether toward a widening of vision; that the student be taught not only how to use the console in the control room, but how to get at, and best use, the console of himself.

Brooks Atkinson once said that it takes most men five years to recover from a college education, and to learn that poetry is as vital to thinking as knowledge. From another point of the compass, but leading to the same conclusion, was Marshall McLuhan's comment that education, in a technological world of replaceable and expendable parts, is neuter.

It is proper to ask whether the average college education in the fine arts is even partially neuter. With the proliferation of the performing arts (almost every college now has courses in TV, film, radio, drama), with tens of thousands of young people enrolling every year in the study of production, direction, writing and acting, it becomes increasingly important that they not be

[3]*The New Yorker*, 2.1.82.

turned into mere extensions of technology—robots in a system of middling, muddling, unoriginal, low-level creativity.

There is first of all the question of priorities. What are the goals? To make a fast buck? If so, then by all means emphasize those techniques by which the fastest buck, and a great many of them, can be made. The surest way is for the student to locate in the scobs of television, and help fill time as a contractor fills a dump, with debris programming. It can turn a tidy profit.

Is the inculcation of ideals a priority? Ah, but then we find that among the many ologies, osophies and isms of this world, idealism cannot be spoken of without a qualm. When we say "ideal" we must either smile, frown, or prepare to explain ourselves. For in the ascendency of the anti-hero, when nice guys finish last, when Kadafi, Khomeini, Marcos, Pinochet and other despots rise to power, when Zenith is a TV set, and Paramount a studio, and Acme a hardware store, and Superior an optical company, and Olympia a beer, when in the Los Angeles telephone directory alone there are 63 companies whose names begin with Ideal, including the Ideal Notion Company, Ideal Tortilla Factory, Ideal Used Furniture, and Ideal Rubbish Company, the adjective has become somewhat less than ideal to carry the weight of its original meaning, which is "an ultimate aim of a high and noble character." No wonder the word suffers from exhaustion.

Most of us agree on what is meant by ideals in the context of arts and media. We mean nothing profounder or more complex than a wish for young, emerging artists to do the best work of which they are capable. Good entertainment, message-free and unencumbered by deep psychological or philosophical implications, is no mean goal itself; but at the same time, one would hope such work will now and then be meaningful and helpful in this inchoate world—work that will serve truth, and perhaps even beauty. To hold to these ideals, no one need wear a suit of mail or fix raptly on the stars. There are such things as worthy goals, and we don't have to split a thousand hairs deciding what constitutes worth.

The question is whether artists emerging from tomorrow's education will be able to believe in what they have been encouraged to do. Pursuit of ideals can be as simple as that. Will they be able to combine what is desirable with what is feasible or attainable, and invest it with imagination, and with something of themselves? Will they be able to distinguish between the impossible dream and the possible one? To brace themselves against dismay or discouragement if the possible dream turns out to be slow-yielding and remote? There is some hope in the growing awareness, on a national level, that the arts can be more than a divertissement, more than an avocation or recreation, more than an escape from the terrors or tedium of reality, more than a juke box that gives us sitcoms and Lawrence Welk and *The Gong Show*.

Before the onset of serious trivialization, before the blight of Reaganism, we were on our way to an increasingly friendly cultural ambience. Notwithstanding the chronic addiction of so much of the public to certified and established mediocrity, we had been encouraged to extend our reach. Never before had the arts been housed so handsomely, in temples and theatres that would have been the envy of Greece and Rome. Never had so many rich foundations underwritten so many artistic enterprises, including the commissioning of new works.

It hardly matters that the Muses, once known as Calliope, Euterpe, Thalia, Polyhymnia, and the rest, are honored now in the names of Oscar, Tony, Emmy and Grammy. The arts, in spite of Reagan and his pruners, have become more than ever a national resource. Given a chance to return to the status they once enjoyed, they could continue to warm our hearts and fuel our spirits long after we have burned our last gallon of oil and consumed the last pellet of uranium.

Meanwhile, if ever there was a time to reinforce the humanities, it is now when they are under attack. The danger is more than that of downgrading our culture—something we can ill afford, considering present levels—but of encouraging anti-intellectualism, which is only a step away from redneckism. Not for nothing were the Know-Nothings in our history called that. Their modern counterparts boldly take on anything—evolution, the constitution, the Bill of Rights, history itself.

For all the sins of movies and TV, they have in their finer moments kept alive a decent respect for history. Nobel laureate Milocz, who was properly concerned about general loss of historical memory, may draw comfort from the fact that the same screen and tube that brought us *Beverly Hillbillies* and *Blood Orgy*, also gave us *Holocaust, Roots, Algiers, The Garden of the Finzi-Continis, The Way We Were, Missing, Gandhi*, and dozens of other conscionable historic canvases.

But the humanities cover much more than history and the memory of history. They deal with philosophy, literature and *all* the arts. There were, after all, *nine* Muses—a big family. And if there is any generative province where birth control should never be practiced, it is in that parish of Elysium. Can there ever be too many art treasures? A too-big library? Were 104 symphonies too many from the hand of Haydn? Do all those Köchel listings— 626 of them—make too much Mozart? Do we plow under Picassos because the old man kept turning them out?

A growing number of social philosophers and commentators feel that our culture has been reduced to vassalage within an imperious co-dominion of film, TV and sports, and that we are now under the flag of Entertainment. (An actor became president; another actor is elected United States Senator; an airport is named after a third actor; a highway is named for a comedian; a school is named after a first baseman; Shirley Temple grows up to be an ambassador). Other commentators are convinced that education is irreversibly on the skids; that it will never recover from Reagan and the attrition of trivialization; that the university of ideas and ideals is doomed.

Yet there is a paradox. Millions of people alive today are older than both film and TV, whereas Academe goes back to a grove in a suburb of Athens where Plato taught. Socrates preceded Sam Goldwyn by two millenia. If film studios and stadia and commercials and anchorpersons were to be swallowed up in some geologic convulsion, the loss would be conspicuous but not fatal. But if a similar catastrophe overtook education, the damage would be irreparable. For the university, with all its bureaucracy, its budget pains, its occasional maladministration, its infighting and intrigue, its legislative, labor and parking problems, is still the prime custodian of the arts and sciences, the preserve of the ologies and osophies, the house of the book, the best-feathered nest of learning, and, ultimately, the last hope for a continuum of reason.

On the seals of Yale and Indiana Universities, stands the motto *Lux et Veritas*. Since the survival of civilization continues to be a race between education and annihilation, light is needed. We must see where we are going. As for truth, it is the best compass man has yet devised. On its bearings we have a fair chance of deflecting our future from a state of unremitting menace toward a reasonable prospect for survival.

32 ✑ Contagions
and Conspiracies

In the service bays of our society, among correctives that people of good intent keep prescribing, is the notion of positive exemplars, of contagions of decency. The rank and decorum of the word "exemplar" itself may be seen in the suggestion of an early philosopher that God created the world "according to exemplars existing eternally in the divine mind." It apparently did not occur to this philosopher that the very concept of God is an exemplar existing in the human mind—but that is another matter.

Example has always had more followers than philosophy, and since our media today are constantly full of examples occurring as news, and most of these examples are bad, and these bad examples are given legitimacy and force by being publicized, and publicity attracts more examples of the same kind, there is set in motion a kind of vast dynamo that generates and renews its own energy, like the batteries of a hurricane.

Exemplars, good and bad, are contagious. It took only one airplane hijacker to infect commercial aviation throughout the world, until today no major airport is without elaborate and costly security apparatus. Contagions are almost as common in society as in pathology. The cycles of fads, fashions, intermittent "crazes," mass hysteria, propagation of religious faiths, political movements, economic upheavals, witch hunts, war psychoses, the rush to imitate successes in art, entertainment, industry, even vogue words and phrases, are fallouts of this process.

There are slow contagions, as expressed in Shelley's "contagion of the world's slow stain," and quick and fulminating ones, as when an event, or, say, an inflammatory speech by a powerful demagogue, triggers a violent response. Trivialization has been in the main a slow contagion, so gradual that, like a tree's growth, change is imperceptible from day to day. But good can be as catching as corruption or malevolence. Serene societies have existed, and even imperial Rome once enjoyed a contagion of peace under a dome of benign rule. Ancient Greece encouraged the spread of genius—witness the burgeoning simultaneously of so many titans of art, drama and statesmanship. In Elizabethan England, there were all at once Shakespeare, Marlowe, Bacon and Jonson. Colonial America enjoyed the communicability of minds like Franklin, Adams, Jefferson, Burr, Madison, Hamilton, Paine.

Obviously there are no easy remedies for the blights of society at any time, and especially at this time, and the few proposals touched on in these pages are hardly mountain-movers. Rescue by fiat is impossible, and the trouble with heroic measures is that they require heroes. Unquestionably, the best chances of reversal depend on attitudinal changes that are seldom advertised or even anticipated; on shifting political and economic climates; on subtle and cumulative effects like the tom-tom and drip-drip indoctrinations of television; on the temper or distemper of whole generations which may be listless, or restless, or angry, or inspired, or culturally numbed, or sensation-starved, or contorted by gimme-ism.

While no existing scenario for our survival as Greatest Nation or World Leader assures us that, if present trends continue, we will not ultimately be swamped in a sea of trivialization, neither is there cause to cover our heads with ashes and, like Job, curse the day we were born. There are still cadres of conscionable and caring people, and so long as they are not muted or exiled, or under house arrest, so long as they keep alert in thought and action, there is a chance, albeit maybe a small one, for a Right-Stuff contagion—moral, not macho—to spread.

A striking confirmation of the viability of this prospect came in a commencement address by Charles Kuralt at the University of North Carolina, Chapel Hill, on May 12, 1985. "A conspiracy of good people," is how he put it. He was speaking to a graduating class in a state represented by Jesse Helms, a senator so far to the right that he makes Reagan look like Fidel Castro. Alluding to his own student days at Chapel Hill, Kuralt said:

> It was on this campus that I first became faintly aware that there is . . . an association of men and women who, while they may not even know one another, might still be called a conspiracy of good people. Carl Sandburg, who was one of them, described them as a "saving minority . . ." Think of our state. From time to time, it has sent scoundrels to represent us in Washington, but always, here at home, the saving minority has returned us to reason, compassion and decency . . . In concentric circles, as if from a pebble tossed into a pond, [their] influence moves outward to the farthest corners of our state, and far beyond . . .
>
> The University says to us here gathered: Now I give you another class, among whose members are those who know, because they learned it on this hill, that there are purposes and undertakings ahead that are decent and compassionate, and unsullied by arrogance, or hostility toward others, or delusions of superiority, or motives of greed, and who will embrace those undertakings as members of the saving minority, the conscience of our country, the conspiracy of good people.

History is on the side of Kuralt's thesis, for in every era, and in all but ironclad theocracies or primitive cultures or utterly monolithic societies, conspiracies of good people have existed. But they are not always a saving minority—no fault of their own. They are sometimes simply overwhelmed. In Nazi Germany, Kuralt's good people were around, but they were destroyed or driven underground, and so could save nothing, not even themselves. The brightest badge of a civilized governance is the freedom of its saving minority to be *allowed* to save. Where that freedom is lacking, or to the extent that it is deprived, benign contagion cannot do the work of spreading good, but is either neutralized or killed off.

Attempts have been made in America to abridge the freedom of conspiracies of good people to conspire. So far they have failed, but it has taken the very elements of which Kuralt spoke—an unplanned association of men and women who may not even know each other—to *see* that they failed. In the dreary innings of McCarthy, McCarran, Mundt, McLaglen, Menjou, and the Motion Picture Alliance for the Preservation of American Ideals (to touch only on M's), the republic stood in danger of subverting itself in the name of fighting subversion, and it required the best efforts of good people, affiliated only by conscience, to return the country to reason and decency. Government itself did not do the job. Indeed when the United States Senate censured Joseph McCarthy, it was not for acts that gave his name to McCarthyism, but for two practically unrelated offenses—his refusal to explain a financial transaction, and for attacking fellow senators.

Cultural erosion itself is not a killing disease, but more like a lingering bad cold which, by weakening resistance, makes the host susceptible to deadly pathogens. The prospects of cure, the remedies and medicines, are in the hands of Sandburg's saving minority, whose members, singly or in concert, are, as Kuralt told his audience of students and parents, "willing to be heard when they have to be heard."

When this book was first published, the question most frequently asked by readers, interviewers and correspondents, was, "What can an individual do about any of this?" There is nothing new either about that question, or the answers to it, since the same appeal is forever being made about grievances beyond those of trivialization; i.e., what can be done about abuses, rip-offs, imbalances, derelictions, lapses, outrages, injustices, official lies, perilous indifferences, professional greed, plunderers, blunderers, warmongering, peace-baiting, galloping Philistinism? And the answer is the same for all: That although the individual can do very little without group affiliation of some kind, whatever he or she *does* do cannot hurt and may possibly help.

On the basis that all outlook, public and private, begins at home, the individual can contribute to well-being in one's physical community, as well as in overlapping communities of art, education, commerce and government, by thinking and acting as a citizen who expects the best from one's country, not a succession of lesser evils; by never debasing one's right to vote by not voting; by never wasting one's freedom to speak by not speaking; by taking nothing for granted, especially the reliability of official handouts, advertising claims, or the integrity of media.

Skepticism is not cynicism, and can be constructive when it identifies flaws in the fabric of a culture that are susceptible of repair. Certain qualities and attitudes that suffer from a bad press, such as impatience, intolerance, resentment, stubbornness, contempt, suspicion, and alarm, have their good uses. It is proper to be impatient with foot-dragging in the redress of inequities and injustices; to be intolerant of intolerance; to resent partisan or professional dictation of patriotism or morality; to be stubborn in the defense of the right to dissent; to hold in contempt courts like that of Webster Thayer, or the one in San Francisco which slapped with a feather the murderer of a mayor and an administrator on the grounds that he had suffered diminished capacity from eating junk food; to be suspicious of simple panaceas like balancing a ravenous budget by lowering taxes and raising military appropriations; to sound alarm, as did the observers quoted earlier in these pages under the heading "General Alarm."

Ultimately it gets back to Whitman's vow, "I swear nothing is good to me now that ignores individuals." Many forces and entities today ignore individuals by trivializing them, but the reverse is also true: masses of individuals ignore the values which make for a healthy society, and that is an even worse form of trivialization. It amounts to a deadly reciprocation which, one can but hope, will be checked in time by those charterless alliances of good people known to the poet as a saving minority, to the broadcaster as an aristocracy of spirit unsullied by arrogance, hostility or greed, and to readers sharing the premises and concerns of these pages, as the conscionable core, the humane marrow of America.

Index